Terrence Malick

Philosophical Filmmakers

*S*eries *editor*: Costica Bradatan is a Professor of Humanities at Texas Tech University, USA, and an Honorary Research Professor of Philosophy at the University of Queensland, Australia. He is the author of *Dying for Ideas: The Dangerous Lives of the Philosophers* (Bloomsbury, 2015), among other books.

Films can ask big questions about human existence: what it means to be alive, to be afraid, to be moral, to be loved. The *Philosophical Filmmakers* series examines the work of influential directors, through the writing of thinkers wanting to grapple with the rocky territory where film and philosophy touch borders.

Each book involves a philosopher engaging with an individual filmmaker's work, revealing how it has inspired the author's own philosophical perspectives and how critical engagement with those films can expand our intellectual horizons.

Terrence Malick

Filmmaker and
Philosopher

Robert Sinnerbrink

BLOOMSBURY ACADEMIC
LONDON • NEW YORK • OXFORD • NEW DELHI • SYDNEY

BLOOMSBURY ACADEMIC
Bloomsbury Publishing Plc
50 Bedford Square, London, WC1B 3DP, UK
1385 Broadway, New York, NY 10018, USA

BLOOMSBURY, BLOOMSBURY ACADEMIC and the Diana logo are trademarks
of Bloomsbury Publishing Plc

First published in Great Britain 2019

Cover image: *The Tree of Life*, 2011 Directed by: Terrence Malick © Collection
Christophel / ArenaPAL

A catalogue record for this book is available from the British Library.

A catalog record for this book is available from the Library of Congress.

ISBN: HB: 978-1-3500-6363-1
PB: 978-1-3500-6364-8
ePDF: 978-1-3500-6362-4
eBook: 978-1-3500-6365-5

Series: Philosophical Filmmakers

Typeset by Integra Software Services Pvt. Ltd.
Printed and bound in Great Britain

To find out more about our authors and books visit www.bloomsbury.com
and sign up for our newsletters.

For György (1934–2016), who set me on the path.

Contents

Preface

This book is about a great filmmaker – Terrence Malick – but also about the relationship between film and philosophy, indeed the idea of film *as* philosophy. Since the release of his first feature, *Badlands* (1973), Malick has come to be recognized as one of the most significant American auteurs of his generation. He has also been described as a 'philosophical' filmmaker, an artist whose work has something valuable to contribute to our understanding of philosophical questions and moral problems. Some have claimed Malick as a 'Heideggerian' filmmaker, principally because of his intriguing background as a scholar of Martin Heidegger's work before abandoning academic philosophy to pursue filmmaking. What does it mean to be a philosophical filmmaker? What is 'Heideggerian cinema'? What is the relationship between film and philosophy? Can cinema 'do ethics'? These questions and concerns have shaped my engagement with Malick's work over many years. But it is Malick's achievements as a filmmaker – the extraordinary beauty of his images, innovative use of sound and music and experimentation with narrative form – that aroused and sustained my aesthetic interest in his work. I approach Malick's films in light of their cinematic qualities, the aesthetic – and philosophical – experiences that they might afford, which always remain, in my view, the touchstones for any theoretical claims one may subsequently develop in response to works of art.

In a broader sense, this book is also an account of my development as a film-philosopher, someone dedicated to the question of film and philosophy, but also open to the possibility that film can teach us about philosophy, or open ways of thinking that have genuine moral and ethical import. I attempt, then, in what follows to present a philosophically and aesthetically engaged account of Malick as a filmmaker *and* philosopher, which also means, in my conception of this relationship, exploring the ways in which Malick's work contributed to my own thinking and outlook on art, ethics and life.

Anyone interested in the art of cinema would appreciate the time and effort involved in studying a filmmaker's body of work, or an important genre in film history, or to understand films from particular cultural traditions. This is especially true of cinema, which as a mass-industrialized artform, one undergoing profound changes thanks to the digital revolution, demands attention not only to the formal qualities of particular works but to their context of production, their cultural and historical background, industrial and technological features and patterns of audience reception. Bringing a philosophical perspective to cinema – or entertaining the idea that cinema might contribute to philosophy – adds another dimension to this already complex situation. One of the challenges, therefore, for anyone working at the intersection of cinema and philosophy is to do justice to both the aesthetic features of a work and its philosophical aspects, while remaining mindful of context and other 'extra-theoretical' considerations.

A filmmaker like Malick poses particular demands on this kind of interdisciplinary inquiry, which I have tried to meet in my work on his films over the past dozen years. One of these is Malick's admirable quality of remaining open to possibility, his willingness to experiment and create, while remaining true to a fundamental aesthetic vision or moral conviction. He is one of those rare artists who becomes more radical the older they get. I admire this ethos, which is not only relevant to art and philosophy but much else besides. This commitment to experimenting with style, coupled with a desire to return to the same ideas in new and unexpected ways, strikes me as one of the hallmarks of a great artist – and this is certainly true of Malick's work.

The price of experimentation coupled with repetition, however, is often misunderstanding or frustration, something readily apparent in the critical reception of Malick's cinema. I take heart, however, from the fact that many of his films at first harshly criticized (including 'classics' like *Badlands* and *Days of Heaven*) have received belated acknowledgement of their artistic achievement. This was quite dramatic, for example, with *The Tree of Life* (2011), which many now regard as his 'masterwork'. For my part, I would not be surprised if Malick's later films – *To the Wonder* (2012), *Knight of Cups* (2015) and *Song to Song* (2017), probably the most demanding in his oeuvre to date – will eventually receive the recognition they deserve, even if that recognition remains selective and even if that point is some years away.

Heidegger once said that all great thinkers only think one thought, but return to it over again, precisely due to its difficulty or inexhaustibility. Something similar might be said of artists, or indeed of filmmakers, who both explore new styles as well as return to the 'one' theme or idea that gives shape and substance to their body of work. Malick strikes me as this kind of filmmaker, one whose originality persists despite his age and one whose body of cinematic work looks, with any luck, far from complete. With another feature due for release later this year (*Radegund*, a Second-World-War drama), one promising a return to a more 'structured' filmmaking style, but also repeating the moral-ethical and spiritual-religious focus of his later work, I expect that the story of Malick's encounter with film and philosophy is far from over. I hope that my modest contribution to this story sheds some light on this remarkable filmmaker and on the philosophical reflections that his films, in their beauty and splendour, continue to evoke.

Acknowledgements

There are countless people who contribute, in ways both implicit and explicit, to the gestation and birth of a book. A book on a challenging filmmaker like Malick, moreover, will provoke myriad ideas, arguments and insights. Indeed, one of the pleasures of working on film-philosophy is the opportunity it provides to engage with philosophers and film theorists whose influence on my own thinking has been immense. A group of colleagues and friends that I think of as 'the Malick crowd' – a group that includes staunch critics of Malick's work – should be singled out for particular thanks. Among others, let me acknowledge the following: Jonathan Beever, Gabrielle Blasi, John Caruana, Mark Cauchi, Vernon W. Cisney, Amy Coplan, Louise D'Arcens, David Davies, Gregory Flaxman, Ross Gibson, Britt Harrison, Stuart Kendall, Noel King, Shawn Loht, Russell Manning, Adrian Martin, John McAteer, Michael J. Mosely, Anat Pick, Murray Pomerance, Ian Rijsdijk, Isabella Rocamora, Martin Roussouw, William Rothman, Steven Rybin, Ilan Safit, Libby Saxton, Paul Sheehan, Daniel Smith, Lisa Trahair, Thomas Deane Tucker, Elizabeth Walden and Jason Wirth. Your conversations, comments, suggestions and criticisms have been both a motivation and a corrective in developing my own thoughts and insights on this remarkable filmmaker's work.

Special thanks are due to John Caruana and Mark Cauchi, whose kind invitation to talk on Malick's *The Tree of Life* at the 'Varieties of Continental Philosophy and Religion' conference held at Ryerson University, Toronto (in 2012), including a wonderful response by Steven Rybin, proved a great spur to my subsequent thinking on Malick's work. I would also like to thank Amy Coplan, whose invitation to give a 2017 keynote address at California State University, Fullerton, where I first presented some of the ideas articulated here on Malick's later films, played an essential role in developing this book. Finally, I am very grateful to Costica Bradatan, as friend and philosopher, for inviting me to contribute to this series on Philosophical Filmmakers and for being such an enthusiastic supporter of this project, and of film and philosophy more generally. The opportunity to talk film and philosophy with friends and colleagues such as these has been one of the great pleasures of my intellectual life.

I have published a number of articles on Malick's films over the past dozen years, and I have revisited and developed this work in writing my book. Some of the chapters in this book draw on material previously published elsewhere. I would like to thank the editors of the following publications for their kind permission to use material from the following texts.

Passages from the Introduction appeared in R. Sinnerbrink (2006), 'A Heideggerian Cinema? On Terrence Malick's *The Thin Red Line*', *Film-Philosophy* 10 (3): 26–37; R. Sinnerbrink (2011), *New Philosophies of Film: Thinking Images*, London and New York: Continuum; and R. Sinnerbrink (2016), *Cinematic Ethics: Exploring Ethical Experience through Film*, London and New York: Routledge. Portions of Chapter 2 drew on R. Sinnerbrink (2006), 'A Heideggerian Cinema? On Terrence Malick's *The Thin Red Line*', *Film-Philosophy* 10 (3): 26–37.

Chapter 3 used material from the following works: R. Sinnerbrink (2009), 'From Mythic History to Cinematic Poetry: Terrence Malick's

The New World Viewed', *Screening the Past*, 26, [Issue on Early Europe], December; R. Sinnerbrink (2011a), *New Philosophies of Film: Thinking Images*, London and New York: Continuum; R. Sinnerbrink (2011b), 'Song of the Earth: Cinematic Romanticism in Terrence Malick's *The New World*', in Tucker, T. D. and Kendall, S. (eds), *Terrence Malick: Film and Philosophy*, 179–186, London and New York: Continuum.

Chapter 4 developed material taken from a number of publications: R. Sinnerbrink, R. (2012), 'Cinematic Belief: Bazinian Cinephilia and Malick's *The Tree of Life*, *Angelaki*, 17 (4): 95–117; R. Sinnerbrink (2016a), '"Love Everything": Cinema and Belief in Malick's *The Tree of Life*', *Symposium: Canadian Journal of Continental Philosophy*, 'Varieties of Continental Philosophy and Religion', 20 (1) (Spring): 91–105; R. Sinnerbrink (2016b), '"Belief in the World": Aesthetic Mythology in Terrence Malick's *The Tree of Life*', in Vernon W. Cisney and Jonathan Beever (eds), *The Way of Nature and the Way of Grace: Philosophical Footholds on Terrence Malick's* The Tree of Life, 89–103, Evanston: Northwestern University Press; R. Sinnerbrink (2016c), *Cinematic Ethics: Exploring Ethical Experience through Film*, London and New York: Routledge; and R. Sinnerbrink (2018), 'Two Ways through Life: Postsecular Visions in *Melancholia* and *The Tree of Life*', in J. Caruana and M. Cauchi (eds), *Immanent Frames: Postsecular Cinema between Malick and von Trier*, 29–46, Albany: State University of New York Press.

Chapter 5 presented some passages deriving from R. Sinnerbrink (2018), 'Love Sick: Malick's Kierkegaardian "Love and Faith" Trilogy', *Paragraph* (forthcoming 2018).

I wish to acknowledge the Australian Research Council (ARC) for their support of the research towards this book, which was funded by an ARC Future Fellowship (FT 130100334, 2014–18) on the topic of cinematic ethics. I owe a debt to my editor, Frankie Mace, at Bloomsbury, who has been wonderful to work with, always professional and supportive. I also owe thanks to my students, both undergraduate and postgraduate, who have been stimulating for my own thinking on the relationship between film and philosophy. Here I would like to acknowledge Ludo de Roo and Philip Martin in particular, as wonderful interlocutors on all issues related to aesthetics, film and philosophy. I owe more than I can say to Louise D'Arcens, my wife as well as my colleague, whose intellectual conversation, emotional support and cinematic companionship have made everything possible for me. Watching and discussing Malick films together has been a singular joy and shared pleasure. I hope that I can do as much for her as she has done for me over the years.

While completing this manuscript, I heard the sad news that Stanley Cavell, Malick's teacher and mentor, had died (on 19 June 2018). Although I never met Cavell, the influence of his work on my own thinking on Malick – and much else besides – has been immense. I would like to acknowledge this wonderful thinker and exemplary philosopher of cinema by dedicating this book to his memory.

Introduction
Terrence Malick – A Philosophical Cinema?

The films of Terrence Malick present unique aesthetic and philosophical challenges. In addition to visionary and poetic, his films have also been described as philosophical and metaphysical. Indeed, he is one of the few directors today who regularly appear in discussions of the idea of 'film as philosophy' (see Critchley 2005, 2009; Davies 2009a; Sinnerbrink 2011) or whose work has been described as 'Heideggerian' (Furstenau and McAvoy 2007; Rhym 2010; Sinnerbrink 2006; Woessner 2011). This is not surprising given Malick's intriguing biographical background (see Critchley 2009; Davies 2009a; Michaels 2009). Before enrolling in the Center for Advanced Film Studies at the American Film Institute in Los Angeles (as part of the inaugural class of 1969), Malick had been set on an academic career. He had studied philosophy at Harvard with celebrated philosopher Stanley Cavell and was awarded a Rhodes Scholarship to undertake a PhD at Magdalen College Oxford, under the supervision of Gilbert Ryle. Malick's thesis was to have been on the concept of 'world' in Kierkegaard, Heidegger and Wittgenstein, but Ryle apparently bristled at Malick's dissertation topic, describing it as 'not philosophical enough'. Disappointed, Malick returned to the United States, having abandoned his dissertation, and began teaching courses in phenomenology at the MIT, replacing Heideggerian expert Hubert Dreyfus (while the latter was on sabbatical). In 1969, he published an important scholarly translation of a key Heidegger text, *The Essence of Reasons* [*Vom Wesen des Grundes*], which offers fascinating insights into Malick's understanding of Heidegger's conception of 'world'. Given this background, surely unique for an American auteur, it is hardly surprising that many critics were quick to pin the philosophical, even 'Heideggerian', label on Malick's unique body of cinematic work.

The first to do so was Stanley Cavell, Malick's erstwhile philosophy teacher. In the 1979 Preface to the expanded edition of his now classic text, *The World Viewed: Reflections on the Ontology of Film* (1971/1979), Cavell singled out Malick for philosophical praise, describing his recently released second feature, *Days of Heaven* (1978), as displaying a beauty in its photographic presentation of nature that invites philosophical reflection:

> Shall we try expressing the subject [of the film] as one in which the works and the emotions and the entanglements of human beings are at every moment reduced to insignificance by the casual rounds of earth and sky? I think the film does indeed contain a metaphysical vision of the world; but I think one feels that one has never quite seen the scene of human existence – call it the arena between earth (or days) and heaven – quite realized this way on film before. (Cavell 1979: xiv–xv)

High praise indeed from the most important philosophers of cinema! But what does Cavell mean? What does it mean to describe film – or indeed Malick's films – as *philosophical*, as containing a 'metaphysical vision of the world', as offering a unique realization of the 'scene of human existence', in an aesthetically powerful way? What does it mean for a philosopher to praise a filmmaker in such terms or to have offered thanks to a filmmaker for helping in the composition of a philosophical work?[1] These are some of the questions that haunt Malick's work, questions that have inspired both his defenders and detractors. They are questions that continue to inspire my own work and serve as guides to Malick's 'cinematic thinking' that I explore in this book.

Let us consider two of these questions further. The first is what it means to describe film as 'philosophical', indeed Malick's films as philosophical, or more particularly as 'Heideggerian'. The second, related issue is to explore what it means for Malick to have turned from philosophy to film, abandoning academic philosophy in favour of filmmaking. One response, the most common, is to suggest that this philosophical background shaped Malick's subsequent career as a filmmaker, such that his films are best understood as attempts to screen aspects of what Heidegger might have thought philosophically. This approach takes Malick's films as cases of artistically applied philosophizing or philosophically inspired filmmaking. An alternative response would regard Malick's films as opening up the question of the relationship between film and philosophy but as a perplexing problem demanding further thought.

Malick may have turned to film because of the limitations of academic philosophy, as practised in institutions like Harvard or Oxford. He may have found this context constraining and hence sought to explore the possibilities of film as a medium with its own aesthetic potentialities – one that may invoke experiences conducive to thought but not reducible to any philosophy as such. Or, as Malick remarks in one of his rare interviews, perhaps he did not feel he was any good as a philosophy teacher, and so turned to another medium and milieu for creative expression.[2] Whatever the case, I contend that the question of the relationship between film and philosophy, especially in regard to a filmmaker like Malick, remains, precisely, *a question*, rather than something assumed or known.

Because of Malick's reluctance to reveal his intentions or offer interpretations, we do not know the answers to these questions. We do know that Malick was wary of the idea that film could 'do' philosophy. As he remarks in an interview from 1975, 'I don't feel that one can film philosophy' (quoted in Morrison and Schur 2003: 97). Even this remark seems ambiguous, for it could mean that cinema has no meaningful relationship with philosophy, hence one cannot film it; or it could mean that cinema and philosophy, in an academic sense, may have a relationship of sorts but not one in which cinema can simply apply philosophical ideas in an illustrative manner. Again, the remark, made in an interview following the release of *Badlands*, reminds us that the question of Malick and philosophy remains just that – a question. In what follows, I shall explore this latter path, taking Malick's body of work as an invitation to think through the relationship between film and philosophy, to explore the possibility that cinema can contribute to philosophical thinking and to consider the ways in which his films have shaped my own views on this relationship.

What follows in this book is a recounting of my apprenticeship in film-philosophy through my engagement with Malick's work. I attempt to think *with* Malick in order to explore how cinema might contribute to philosophical understanding by aesthetic means. Indeed, I offer an alternative response to the question of philosophical cinema by suggesting that Malick's work is best understood in relation to ethics – as evoking ethical experience, taken in an expansive sense. Rather than remaining bound to the narrower debate over whether films can do philosophy, Malick's work belongs to what I call *cinematic ethics*: the idea that the aesthetic medium of film has the potential to express and evoke ethical experience in ways related but not reducible to philosophical discussions of ethical questions and moral problems (see Sinnerbrink 2016). I shall approach Malick's body of work as a case study in cinematic ethics – a distinctive way of evoking experiences of ethical complexity that are resistant to philosophical paraphrase but conducive to ethical reflection. In doing so, I also reflect on how his work has shaped my responses to the question 'Can films contribute to philosophical understanding?' For my encounter with Malick's cinema has prompted me to transform my own thinking, to explore different paths, to experience a different way of viewing the world.

Can films do philosophy?

In one of his rare early interviews, Malick expresses doubts as to whether one can 'film philosophy'. Yet Malick's former teacher and celebrated film-philosopher Stanley Cavell claims that *Days of Heaven* (1978) presents, through moving images, the play of presence and absence that reveals the luminous being of things. Malick questions whether one can film-philosophy, whereas Cavell claims that Malick has done just that, revealing through cinema what Heidegger explores in his thinking of being. What are we to make of these conflicting views? Some philosophical film theorists (Mulhall 2008; Sinnerbrink 2011; Wartenberg 2007) have argued that film can explore philosophical ideas via cinematic means – the idea of film *as* philosophy. Philosophers defending the 'film *as* philosophy' thesis have argued that movies can screen philosophical thought experiments (Wartenberg 2007); that film can philosophize on a variety of topics, including reflection on its own status, in ways comparable to philosophy (Mulhall 2008); or that cinema has its own aesthetic ways of thinking that challenge the manner in which thought can be communicated (Frampton 2006). Critics of the idea, by contrast, have argued that such claims are merely metaphorical: film, as a visual narrative art, does not give reasons, make arguments or draw conclusions, so it cannot be understood as 'philosophical' in the proper sense (Baggini 2003; Russell 2006). Or given the ambiguity of film narrative, whatever philosophical aspects there are to a film are usually subordinate to its artistic and rhetorical ends (Smith 2006). Alternatively, critics argue that any philosophy to be gleaned from a film is either due to the philosophical acumen of the interpreter, or else is confined to the expression of an explicit aesthetic intention on the part of its maker(s) (Livingston 2006, 2009), neither of which would qualify the film itself as original source or exclusive medium of philosophical thought.

The difficulty with such contentions, however, is that they assume a narrow or reductive conception of what counts as philosophy or fail to reflect adequately on the various ways in which film and philosophy can be related. Arguments over film and philosophy, especially the claim that films can 'do philosophy', typically assume a given conception of what counts as philosophy, and hence how cinema may or may not contribute to philosophical understanding. If we take 'philosophy' to refer to the practice of 'professionalized' academic discourse – comprising the framing of arguments, the giving of reasons, analysis of concepts, articulation of objections, criticism of conceptual frameworks, all aiming at rationally justified conclusions – then the idea of 'film as philosophy' would seem controversial or implausible. Film, as an audiovisual medium deployed for narrative purposes, seems ill-suited to the conceptual argumentative work of philosophy, a linguistic medium par excellence. If, however, we take philosophy in a broader sense, as a practice of thinking contributing to human flourishing (to living the 'good life' or what the Greeks called *eudaimonia*), then the idea that film might be an art contributing to philosophical understanding – or to living a philosophical life – appears more persuasive. This is especially the case, as I argue below, if we take film as a medium with the potential to elicit and express ethical experience. Indeed, Malick is one of those filmmakers, I contend, whose work contributes to deepening our capacity for imaginative moral experience, to expanding our horizons of ethical meaning and to sensitizing our capacity for ethical engagement, even moral self-transformation.

In short, the 'film as philosophy' debate is an aesthetic as well as a meta-philosophical dispute: one that challenges us not only to think through the philosophical significance of cinema but also to entertain the possibility that cinema might expand our conception of philosophy. From this point of view, the idea of film as philosophy seeks to explore the novel ways in which conventional views of philosophy – and receptivity to philosophical experience – might be transformed through our encounter with film. We may even come to regard cinema as expressing thought in a distinctively cinematic manner that has philosophical significance or invites philosophical reflection. Film and philosophy can thereby enter into a dialogue – a relationship or 'marriage' with the potential to transform both partners – without subsuming cinema into philosophy or rendering cinematic art as the passive object of philosophical inquiry. From this perspective, it will be cinema with the capacity to evoke complex forms of aesthetic experience, to engage spectators emotionally and imaginatively, while also prompting reflection or questioning, which will be the most ethically significant.

As I shall argue in this book, Malick's cinema prompts us to consider how we might think through the question of film as philosophy and offers fascinating case studies to explore the idea of cinematic ethics. It is no surprise that his films have been understood as 'Heideggerian' – or as a 'best case' example of film as philosophy (Neer 2011). At the same time, they have been used to debunk claims that films can screen philosophy or to argue that film-philosophical interpretations of cinema amount to reductive acts of hermeneutic instrumentalization (Neer 2011) – a kind of philosophical abuse of cinematic art. The challenge is to think through the 'matter for thinking' (Heidegger) posed by Malick's work and to do so by avoiding two temptations: (1) *philosophical dogmatism* (assuming that Malick's films simply are 'philosophical' or 'Heideggerian' or else that they could not possibly be so) and (2) *aestheticist mysticism* (the view that any attempt to ascribe philosophical meaning to his works instrumentalizes their aesthetic beauty and cinematic complexity).

It is striking to see how often film theorists warn against instrumentalizing Malick's films for philosophical purposes, yet also draw upon philosophical ideas, concepts and perspectives in analysing his work. To borrow a phrase from a recent article (Roussow 2017), there is 'something about Malick' and philosophy that continues to fascinate, perplex and disconcert, even if Malick's most recent films, with their more overtly spiritual/ religious sensibility, seem to resist such philosophical readings. Philosophers enamoured of 'Heideggerian' readings of Malick and cinephiles sceptical of philosophical speculation may yet have something to learn from each other, thanks to the ethical quality of Malick's work.

There are both aesthetic and philosophical reasons why Malick's work presents a challenge for a philosopher of cinema. As remarked, he is a filmmaker trained in philosophy (an expert on Heidegger and existential phenomenology), whose background implies a sharply philosophical mind. He is also a distinctive cinematic artist whose films, with their eschewal of narrative conventions (such as strong or well-defined characters, psychologically motivated plot development and foregrounding of emotion and action), have attracted critical responses that emphasize the poetic, abstract and impressionistic style of his work. Some critics have argued that Malick's is a 'Heideggerian cinema' (Furstenau and McAvoy 2007; Loht 2017; Silverman 2003); others claim that his films must be understood independently of philosophy in order to appreciate their distinctive aesthetic qualities (Cousins 2007; Martin 2007; Neer 2011). For many, however, it is precisely the aesthetic experience of Malick's films that prompts one to reach for philosophical ideas in order to comprehend and communicate this experience. Such films invite a philosophical response, which does not mean that Malick explicitly intended to communicate philosophical ideas via moving images. This would be a benign case of 'film as philosophy', namely 'film as inviting philosophy', thanks to the aesthetic experiences Malick's films evoke. His work offers viewers an invitation to thinking, extended via poetic cinematic means.

This may sound persuasive but it does not really track the reception of Malick's work. Malick's first two films, *Badlands* (1973) and *Days of Heaven* (1978), for example, were not received as philosophical works but as impressive offerings by a young 'New Hollywood' director experimenting with various genre conventions (the 'lovers on the lam'/true crime story/road movie in the case of *Badlands* and the mythic romantic love triangle/agrarian 'Western', in the case of *Days of Heaven*). Malick's unusual background as a philosopher is noted but not made intrinsic to the reception of these films (see Woessner 2011). It is only after Malick's return to filmmaking (after a twenty-year hiatus) with the release of *The Thin Red Line* (1998) that the 'paradigmatic shift' from genre studies to 'film as philosophy' (or even 'Heideggerian cinema') took hold in the critical reception of his films (see Rhym 2010; Woessner 2011).

It is not difficult to see why there was such philosophical enthusiasm for *The Thin Red Line*, with its 'philosophical' voiceovers and 'Heideggerian' (but also Emersonian) overtones. Here was an existential war movie – differing sharply from Spielberg's *Saving Private Ryan*, released the same year – with poetic splendour, phenomenological richness and existential complexity. Here was a film encompassing metaphysical ruminations on finitude, mortality, violence and love, while offering a poetically rich presentation of disparate ways of being-in-the-world amid an indifferent but expressive nature (see Critchley 2005; Pippin 2013; Silverman 2003). Little wonder that philosophically minded critics were swift to claim the film as Heideggerian cinema (Furstenau and McAvoy 2007; Loht 2013), thereby enshrining Malick as a bona fide 'philosophical' filmmaker – along with auteurs like Bergman and Tarkovsky – whose work could be said to bring philosophy to the big screen.[3]

Many theorists (myself included), however, were quick to point out the risks and pitfalls of a too hasty declaration of Malick as a 'Heideggerian' (Sinnerbrink 2006). Simon Critchley (2005), for example, warned of the dangers of slipping on various 'hermeneutic banana skins' (Malick the Heidggerian, Malick the tortured genius, Malick the romantic mystic), cautioning against imposing one's own philosophical assumptions or conceptual frameworks onto the film. Articulating what Thomas Wartenberg (2007) has since called the 'imposition objection', Critchley's warning proved difficult to heed, especially in the case of *The Thin Red Line* (as I discuss further in Chapter 2). Critchley's own reading of the film, for example, relies heavily on the three thematic relationships (concerning love, nature and war) articulated in the narrative. It ends up affirming Witt's acceptance of finitude and mortality in facing the violence of battle with an existential calm and contemplative ethical attitude of 'letting be' towards nature and the world – an idea that recalls the later Heidegger's *Gelassenheit* or releasement (see Loht 2017;

Sinnerbrink 2006 for a critique of Critchley). Bersani and Dutoit (2004), often quoted as exemplary critics of *The Thin Red Line* for their attention to cinematic presentation, draw on ideas from Freud's *Civilisation and Its Discontents* and a quasi-Deleuzian vitalist ontology in their 'non-philosophical' reading of the film. They argue that Witt's wide-eyed gaze signals an openness to the world, revealing a cinematic relational ontology expressing a 'subjectless' experience of being in which we encounter 'all things shining' (Bersani and Dutoit 2004: 163–171).

Richard Neer's critical discussion of the film (2011) is framed by a critique of film-philosophers who insist on imposing a 'Heideggerian metatext' onto the film at the expense of its cinematic compositional strategies (Malick's flowing mobile camera and remarkable presentation of world perspectives combining natural light, widescreen format, with depth of field). He rightly emphasizes the film's thematic exploration of the concept of 'world', but to elaborate this idea has recourse to Malick's own critical interpretation of Heidegger's *Vom Wesen des Grundes* and the concept of world-disclosure at its heart. Having criticized philosophers for their imposition of Heideggerian philosophy onto Malick's work, Neer elaborates his close analysis of the cinematic framing and disclosure of world horizons via Malick's own philosophical reading of Heidegger. At the same time, Neer is careful not to assert that such ideas offer anything more than hermeneutic guides to engaging with the film's stylistic elements. This is not to fault Bersani and Dutoit, Neer or Critchley – all of whom are aware that movies are embedded in cultural and historical contexts including philosophical ideas – but rather to note that there are two risks for philosophical film critics to navigate here.

The first is the reductive, uncritical imposition of a 'Heideggerian' (or any other philosophical) perspective, as though this provided a hermeneutic grid that would reveal the film's philosophical significance. The second is the 'formalist' demand to 'bracket' any such theoretical prejudices (in the hermeneutic sense) as though one could simply attend – in a manner recalling the phenomenological *epoche* or suspension of 'theoretical' assumptions underpinning ordinary consciousness – to the pure givenness of the film itself. Such an approach, however, proceeds as though we can simply suspend context, cultural-historical setting and discursive traditions through an act of formal-aesthetic appreciation coupled with 'theory-free' critical analysis. Indeed, Malick's films provide an exemplary case study to show how difficult such a demand turns out to be; how it is precisely in the interplay of these contextual, formal-aesthetic and philosophico-ethical elements that the real cinematic and philosophical richness of his work can be found.

As an alternative to both the 'Heideggerian cinema' approach and the 'non-philosophical formalist' approach, I propose that we are better off articulating the relationship at issue as a 'hermeneutic parallelism': a productive parallel or critical exchange between philosophical ideas, themes or theories and aesthetic elements, cinematic techniques, and narrative features of Malick's films. Such an exchange can lead to new ways of thinking about both film and philosophy. Malick's films elicit and evoke forms of experience that often invite metaphysical reflection or prompt one to seek comprehension by having recourse to philosophical reflection. Philosophical ideas, in turn, can serve as heuristic devices to help open up or articulate aspects of the film or the significance of the experiences – aesthetic, ethical or metaphysical – to which it gives rise. This does not mean that one 'reads into' a film philosophical themes or ideas associated, for example, with Heidegger, but rather that a 'Heideggerian' way of thinking, for example, offers one way of articulating the kind of thought-provoking aesthetic experience to which Malick's films give rise (and there may be many others, which emphasize different aspects of these films). This receptivity to aesthetic experience that invites thought justifies the claim that his films are in some ways philosophical, without thereby claiming that they are 'Heideggerian' as such.

As it happens, the 'Heideggerian' approach that was so prominent with regard to *The Thin Red Line* began to wane with Malick's subsequent films. *The New World*, for example, left some Malick critics deeply perplexed.[4] Nonetheless, the film did explore themes of nature, authenticity, power, earth and dwelling, which could be linked with a Heideggerian way of thinking, now coupled with a new emphasis on the founding myths of (American) colonialism and the possibility of articulating a neo-romantic (historico-poetic) mythology. The 'Heideggerian' approach to Malick continued but reached a watershed with the release of *The Tree of Life* (2011). It began to falter as it became more difficult to ignore the film's Christian religious/theological strands together with its historical, metaphysical and moral aspects. Indeed, the discourse of 'Heideggerian cinema' appears to have receded in response to his later works (since *The Tree of Life*), which have been dismissed by philosophical critics as regressive and repetitive rather than visionary or transformative. These are claims that I shall question in later chapters, exploring the shift – or expansion – in the modes of ethical experience opened up by these works, one that includes spiritual-religious forms of moral-ethical responsiveness to the aesthetic experiences afforded by cinema.

The dismissal of these later films overlooks the illuminating journey mapped out by Malick's development: from 'naïve' poetic genre works (in his early films) to more philosophical-aesthetic meditations (in his 'middle works') to post-philosophical, poetic narrative experimentation (in his later works). All of his films, however, are concerned with both aesthetic and ethical experience. This is true even in the 'negative' mode of presenting apparently unmotivated acts of violence, refusing to 'explain' these in terms of character psychology or social situation, thus prompting the viewer to reflect on the sources and significance of such violence (an important feature in Malick's earlier films and in *The Thin Red Line*). Here I would like to introduce the relevance of cinematic ethics for understanding Malick's work, an idea that offers a more aesthetically attuned way of exploring the question of film as ethics.

Malick's cinematic ethics

Cinema has an ethical potential – for exploring moral issues, ethically charged situations or moral thought experiments – that has often been neglected in film theory. In more recent years, however, film-philosophy has been undergoing what might be described as an 'ethical turn', examining ethics in cinema from a variety of philosophical perspectives (Mulhall 2008; Shaw 2012; Wartenberg 2007) or exploring how filmmakers can be approached as engaging in ethics through film (Cooper 2006; Downing and Saxton 2010; Stadler 2008; Wheatley 2009). For the most part, ethical approaches to film tend to focus on one of three aspects of the relationship between film, spectator and context (Sinnerbrink 2016: 10–14). The first is ethics *in* cinema (focusing on narrative content such as dramatic scenarios involving morally charged situations, conflicts, decisions or actions). The second is the ethics *of* cinematic representation (focusing on the ethical issues raised by elements of film production and/or audience reception, e.g. debates in documentary theory concerning the ethics of informed consent in filming subjects or the ongoing debates in film and media theory over the effects of depictions of screen violence). The third is the ethics of cinema *as* a cultural medium expressing beliefs, social values or ideological perspectives (such as feminist film analysis of gender, examinations of 'race' in popular film or Marxist analyses of ideology in popular cinema). To these three perspectives we can add a fourth: the *aesthetic dimensions* of cinema as a way of evoking ethical experience and thereby expressing ethical meaning (the ethical significance, for example, of the use of long takes or non-narrative sequences drawing attention to perception, time or nature in slow or contemplative cinema).

All three aspects of ethics in relation to film are relevant for exploring Malick's work as a case of what I call 'cinematic ethics': the idea of cinema as a medium of ethical experience with a transformative potential to shift our horizons of meaning and thus deepen our moral understanding (see Sinnerbrink 2016). The idea of cinematic ethics can bring together all four dimensions of the cinema-ethics relationship: ethical content in narrative cinema; the ethics of cinematic representation (from filmmaker and spectator perspectives); the ethics of cinema as symptomatic of broader cultural, historical, ideological concerns; and the 'ethics of cinematic form' as exploring the ethical significance of cinematic aesthetics.

What do I mean by 'ethical experience' in the cinema? There are three strands to this idea. First, the shared cinematic experience of engaging with the perspectives, responses, actions or experiences of others (fictional characters) depicted in complex interpersonal, social, moral or political situations. Second, responses to the cinema where the viewer or spectator is moved to reflect ethically on what they are viewing, through their experience of emotional engagement, moral sympathy or critical reflection. And third, responses to cinematic experience that are brought about by aesthetic means and that aim at broadening our ethical horizons of meaning and deepening our moral understanding, typically by questioning or challenging the viewer's opinions, beliefs or attitudes.

From this point of view there is also the possibility of a film engaging in what we might call a 'negative ethics', that is, refusing to show or express any particular moral perspective, but to depict, rather, an ethically charged or morally challenging situation without either offering moral-psychological reasons to explain character actions or providing ethical judgements concerning their conduct. In such cases, the ethical experience evoked in the spectator is one of perplexity or confusion, a moral-cognitive dissonance that can provoke critical reflection or a reframing of one's moral-ethical assumptions, perhaps even a transformation in one's attitudes or beliefs.

In Malick's work, the ethics of cinematic form offers the most productive way of approaching his films. At the same time, his earlier as well as middle period works also offer cases of negative cinematic ethics foregrounding inexplicable expressions of violence coupled with emotional distance, the evocation of mood and poetic modes of cinematic presentation. In his later works, Malick offers a more 'positive' ethical perspective, one imbued with both existential-metaphysical and spiritual-religious overtones. It is through evoking experiences of wonder and perplexity, grace and confusion, or immanence and transcendence that his films not only offer aesthetic pleasure but also cultivate our moral imaginations and pose questions for ethical consideration. Let us consider Malick's first two films in this philosophical light, exploring how they evoke ethical concerns through their distinctive aesthetic style.

1

Approaching Cinematic Ethics: Badlands *and* Days of Heaven

I t is not uncommon for great art to be ignored or misunderstood when it first appears in the world. This has proved true for Malick's work as an artist. Hailed as an American classic today, Malick's first feature, *Badlands* (1973), was praised by many critics (its premiere at the New York Film Festival was favourably received), but it also met with mixed reviews, including negative ones, upon its commercial release. Pauline Kael, for example, declared it a self-conscious art movie that hints at things unspoken but we cannot really say what they are.

> The film is a succession of art touches. Malick is a gifted student, and 'Badlands' is an art thing, all right, but I didn't admire it, I didn't enjoy it, and I don't like it. (Kael 1977)

Kael's complaint concerns what she takes to be the film's 'negative' critique of mass culture and its deadening effects on youth, a rather literal and reductive interpretation of the film that misses what makes it aesthetically distinctive and ethically significant. *Days of*

Heaven (1978), his next feature, received praises for its beautiful cinematography (by Nestor Almendros, along with Haskell Wexler) and poetic presentation of landscape, but it was also criticized for being not only too 'pretty' but too emotionally distant to be a successful narrative film. Kael, again, dismissed the film as empty, lacking in character depth or narrative focus, remarking that, like a Christmas tree, 'you can hang all your dumb metaphors on it' (1982: 137). Kael's complaint echoes a long line of Malick critique that commenced with *Badlands* and *Days of Heaven* and continues – in increasingly harsh tones – to the present day: namely, that Malick films strip back narrative content, character presentation and plot development far too much, replacing these standard elements of narrative film with an emphasis on cinematic mood, poetic atmospherics or metaphysical themes. Although critics readily acknowledge the beauty of Malick's imagery, the success of his works as narrative films often remains in doubt.

One could respond to this charge in a number of ways. One could argue that, rather than fault Malick for not making conventional movies, we should praise him as a filmmaker exploring, indeed extending, the possibilities of narrative cinema, while working within, yet transforming, conventional genres. Or one could argue that Malick's films are essentially poetico-philosophical meditations and are thus best treated as non-conventional forms of narrative cinema with a distinctively existential slant. Or one could adopt a more radically aestheticist stance, arguing that Malick's films are first and foremost exercises in cinematic poetics, exploring the possibilities of cinematic style within highly abstracted narrative formats, and so should not be viewed as either conventional dramas or as philosophical narratives but rather as bold experiments in cinematic form.

Although there is truth in all three perspectives, I shall focus in what follows on Malick's films as cases of cinematic ethics, exploring and evoking ethical experience by distinctive aesthetic means. Indeed, even his early works, not generally regarded as 'philosophical', offer complex forms of ethical experience. Their fascinating combination of impressionistic character portrayal, minimal plot development and poetic disclosure of nature offers compelling ways of evoking varieties of ethical experience expressed in mythic and poetic form. Malick's first two films, moreover, also show a surprisingly consistent concern with moral questions concerning existential choice, the nature of love and the meaning of violence. They explore mythological, cultural, moral-religious and philosophical themes that will recur in Malick's oeuvre. With their lyrical voiceovers, mythical overtones and poetic moods, they offer striking cases of how cinema can explore ethical experience through aesthetic means.

'I got some stuff to say' (*Badlands*)

Consider Malick's directorial debut, which I saw as a student and have revisited many times over the years. I remember it being discussed in a university film class, which was supposed to explore the idea of aesthetic experience. My teacher, a well-known Australian cultural theorist, was trying to persuade his sceptical charges that beauty and aesthetic pleasure were not merely cultural constructs, addictive opiates peddled by a hegemonic ruling class. He cited *Badlands* and Ozu as cases of pure aesthetic pleasure, a counter-example to the postmodernist, 'cultural studies' scepticism towards art and beauty that was prevalent in the 1990s. My peers appeared unmoved by the *Badlands* clip he showed, but the scenes I saw were stunning; the movie has resonated with me ever since, along with a desire to communicate something of this experience.

The film is loosely based on the case of 20-year-old Charles Starkweather and 14-year-old Caril Ann Fugate – recast in the film as 25-year-old Kit Carruthers (Martin Sheen) and 15-year-old Holly Sargis (Sissy Spacek) – a young couple who go on a killing spree through the American Midwest during 1958–59. A number of generic features might strike the viewer on a first viewing. On the one hand, this is a 'true crime' story, combining elements of the Bonnie and Clyde/lovers-on-the-lam narrative. It is also an impressionistic road movie set in a very distinctive historical and geographical setting (the South Dakota town of Fort Dupree in 1958, following the fugitive couple all the way to the 'Badlands of North Dakota', as Holly tells us). On the other hand, it retains a personal, subjective quality, emphasized in Holly's naive, incongruous voiceover. This is combined with a mythic 'fairy tale' atmosphere that removes the story from its historical-factual setting and opens up a fantasy world in which psychological and social realism gives way to poetic reflection and mythic resonance. At the same time, the film comments on its cinematic references (Arthur Penn's *Bonnie and Clyde*), literary influences (Treasure Island, Tom Sawyer, Huckleberry Finn),[1] and on myths of American freedom and cultural history (Holly's immersion in teen romance stories, her naive speech and mundane reflections reflecting a 1950s Southern upbringing, Kit's idolization of James Dean, the 'gun crazy' theme marking their story and so on). Finally, it is Malick's arresting images of nature, place and landscape, evoking a densely textured world imbued with a mythic sense of unreality, which made this film so original and impressive. This unique combination of history and myth, romantic naivety and cinematic self-reflection, made *Badlands* a landmark in contemporary American cinema (see Campbell 2007; Patterson 2007).

It is clear, nonetheless, that *Badlands* is not often regarded as a philosophical, let alone 'Heideggerian', film in the ways that Malick's later efforts (after *The Thin Red Line*) would be.[2] At the same time, it is difficult to ignore the obvious moral question at the film's heart: What prompts an ordinary young romantic couple to go on a remorseless killing spree? What does this story of casual killing in the pursuit of freedom on the road encapsulate about late 1950s American culture? Although it does not offer any direct answers, *Badlands* addresses the mythic themes of freedom, authenticity, the pursuit of happiness and self-assertion through violence, which together define the mythology of American individualism and its role in American cultural-historical self-understanding. *Badlands* is, in this respect, an historical film with a strong focus on cultural mythology, as mediated via cinema and popular culture; moreover it is a film that reflects on its own status and condition as a cinematic work dealing precisely with such themes. Kit both resembles and emulates James Dean, as remarked by Holly in voiceover and by one of the state police who captures him. Holly's father (played by Warren Oates) is a commercial sign writer and is shown painting signs, painting a billboard in the isolated plains during one of the film's standout sequences and looking through his stereopticon viewfinder, which Holly also ruminates upon, wondering about her contingent existence in the world. Practices of image-making, perceiving images and projecting self-images abound in the movie, which retains a subtly self-reflexive character despite its obviously impressionistic tone and poetic atmosphere.

The film echoes scenes and motifs from Arthur Penn's *Bonnie and Clyde* but presented in a deadpan manner, staging while deflating the romantic myth of the fugitive couple, whose killing is bound up with their outsider status and 'forbidden' romance (Michaels 2009; Orr 2007). Although this theme is also foregrounded in *Bonnie and Clyde*, *Badlands* renders it in a far more deflationary manner. Holly remains passive and undemonstrative throughout the story; Kit's expressions of desire and affection are clichéd, flat and rudimentary.[3] Neither Kit nor Holly appears to have any emotional maturity or psychological insight into their predicament. Indeed, Kit may be emotionally disturbed, as Holly remarks; after Kit shoots his friend Cato (Ramon Bieri) in the stomach and deposits his body in a storage shed, we see Kit pacing up and down in front of the shed, violently flailing his arms and remonstrating with himself. Both characters are lacking in affect and emotional involvement, in critical self-reflection or moral conscience; they seem to be in a state of depression or despair, yet unable to communicate a condition that remains opaque even to themselves. Kit and Holly both appear to be drifting through life in search of meaning or purpose, finding it in a personal mythology of love and violence – characters that we might describe as in states of existential despair.[4] Although *Badlands* evokes some of the cinematic and cultural myths of outsider romantic couples, expressing their passion through violence, their fate as doomed to die through their self-chosen confrontation with society, it refuses to celebrate or romanticize this myth. Instead, the film deflates or ironizes it, offering an existential fable rather than a romantic critique. In place of aesthetic fascination with the outsider couple, we are offered an emotionally distanced, mood-evoking, cinematic meditation on the nature of this myth promulgated via Hollywood.

Badlands, moreover, reflects upon its own complicity in such cinematic mythmaking. Malick himself appears in an intriguing scene, playing an architect carrying blueprints, who has come to visit the rich man's house, where Kit and Holly are holding the occupants captive. He passes on a written message to Kit, who promptly throws it away (a wry joke on authorial intent and the search for 'meaning' in film). Kit then steals the rich man's hat and jacket, clearly imitating the Malick/architect figure as they flee in the rich man's Cadillac. In this respect, *Badlands* would qualify as a case of what Stephen Mulhall has called 'film in the condition of philosophy': films that reflect upon their conditions of possibility or that draw attention to – hence reflect upon – their own status as cinematic works presenting ideas via the medium of cinema itself (2008: 6–8). This concern with reflexively marking the status of the medium, while rendering cinematic mythmaking in aesthetically rich form, will continue to be a distinctive feature of Malick's oeuvre. None of these features are presented in an historical realist mode or as a modernist form of self-reflexivity but rather in a subjective, impressionistic, mythopoetic manner that Malick will develop further.

The opening sequence of *Badlands* includes many elements of what has since become recognizable as Malick's signature style. The opening shot depicts Holly on her bed playing with her beloved dog as the camera slowly moves from left to right around her, revealing her room, and accompanied by George Aliceson Tipton's melancholy score. Her voiceover, an artless, naive, deadpan narration, has been aptly described as vernacular poetry.

> My mother died of pneumonia when I was just a kid. My father had kept their wedding cake in the freezer for ten whole years. After the funeral he gave it to the yardman. He tried to act cheerful but he could never be consoled by the little stranger he found in his house. Then, one day, hoping to begin a new life away from the scene of all his memories, he moved us from Texas to Fort Dupree, South Dakota.

During Holly's voiceover, the film cuts to two wide street shots of Fort Dupree, in early morning stillness, an anonymous, sleepy, small town with little to distinguish it. A garbage truck rolls into view, and we are introduced to Kit, sporting a James Dean haircut, white T-shirt, jeans and boots and leaping off the truck. He is shown peering at a dead dog, asking his colleague (Cato) whether he'd eat the dog for a dollar. Kit's indifferent curiosity towards the dead dog contrasts sharply with

Holly's playful embrace of her beloved pet. He will be shown engaging with several other dogs (throwing an apple to one during his garbage round), later stepping on a dead steer, again with indifferent curiosity, while working at the cattle feedlot, whereas Holly's dog will be shot and dumped in the river by her father as punishment for seeing Kit. As for Holly, the one thing she mentions with regret, narrating her experiences with Kit from the perspective of the future, is that she threw out her sick catfish, which made her feel bad. The characters' curious proximity with animals and simultaneous indifference towards nature, contrasting with the sublimity of the landscapes they journey through, sets up a visual and narrative tension marking the entire film.[5]

After breaking off during the middle of his garbage round, Kit leaves Cato and wanders off aimlessly towards town, balancing an old mop on one hand and kicking cans around, before coming across Holly, practising her baton-twirling routine in the yard before her house. A mid-shot of Kit, as he spots Holly, shows him glancing furtively around to see if anyone is looking, then heading towards her to engage in conversation. As he approaches the house, the title 'Badlands' is superimposed over a long shot of the twirling Holly to the left of screen, with Kit wandering towards her from screen right, against the solidity of the family home in the background. All the key elements of the film are condensed in this shot, accompanied by Carl Orff and Gunild Keetman's 'Gassenhauer' (Street Song), a whimsical tune, arranged for children, that serves as a leitmotif for the film (it is adapted further in George Aliceson Lipton's score, which includes a piece mistakenly attributed to Orff).

These two characters, stripped back to the barest, minimal features, given little if any backstory, whose inner lives are left opaque, are presented in a lucid, non-judgemental light. Their actions and responses are depicted with an expressive clarity but without revealing their inner psychology, familial history or social background. As will become more pronounced in Malick's later films, they are presented more as mythical or allegorical figures than as psychologically developed, concretely individuated characters. Their stories take on the quality of myth, presenting the physical landscape and character's environment as expressive of their states of mind, while concealing their inner feelings or psychological responses. The central question posed by this mythic tale – Why do Kit and Holly go on their murderous crime spree? –remains unanswered throughout the film. Holly's voiceover, which combines naive artlessness and moments of lyrical poignancy with callous indifference and vacuous cliché, obscures rather than reveals the meaning of their violent adventure. Her romantic fantasies and adolescent naivety never fully grasp the measure and meaning of her own experiences. Kit's dialogue remains stilted and hackneyed, a combination of movie clichés, James Dean posturing and small-town truisms worthy of an 'Eisenhower conservative', to use Malick's phrase describing Kit's personality and outlook.[6]

The way the film presents Holly's father's killing (played by Warren Oates) is a case in point. In one of the most commented on scenes in the film, Kit drives out to a desolate sunlit plain in order to talk to Holly's father, who clearly disapproves of Holly's meetings with Kit. In a stunning sequence of long shots, showing the lurid farm advertisement billboard incongruously placed in an desolate empty plain, blasted with harsh sunlight, Kit asks permission, as it were, to see the man's daughter but is brusquely rebuffed. The film lingers on the father's attempts to ignore Kit's presence, refusing to look at him and focusing intently on the billboard patches he is painting. The billboard itself, a local advertisement featuring a garish, homely farm scene, has a missing panel through which we can see a patch of bright blue sky. The father finally turns to Kit and warns him to stay away from his daughter, a warning that Kit politely refuses, setting up the expectation of some kind of conflict. Kit leaves, only to learn that he has been fired from the garbage route, which releases him from his remaining tenuous links with the social community.

He returns to Holly's family home (a gun stuffed down the back of his jeans) apparently intending to take Holly away with him and prepared to use the gun if confronted. Kit's unnerving combination of folksy politeness and callous indifference is amply on display in this sequence, which shows the father confronting Kit, standing atop the staircase, noticing his gun and warning that he will have to call the police. The father turns and heads off-screen, pursued by Kit, who shouts and fires two shots into his back from close range. Cut to a shot revealing the father lying inertly on the ground, shocked and silent, attended by a mutedly distressed Holly, silent witness to the shooting, too stunned to comfort him.

Kit's reaction is extraordinary: a combination of indifference and irritation that the dying father presents an inconvenience, vaguely defending his action because of the threat to call the cops and half-heartedly apologizing to Holly for the unfortunate turn of events. In one of the few scenes where Holly responds through action, she slaps Kit, but remains silent, a strange pantomime of romantic tiff and immature playacting. Despite her pretence of anger, she soon meekly falls into line, follows Kit's instructions to help move her dying father to the cellar, before they resolve to burn down the house. This sequence that follows, commenced by Kit angrily dousing the piano and furniture with kerosene, turns powerfully poetic as the flames take hold, consuming Holly's 'childish things', her domestic space of family and memory, in a ritualistic destruction of the past through fire. The beautiful but terrifying conflagration, consuming toys, objects, furniture and the building, accompanied by Orff, takes on a sombre and funereal quality. We are witnessing an esoteric rite, a symbolic death and rebirth of Kit and Holly as placed outside the law, existing in their own private mythic world, a child's fairytale version of existential freedom and flight into the wilderness. They flee the burning house, now on the verge of collapse, rescuing some obscure domestic items (like a lamp). Kit leaves a surreal calling card, his fake suicide message recorded on a vinyl record recording (a popular means of recording testimonials to which Kit will have recourse again later in the film, at the height of their killing spree). The idea of recording himself, of leaving a message to posterity, of communicating something of import to the world ('I've got some things to say') is a recurring motif in the film. In the end, Kit communicates not through words but acts of violence – and a concern with images (above all, his own self-image).

Kit mediates his relationship with the world by using his gun, which, according to Malick, he thinks of as a 'magic wand' allowing him to get what he wants (quoted in Martin 2006). What Kit really wants, however, or for that matter what Holly does, remains obscure and confused throughout the film. He wants recognition of his unique individuality, but seeks it through cliché and stereotype. He wants to experience a romance with Holly, but remains indifferent and distant with her during their most intimate moments (their painfully passionless sexual encounter by the river). He wants notoriety as an outlaw but also regards his capture as an opportunity for celebrity attention, an obscure reward before being banished to prison and eventually executed.

Holly's desire remains even more opaque, despite her nominal role as narrator of the story. All she tells us is that Kit was strange, that he wanted her to scream out his name when he died; their parting of ways is as flat and desultory as their initial encounter. Holly, as she narrates, ends up marrying the son of her attorney. The romantic myth of achieving authentic identity by rejecting

convention through forbidden romance and moral transgression
has rarely been deflated more effectively. As the plane carrying Holly
away from the Badlands ascends through the clouds, their mythic
adventure ends inconclusively and anti-climatically. There are no
answers offered concerning why Kit and Holly act as they did, no
obvious critique of the social reality in which they find themselves
or no moral criticism of the deadening effects of mass cultural
distraction or the romanticization of violence. What persists is a
poetic, thought-provoking existential-moral fable on love, one that
both deflates romantic myths while also staging and exploring these
in cinematic terms. This fascination with romanticism, myths of
love and an opaque allegory of cultural history and memory will be
explored more explicitly in Malick's next film, *Days of Heaven*, which
adds a dimension of religious/theological allegory to the romantic
myth of lovers outside the law. It also anchors this mythic treatment
in a definite historical moment, while at the same time retaining a
remarkably mythic, timeless, sense of beauty and tragedy.

'God don't even hear you' (*Days of Heaven*)

Malick's second feature, *Days of Heaven* (1978), offers another mythically
rendered tragic love story with strong theological resonances.[7] Set in
the Texas Panhandle just before the First World War, and combining
poetic landscape and historical realism with expressive anachronism,
the film also draws attention to our mediated relationship with the
past and to its own status as a cinematic artefact presenting a stylized
fictional world. It opens with a remarkable title sequence, set to Saint-
Saëns whimsical, melodically haunting piece, 'Aquarium' (the seventh
movement of the 'Carnival of the Animals'). It consists of a sequence
of sepia-toned photographic images from the turn of the century,

including a stunning shot of a man leaping across a rocky abyss, anonymous historical streetscapes and naturalistic portraiture. As Kendall notes, this opening sequence is clearly modelled on a series of iconic turn-of-the-century photographic images – including images by Lewis Hine, H. H. Bennett and others – and includes allusions to iconic American painters whose work provides direct models for particular shots, including 'Andrew Wyeth's *Christina's World* and Edward Hopper's *The House by the Railroad*, as well as images and situations reminiscent of paintings by Pieter Bruegel the Elder, Gustave Courbet, and Jean-François Millet' (Kendall 2011: 150–151). It concludes with an imitative fictional image of a street urchin, a girl who turns out to be the narrator Linda (Linda Manz), staring warily at the camera. Coupled with the title, a biblical quotation from Deuteronomy,[8] the opening announces what follows as combining historical authenticity, aesthetic mediation and mythic-religious allegory.

The opening scene is similarly arresting but also disorienting. The protagonist, Bill (Richard Gere), is working in a steel factory depicted as a cross between industrial 'satanic mill' and elemental cauldron of suppressed energies. He gets into an argument with the foreman, the nature of which remains unclear, and strikes the man in a fit of anger, apparently injuring or killing him. He flees the mill, watched mutely by his co-workers, his actions marked by a deafening cacophony of machine and fire, the whole sequence presented in a psychologically flat, distanced manner, visually striking but aurally assaultive, confusing, devoid of dialogue or orienting narrative background. He is shown finding solace with his beloved, Abby (Brooke Adams), accompanied by his younger sister Linda (Linda Manz), the unreliable narrator of the film. Her voiceovers, far more nuanced, insightful and engaging than Holly's flat narration, will both comment upon and come into tension with the images we see on screen. She is perceptive and observant, with rich descriptions suggesting a kind of vernacular poetry, despite the limited perspective defining her narration as the film unfolds.

> Me and my brother – it just used to be me and my brother. We used to do things together. We used to have fun. We used to roam the streets. There was people sufferin' of pain and hunger. Some people, their tongues were hangin' out of their mouth. ... I met this guy called Ding Dong. He told me the whole earth is goin' up in flames. Flames will come out of here and there ... and they'll just rise up. The mountains are gonna go up in big flames. The water's gonna rise in flames. There's gonna be creatures runnin' every which way ... some of them burned, half their wings burnin'. People are gonna be screaming' and hollerin' for help. See, the people that have been good, they're gonna go to heaven ... and escape all that fire. But if you've been bad, God don't even hear you. He don't even hear you talkin'.

The three fugitives, anonymous representative of a whole class of itinerant, pre-industrial workers, join the seasonal movement of wheat pickers heading towards the wheat fields to work at harvest time. The film lingers on breathtaking pastoral landscape shots – the beautifully composed wide shot image of a train crossing a wooden box bridge suspended high over an abyss, an emblematic image of the tragic love myth to follow – poignant images of travelling itinerant workers and the excitement of the new technological world (the railway) confronting the mythical premodern agrarian cycles of nature (the fields and harvest time).

These opening sequences also offer an expressive portrait of Bill, Abby and Linda that again presents them as allegorical types within a modern morality tale set at the mythical threshold of the twentieth century, rather than distinctive characters with a personal psychological world embedded within a definite historical time and place. The final character in the story, another allegorically presented personage, known simply as 'the Farmer' (Sam Shepard) is the lonely and distant owner of the farm, overseeing his crops and workers like a benevolent director or master of ceremonies. The basic elements of the mythic love triangle are now in place, articulated with visual complexity, musical mood setting, evocative voiceover and expressive use of light, colour and movement.

Although the film begins with a dramatic event, motivating the flight of the trio and marking their outsider status, much of it focuses more on revealing or expressing, through mood and affect, the world they inhabit. Narrative drive is subordinated to poetic expression. We are shown the brutality of the factories; the lure of the open road; the beauty of the landscape; the physical labour involved in harvesting; the pleasure in nature, movement and existence; and all the ambiguous insinuations of romantic love. Bill, Abby and Linda's journey to the wheat fields, for example, joining an anonymous group of itinerant workers, focuses on the mass of humanity they are part of, packed into trains and braving the elements. It features stunning landscape shots reminiscent of Bruegel and Hopper (*The House by the Railroad*), mostly shot at the 'magic hour', which add an elemental poetry and lyrical poignancy to the mythic tale unfolding before us. Elements of realism are mixed with romanticism, historical detail with mythic allegory; psychological realism gives way to poetic expression, social realism to mythic poetry, historical drama to religious allegory – an aesthetic movement apt to reveal, in cinematic splendour, 'the days of heaven upon the earth'.

The story, elemental and mythic, recalling the biblical tale of Ruth, depicts the outlaw couple, colluding to deceive the farmer, who is dying of an undisclosed disease.[9] Abby courts his attention and subtly feeds his attraction, while maintaining her secret relationship with Bill, the two planning to benefit from the farmer's imminent demise. Things do not go as planned, however, as suspicions around the trio begin to grow:

co-workers provoke Bill about his clandestine 'incestual' relationship, while the farmer's taciturn foreman (Robert J. Wilke) suspects the pair are plotting to deceive the farmer, warning Bill, in a chilling scene, that he knows what the pair are doing. Tensions mount between the clandestine lovers as Abby realizes she is falling in love with the farmer, fuelling Bill's jealousy. The farmer also begins to suspect something disturbing about the pair's intimacy with each other, setting the two men on a tragic collision course that can only end in death.

Like *Badlands*, the dramatic arc of *Days of Heaven* is organized and expressed in elemental terms. Landscape stands for the expression of character emotion and mental states, while the characters themselves appear as figures inhabiting a landscape that transcends and frames their personal situation. Like *Badlands*, the dramatic turning point or caesura is marked by catastrophic fire, marking the transition from love triangle to tragic myth. Indeed, as though to mark the violation of which they are guilty in their deception of the farmer, a biblical plague of locusts descends on the farm, sparking a panicked attempt to use fire to drive the pests away and restore disrupted natural, social and moral orders. What follows is a tragic personification of suppressed emotions, a biblical conflagration, caused by the farmer lighting crops to drive out the dreaded locusts, his suspicions and jealously towards Bill having reached incendiary proportions. The two men clash against a fiery backdrop, the farmer unleashing the flames as the two men confront each other, consuming fire personifying their violent antipathy. In a contingent moment of anger, ostensibly in self-defence, Bill stabs the farmer, fatally wounding him. Like *Badlands*, the fugitive lovers (and their 'child') now have to flee, forced out of their Edenic garden – the farmer's bounteous property between harvest times – before being expelled and then pursued by the law.

Malick's pointed use of the natural elements – earth, fire, air/sky and water – gives film a mythic quality, in contrast with the elements of historical realism punctuating the film. Again like *Badlands*, the mythic love story is combined with moments of reflection on the manner in which this film narrative and its world are represented. A good example is the remarkable sequence where a contingent of travelling circus performers – arriving in the fictional guise of First World War biplane fighters – momentarily suspends the increasing tension in the farmer's household. The performers stage impromptu plays for the trio, their playacting and veiled innuendo suggesting an awareness of what is happening. They organize a screening of Chaplin's *The Immigrant* (1917) in a pointed moment of allegory – the performances perhaps suggesting a cuckolding scenario – that not only alludes to the lovers' deception but marks a moment of the film's self-reflection concerning the cinematic status of myth, romance and tragedy, to which we are witness.

Again like *Badlands*, the protagonists are more like allegorical personages than fully fleshed characters with a complex psychological life and intelligible motivations. Actions occur spontaneously, in the heat of the moment, rather than as the expression of firmly held beliefs or rationally elaborated plans. The biblical resonance adds an allegorical dimension to this historical tale that lends its tragic denouement both moral-spiritual and cultural-historical significance. Bill's tragic capture and death (shot in the back as he flees, his face plunging directly into the water) ends the myth and returns his lover and his sister to social reality. The story ends, on an open note, with Abby now inheriting the farm; Abby brings Linda into town depositing her at a boarding school, from which she almost immediately escapes, off to have new adventures.

The film leaves us with questions rather than answers, mood-like evocations of atmosphere rather than articulated plot development or satisfying narrative conclusions. No explanation of Bill's actions is given other than the affective pressure and contingent motivation of the particularities of the moment and the ambiguous dynamics of his relationship with Abby. Instead of a psychologically driven drama or tragic love story, the film offers a poetic reflection on love and loss in the form of historically situated poetic myth. The film both stages and subverts the myth of America as the land of opportunity, where everyone can find liberty and happiness and where lovers can find meaning and purpose in their adventures on the road. The mythic form itself is revealed as part of what defines the opaque and unstable identities of these ephemeral personages. More akin to allegorical figures than dramatic characters, their relationship with the world remains rootless and contingent, driven hither and thither by the whims of desire and circumstance.

Again, like *Badlands*, *Days of Heaven* was criticized for the tension it sets up between beautiful imagery and abstract narrative, its emphasis on the poetics of mood rather than the psychology of emotional engagement. Its meditative qualities hint at allegorical significance, exposing while exploring myths of nature and of America; but it also offers subtle reflections on the potential of cinema as medium of mythopoetic evocation and aesthetic expression. There is, however, no particular moral message the film seeks to convey; rather, it offers the possibility of morally charged reflection in response to the aesthetic pleasure in visual presentation and an indeterminate cathartic release through the evocation of mood. The desolate beauty of the landscape shots is coupled with the tragic resonances of the mythic love triangle, all of these visual and narrative elements resonating in a stylized mythic space that is at once historical and existential.

In both of these films, the mythic rendering of a love story with existential overtones anticipates much of Malick's later work. It is also striking, viewed from the vantage point of Malick's later films, that these are both love stories involving existentially groundless, 'weightless' characters who fail to imbue their own experience with any social substance or moral insight. Both of these films feature tragic love stories that are resolved through violence, where the quest to find fulfilment through romantic love ends in violence, isolation and self-destruction (for the male character) or uncertain liberation (for the female character). The two couples' quest for Edenic redemption by fleeing into the wilderness to escape the fallen world of modernity is thwarted by the tragic return of law, judgement and secular justice, but also tinged by the fragile possibility of renewal or rebirth. There are no religious or spiritual forms of reconciliation to be found here, just the mythologically charged attempt to elevate a flawed, naive conception of romantic love to the level of existential and moral redemption by means of violence or escape. This theme will return in Malick's later films, which adapt and explore quite different genres (war film, historical myth, family melodrama/memory film, contemporary experimental love story). The theme of the insufficiency of romantic love will be broadened and contextualized by transposing the mythic dimension towards more explicitly philosophical, historical and theological sources of allegorical meaning.

Malick's style

From a cinematic perspective, these two films lay down the foundations of Malick's visual style, which will be developed and modified over his career and taken to an extreme pitch in his later films. There are six that I shall highlight here. (1) A minimalist presentation of character, with little offered by way of psychological or social background, and a corresponding diminution in the presentation of psychological interiority in favour of gesture, physical movement and emotional ambiguity. (2) An emphasis on place and location, whether landscape, urban environment or domestic interior, which provide not just a backdrop but an aesthetic expression of these character's opaque moods and inchoate feelings, where these moods both link and express world and character. (3) A pointed use of voiceover, which often does not correspond with what we see on screen, offering a complicating counterpoint or ambiguous self-reflection rather than a psychologically revealing insight into the character's subjective states. (4) An attenuation of narrative form into loose episodic sequences, structured mainly by visual, aural and musical motifs, the capturing of contingent moments and the expression of mood rather than by character action, psychological motivation or teleological plot development. (5) The use of an ever mobile, questing, flowing camera, whose perspective not only provides a sense of animated witnessing, a 'spiritual' (disembodied) presence, rather than a conventional narrative point of view or character display structuring action, modulating emotional engagement and organizing viewer attention. Finally (6), a mise-en-scene emphasizing the life of objects, the 'elemental' presentation of earth, sky and fire, with a ubiquitous focus on light, an encompassing, enveloping atmospheric and expressive medium of aesthetic as well as spiritual value. The latter again stands in not only for the expression of character states of mind but for an atmospheric disclosure of their shared world and its existential significance.

Taken together, we have all the elements of Malick's 'signature style' already appearing in his earliest feature films, which are both love stories combined with cultural-historical myth, poetic allegories with existential resonances, cinematic meditations on subjectivity and world. After these two remarkable debut films, however, Malick more or less disappeared from public view. It would be twenty years before the release of Malick's next feature, *The Thin Red Line*. This was a film that, for me, genuinely opened up the question of film as philosophy.

2

Philosophy Encounters Film: The Thin Red Line

When I was a graduate student in the 1990s, going to the movies was a regular feature of my weekly routine. Not only did Sydney have, at that time, a lively film scene with a range of independent cinemas; there were also weekly 'Cinematheque' screenings at the Chauvel Theatre in Paddington (named after a famous Australian cineaste), a venue where one could gain a decent understanding of film history thanks to weekly screenings covering different genres, periods and styles. I had first seen *Badlands* at one of the weekly sessions dedicated to American independent cinema of the 1970s and had been mesmerized. I hadn't seen *Days of Heaven* until a dinner invitation one evening to a friend's house near the university (a well-known American Deleuzian scholar living in Sydney at the time). After a lovely dinner we enjoyed a communal viewing of Malick's second film with our friends over wine, one of the few films I could imagine working well in such an intimate, convivial atmosphere.

At that time I was deeply immersed in my doctoral research, having returned after six months in Berlin as a graduate student, where I had been busy attending seminars on Hegel, Heidegger and aesthetics. After my return I had been involved in various postgraduate reading groups, one of which focused on Deleuze's two *Cinema* books. I enjoyed this experience a great deal but was slightly troubled by the tendency to subordinate cinema to philosophy, reducing complex films to apt examples of Deleuzian concepts. The idea of 'film as philosophy' was still no more than an intuition at that point, but I had the sense that cinema had a more independent contribution to make to philosophical thinking. In the (antipodean) Summer of 1999, I went to a screening of *The Thin Red Line* at a local cinema with some postgraduate friends, having heard that Malick's film was a highly unusual war movie, far more experimental than Spielberg's *Saving Private Ryan*, which had also screened over the summer. I didn't really know what to expect but was keen to see the film, given my growing interest in film and philosophy coupled with what I had heard about the reclusive Malick, having emerged out of a twenty-year obscurity since his last film, *Days of Heaven*.

From the opening images of a crocodile descending into murky green waters, light filtering through a rainforest canopy, to shots of children playing and diving into the ocean – accompanied by the 'In Paradisum' section of Faure's Requiem – I was captivated and amazed by what I saw on screen. The first voiceover in the film, famously misattributed to Witt (but recited by Train, a fact that is impossible to discern on first viewing the film[1]), was unlike anything I had seen or heard in a war movie:

> What is this war at the heart of nature? Why does nature vie with itself? The land contend with the sea? Is there an avenging power in nature? Not one power, but two?

More than twenty years after that initial viewing, this opening sequence still moves me, even though I have watched the film many times since. At the time I wondered about my response to *The Thin Red Line* – why I found it so powerful; I wanted to reflect on how it made me feel and what it made me think. I also pondered what seemed to be the movie's merging of a distinctive aesthetic style with pervasive 'philosophical' resonances: its use of music and tableau shots; its slow pacing, meditative images of nature interspersed between scenes of battle; its poetic, questioning voiceovers; and its existential reflections on the meaning of war, violence and mortality. On the other hand, some of my friends who had also seen the film were irritated, sceptical or disparaging towards it, reflecting common responses to the movie at the time, split between passionate devotees and sceptical critics. I remember the awkward and unpleasant experience of walking out of the cinema after the movie had ended, still awash with the mood and feeling of the film, in that heightened state of awareness and aroused sensibility characteristic of aesthetic experiences, only to find my companions complaining about the film, mocking its pretensions and clearly relieved it was over.

What was going on? How could a film that had moved me so much, prompting all sorts of reflections, have had such a different effect on my peers? This experience of aesthetic wonder and philosophical perplexity has stayed with me ever since. It helped shift my focus and perspective in philosophy and to question how it might be pursued, especially in relation to art and to cinema. After completing my PhD (on Hegel and Heidegger) in 2001, and being fortunate enough to secure an academic position, I felt freed up to find my own path, to explore my own questions, those for which I was best placed to respond. I began to write about the relationship between philosophy and film in the early to mid-2000s (coinciding with the release of *The New World* in 2005) in many ways inspired by, and working through, my experience of *The Thin Red Line*. Malick's films were an essential catalyst and motivation for that journey; *The Thin Red Line* was what prompted me to consider more seriously the question of the relationship between film and philosophy. Indeed, the book you are reading provides an opportunity to explore some of the questions that first set me on this path twenty years ago – inspired by that viewing of *The Thin Red Line* – and that still inspire my passion for how film might be regarded as contributing to philosophy by cinematic means.

One of the articles that motivated me to consider the problem of film and philosophy in depth was Simon Critchley's 'Calm – On Terrence Malick's *The Thin Red Line*' (2002) published in the online journal *Film-Philosophy*. Resonating with ideas from Stephen Mulhall's recently published *On Film* (2002), exploring the idea of film as philosophy via the *Alien* tetralogy, I became fascinated, thanks to these texts, by the idea that cinema might be a means of philosophical engagement, even a way of exploring thought through images. Critchley's discussion of *The Thin Red Line* as both inviting and eluding philosophical comprehension inspired me to engage with the film philosophically. Of course the fact that *The Thin Red Line* had been described as 'philosophical', indeed as 'Heideggerian', naturally piqued my interest. As a graduate student I had often borrowed our library's copy of Heidegger's *The Essence of Reasons*, noting vaguely that the translator's name was the same as the filmmaker; yet I unthinkingly assumed that they must have been two different individuals, the one a filmmaker, the other a philosopher. It was only much later that I realized, to my chagrin, that they were one and the same person: Terrence Malick, filmmaker *and* philosopher.

What is 'Heideggerian cinema'?

A filmmaker who is also a philosopher is a strange and intriguing creature. One who had translated Heidegger, and lectured on his work, was even more so to me; but what was one to make of this intriguing connection? Had Malick's background in phenomenology, in particular Heidegger's philosophy, influenced his approach to filmmaking? Did it play an important role in *The Thin Red Line*? These questions presented themselves to me (and many others) in response to this remarkable film, which was not only aesthetically powerful but also philosophically suggestive (see Rhym 2010 and Woessner 2011). At the same time, the conjunction of Heidegger and cinema seemed peculiar, even confusing. I knew there was little that Heidegger had actually written concerning cinema, and the few remarks on the subject one can find make it clear that he considered cinema and photography to be forms of technical image-making signifying the 'end of art' in the age of technology.[2] Given Heidegger's scepticism concerning film, what was one to make of the frequent talk of 'Heideggerian cinema' that *The Thin Red Line* seemed to provoke?

I found myself oscillating between linking Malick to Heidegger and then wondering what this might actually mean, or even whether it was aesthetically or philosophically legitimate. For some Malick scholars, however, there was no question here to ponder; Marc Furstenau and Leslie MacAvoy, for example, argued that Malick's *The Thin Red Line* offered a paradigmatic case of Heideggerian cinema (2003). For one thing, there was Malick's background in philosophy and expertise on Heidegger: he had studied philosophy with Stanley Cavell, taught philosophy at the MIT, teaching courses for noted Heidegger scholar Hubert Dreyfus, and had produced, as we know, a scholarly translation of Heidegger's *Vom Wesen des Grundes* (Malick 1969). Malick seemed set on a promising academic career as a phenomenologist when he abandoned philosophy to become a filmmaker. Drawing on these biographical facts, Furstenau and MacAvoy argued that Malick clearly 'transformed his knowledge of Heidegger in cinematic terms' (2003: 175), a knowledge that came to fruition in *The Thin Red Line* (1998).[3]

A stronger reason to regard Malick's films as Heideggerian, for Furstenau and MacAvoy, is their philosophical complexity and aesthetic texture. Citing Cavell, they point to Malick's philosophical concern with the self-reflexive character of the cinematic image, the way the structures of presence and absence that shape metaphysical thinking are re-enacted through the technology of the cinema. According to Cavell, Malick artistically explores this play between presence and absence, or the difference between (present) beings and their (concealed) Being. Already in *Days of Heaven*, Malick explores the parallel, important for Cavell's own work, between metaphysical and cinematic representation (Cavell 1979: xiv–xv). As Cavell remarks, *Days of Heaven* does indeed have a metaphysical vision of the world, but 'one feels that one has never quite seen the scene of human existence – call it the arena between earth (or days) and heaven – quite realized this way on film before' (1979: xiv–xv). On this Cavellian-inspired approach, it is the conscious exploration of this parallel that makes Malick an exemplary philosophical filmmaker: 'The task of a philosophically engaged cinema', Furstenau and McAvoy maintain, 'is to address both the inherent reflexivity of the film image, as well as the potential consequences of the transformation of the world into image' (2003: 176).

Malick's Heideggerianism, however, is not just a matter of the reflexivity of his cinematic work, or even a consequence of the technological transformation of reality into a stock of representational images. Echoing Heidegger on Hölderlin, Furstenau and McAvoy suggest that we should regard Malick as a cinematic poet responding to the forgetting of Being characteristic of the modern age: 'Malick has assumed the role of poet-philosopher ... revealing through the use of poetic, evocative imagery the cinema's unique presencing of Being' (2003: 177). Much like Hölderlin and Rilke, Malick's cinema can be taken as a form of poetic revealing or bringing-forth, a way of reawakening our lost sense of Being, of finitude and mortality, in a technological world that reduces the presencing of Being to a stock of representational world-images.

I have always found this approach to Malick tempting, especially in regard to *The Thin Red Line*; at the same time, I remained somewhat sceptical of the assumption that a 'Heideggerian cinema' is something that goes without saying. As Critchley remarks, we should be wary of reading the film solely through the lens of Malick's biography (2002); the fact that Malick studied Heidegger does not necessarily imply his films must be Heideggerian (whatever that should turn out to mean). Moreover, even if we can recognize 'Heideggerian' aspects in his films – such as a focus on mortality and finitude, the possibility of authentic existence and our relationship with Being – this should not blind us to other dimensions of their aesthetic and philosophical complexity. It seemed to me also important to note that Malick's work has affinities with the tradition of American transcendentalism, embracing figures such as Emerson and Thoreau, not to mention Cavell (combining Heidegger, Wittgenstein and Kierkegaard, as in Malick's failed dissertation topic). Rather, it seemed more important to reflect on the question of the relationship between Malick and philosophy, in particular the relationship between Heidegger and *The Thin Red Line*, rather than assume this connection as the key for any philosophical reading of his work. As ever in film-philosophy, we need to attend to the film and not just the philosophy, focusing as well on the relation or connection – signalled by the hyphen – between them. For in searching exclusively for the philosophical significance of a work, what risks disappearing from view is the film *as a film*: the detail of its narrative structure, the significance of its characters and their situation, the complexity of its sound and imagery, which is precisely how all of the former is established and communicated. Malick's work emphasizes this so starkly that any attentive philosophical viewer must come to grips with what it means to find philosophy expressed in such poetically rich audiovisual form. At the same time, the question as to why *this* particular style of cinematic presentation is expressive of certain philosophically suggestive motifs also presents itself insistently. This dual concern – with Malick's distinctive audiovisual style and intriguingly philosophical thematics – returns repeatedly in the critical literature on his work.

Malick as phenomenologist of finitude

Despite recognizing the importance of this insight, there was 'something about Malick' (to quote a recent article on the topic) that kept me returning to the Heideggerian question, especially in the case of *The Thin Red Line*.[4] Another piece that impressed me, arguing that this was indeed Heideggerian cinema, was Kaja Silverman's essay, 'All Things Shining' (2003), in which she emphasizes Malick's Heideggerian existential phenomenological vision of mortality and finitude. If Furstenau and MacAvoy read Malick as a Heideggerian poet in destitute times, Silverman interprets Malick as a Heideggerian existential phenomenologist concerned to evoke 'the Nothing' (*das Nichts*) in our experience of finitude and indeed of Being itself. While Furstenau and MacAvoy rely on the later, post-turn (post-*Kehre*) Heidegger of 'What are Poets For?' ' … Poetically Man Dwells … ' and 'The Question Concerning Technology', Silverman focuses instead on the Heidegger of *Being and Time*, Division II and the famous 1929 Freiburg lecture, 'What Is Metaphysics?' (Heidegger 1993: 93–110). For Silverman, it is clear that Malick's concerns are more philosophical than conventionally narratological (2003: 324), which explains the perplexity many critics and viewers experience when confronted with this idiosyncratic version of the war film genre. For Silverman, this means we should take *The Thin Red Line* to be principally a philosophical work, according to which Heideggerian thinking provides the key to understanding the film.

I think this observation provides a clue to the mystery (why take this film to be Heideggerian?), which I did not perceive until much later. It is because of the perplexity induced by this very peculiar take on the war film genre that many critics and theorists reached for philosophy to provide a hermeneutic frame of reference for understanding the film more generally. It is because of the powerful aesthetic experience the film solicits, with its strongly existentialist resonances, that many critics and theorists turned to philosophy, or in this case Heidegger, in order to articulate this experience by means of philosophical concepts. This of course leaves open the justification for turning to philosophy in order to make sense of one's experience of film. It also leaves open whether the account of the film one offers reveals something important about it or falls prey to Wartenberg's 'imposition objection' (2007: 25 ff.): that philosophers tend to impose, rather than find or uncover, a philosophical framework onto a film, which provides a hermeneutic basis for the claim that the film is philosophical. At the same time, I had (and continue to have) the strong impression that it is not simply a matter of blind imposition on the part of philosophers, who are typically charged with being insensitive to aesthetic expression or to cinematic style. Rather, we are dealing here with cases of philosophical film interpretation, analysis and criticism that aim to account for both the film's aesthetic impact *and* its philosophical suggestiveness.

Like Furstenau and MacAvoy, Silverman too regards *The Thin Red Line* as philosophy, a vision grounded in Heidegger's account of authentic being-toward-death (as explored in *Being and Time*, Division II) and his arresting reflections on the anxiety-inducing encounter with 'the Nothing' (examined in Heidegger's 1929 essay, 'What Is Metaphysics?'). As she explains, Heidegger's being-toward-death is less an account of a limit to existence than a way of existing in the world as a finite being, as a contingent self that is grounded in 'the Nothing' (Silverman 2003: 334). We could describe it less as a way of embracing death than a way of affirming life by 'living toward' our finite end. It is this aesthetically mediated experience of existential confrontation with *mortality* – of 'an almost unbearable negativity' evoked by the film – that prompts her recourse to Heidegger's thinking (2003: 324).

Indeed, *The Thin Red Line*, Silverman suggests, takes phenomenology to a place where Heidegger himself was not capable of bringing it: namely 'the battlefield' (2003: 326). It is here that we encounter finitude in its rawest sense; the experience of 'the nothing' that dissolves our spurious independence, our inauthentic everyday self (*das Man-Selbst*), and radically individualizes us to a core existential self, revealing our 'groundless' mortality or temporal finitude. Far from exulting in negativity and violence, however, Malick's explorations of mortality are oriented by philosophical, ethical and spiritual concerns.[5] For Silverman, Private Witt's journey is one that transpires through an authentic affective relationship to his own mortality, his 'confrontation with the nonbeing that grounds him' (Silverman 2003: 331). Like Critchley (2002), she argues that this confrontation is manifested through his affective relationship with death, that is, through the affective state or mood of *calm*, or what the later Heidegger called *Gelassenheit* or releasement towards things. The metaphysical dimension of *The Thin Red Line*, Silverman argues, is centred on this affective encounter with non-being and finitude – an affective experience, disclosed through cinematic images, that might reawaken a sense of Being itself in its plurality and plenitude.

The film's opening question, in voiceover, sets the scene for this meditation on violence and mortality: 'What is this war at the heart of nature?' Silverman describes what follows as Witt's phenomenological journey, his experience in locating the conflict first in nature, then attributing the conflict to an external invading force, this 'evil' that possesses us, 'mocking what we might have known', as Witt (but actually Train) says. For Silverman, Witt learns, however, that this violence that stains our being is not due to a nature at odds with itself or to a corruption of our own nature; rather, it is due to our failure to confront our own mortality, our finitude as beings defined by our living-toward-death. War has an existential-ontological basis, rather than a psychological, historical or political one: 'we kill each other like this because we have not yet succeeded in apprehending in the indeterminateness of the "nothing", the indeterminateness of being' (Silverman 2003: 337). Cut off from Being, 'like a coal thrown from the fire', we revert to this brutal violence as a way of making manifest the disturbing, uncanny nature of 'the Nothing' from which we flee or from which we distract ourselves, trying to negate this insight through violence.

The counterpoint to violence is wonder, the openness to Being, manifested in Malick's extraordinary images of nature that punctuate the film, granting it a unique poetic resonance and contemplative mood. The Nothing that appears to be the source of life and death, however, can also give rise to what makes us most human, to the 'affirmative affects': to 'glory, mercy, peace, truth ... calm of spirit, understandin', courage, the contented heart' (Silverman 2003: 337). This is not merely a psychological feeling or private emotion so much as a shared Heideggerian *Stimmung*: a world-disclosing mood that is also a mode of understanding and of practical engagement. *The Thin Red Line* evokes many such moods – anxiety, boredom, dread, despair, wonder, joy, love – as ways of disclosing our being-toward-death, which, as Silverman repeats, is less a way of dying than of living through our mortal end.

The affect of *calm*, for example, provides the appropriate mood or *Stimmung* for apprehending our finitude; a mood pervading the sequence depicting the death of Witt's mother and Witt's own confrontation with death in saving his fellow soldiers. Witt's death is the conclusion of his phenomenological journey; having understood the nature of this mortal conflict at the heart of nature, which is a conflict with our own mortal nature, Witt literally 'runs forward' into death (recalling Heidegger's 'anticipatory resoluteness'), embracing it as of a piece with the life of the jungle forest clearing in which he is shot. 'O my soul, let me be in you now' an unattributed narrator intones,[6] over images of the wake of the patrol boat departing from the island over dark waters. 'Look out through my eyes. Look out at the things you made. All things shining.' With these final words, as Silverman remarks, we are returned to the finite world, now illuminated by wonder. The film's final lesson is profound: we can affirm Being, encounter the Nothing, only by experiencing this phenomenal world and our own mortality within it; moreover, this philosophical or existential insight can only be experienced affectively from a particular point of view, which the film excels in presenting with illuminating power and clarity. As Silverman puts it, *The Thin Red Line* literally shows how 'we can affirm the world only through a very particular pair of eyes' (2003: 340) – where these particular eyes merge with a shared experience of mortality, of our finite, precarious existence.

The mood of calm that pervades the film is an important insight, as I discuss presently, and certainly underlines the existential *Stimmung* of the film. At the same time, however, Silverman's approach assumes that we can talk about Malick's cinema, and *The Thin Red Line* in particular, as 'Heideggerian' in a straightforward sense. Although they emphasize different aspects of Heidegger's thought, Furstenau, MacAvoy and Silverman all assume that we can subsume the film within a philosophical framework that would explain its thematic content and aesthetic style. This strongly 'Heideggerian' approach applies philosophy to film or reads film in light of a given philosophical framework, without, however, raising the question of the relationship between philosophy and film, which is what a reading in the spirit of Heidegger's thought, it seemed to me, might be expected to do.

Malick as cinematic philosopher

So how should one approach *The Thin Red Line*, given its existentialist mood and Heideggerian resonances? Addressing this question drew me to Simon Critchley's highly influential piece on *The Thin Red Line* (2002), one that was decisive for my reflections on film and philosophy in Malick's work.[7] How to approach a film that is both aesthetically challenging and invites philosophical reflection? What was the relationship between these two aspects? Critchley's piece focuses on the question of cinema and philosophy, counselling caution or even scepticism towards the idea that philosophy provides a preferred way of understanding Malick's film (or indeed any film). Indeed, Silverman, Furstenau and MacAvoy, all risk slipping on what Critchley dubs the three 'hermeneutic banana skins' that confront philosophical critics of Malick's work: (1) fetishizing Malick the enigmatic auteur, (2) being seduced by Malick's intriguing relationship with philosophy and (3) reducing the matter of Malick's film to a philosophical meta-text that would provide the key to its meaning. Doing film-philosophy, as Critchley observes, is a risky undertaking: 'To read from cinematic language to some philosophical metalanguage is both to miss what is specific to the medium of film and usually to engage in some sort of

cod-philosophy deliberately designed to intimidate the uninitiated'
(Critchley 2005: 139).

This was a powerful insight, outlining a danger I was conscious of
trying to avoid, while remaining perplexed as to why the film seemed
to elicit philosophical responses. Critchley's point, however, was to
emphasize the cooperative nature of this encounter: a philosophical
reading does not mean reading *through* the film to a framing
philosophical meta-text, but presenting a reading *of* the film as itself
engaged in philosophical reflection. A philosophical reading does
not rely on a pre-given philosophical framework but, in the spirit
of phenomenology, remains responsive to the cinematic matter at
hand or *die Sache selbst*. This 'film as philosophy' approach takes film
seriously as 'a form of philosophizing, of reflection, reasoning, and
argument' in its own right (Critchley 2005: 139). This claim resonated
strongly with Mulhall's oft-quoted remark that film offers a way of
engaging with philosophy via cinematic means:

> I do not look to these films as handy or popular illustrations of
> views and arguments properly developed by philosophers; I
> see them rather as themselves reflecting on and evaluating such
> views and arguments, as thinking seriously and systematically
> about them in just the ways that philosophers do. Such films are
> not philosophy's raw material, nor a source for its ornamentation;
> they are philosophical exercises, philosophy in action – film as
> philosophizing. (Mulhall 2002: 2)

Both Mulhall's and Critchley's comments influenced my own
approach to the film as philosophy question, which I would write
about at length in my book *New Philosophies of Film* (2011). At this
point, however, the question of film as philosophy in Malick presented
itself with an arresting urgency, especially with such an aesthetically
impressive and philosophically beguiling film as *The Thin Red Line*.

Critchley's 'film as philosophy' approach to *The Thin Red Line* offers a strongly immanent reading of the film, avoiding explicit recourse to given philosophical frameworks, while foregrounding its textual, thematic and narrative elements.[8] At the same time, like most other commentators, he emphasizes the stylistic elements of Malick's use of landscape, nature images and the contemplative mood of calm that backgrounds much of the film. The narrative itself, Critchley suggests, is organized around three central relationships, each consisting of a conflict between two characters, and each articulating one of three related themes. First, *loyalty*, the conflict between Colonel Tall (Nick Nolte) and Captain Staros (Elias Koteas) over loyalty towards the commands of one's superiors versus loyalty towards the men under one's command. Second, *love*, explored in Private Bell's (Ben Chaplin) devotion to, and ultimate betrayal by, his wife Marty (Miranda Otto). Third, the question of metaphysical *truth*, an argument, in a philosophical sense, between Sergeant Welsh (Sean Penn) and Private Witt (Jim Caviezel), spanning the entire film.

For Critchley, the most important philosophical theme is that of *truth*, the search for which shapes the complex relationship between Welsh and Witt. The question they clash over, as Critchley puts it, is whether there is a transcendent metaphysical truth or whether truth is something of this world: 'is this the only world, or is there another world?' (2005: 140). In their first encounter, Welsh remarks to Witt that 'in this world, a man himself is nothing ... and there ain't no world but this one'. Witt disagrees, replying that he has seen another world, beyond the merely physical realm. 'Well', Welsh replies, 'you're seeing something I never will.' This argument is elaborated throughout the course of the film. Welsh maintains that the war is ultimately about 'property', which means that the best a man can do is to 'make himself an island' and survive. Witt, by contrast, claims to see beyond the lie of war, finding amidst the violence and brutality the possibility of selfless sacrifice; he seeks an encounter with 'the glory', which for Critchley means the moment of immortality that arrives in facing one's death with calm.

Their relationship thus takes on the character of a philosophical disputation, Welsh's 'nihilistic physicalism', as Critchley describes, clashing with Witt's 'metaphysical panpsychism' (2005: 141). It is worth pausing over these descriptions. It is not clear, for example, that Welsh is a nihilist and that 'physicalism' (generally referring to a kind of scientific naturalism) is the right term for his sceptical, even cynical defence of rational self-interest in the face of the madness of war. Welsh both admires Witt's independent spirit and is troubled by Witt's insubordination and lack of concern for duty (in the narrower sense of obeying commands, such as going AWOL when the mood takes him). Witt, for his part, recognizes something in Welsh, a core of value, even a light or spark, and senses a kinship and rivalry between them, less to do with military status or heroism and more to do with moral or existential authenticity, which does not fit well with Welsh being a nihilist. Witt's outlook could be described as 'metaphysical' but not necessarily as panpsychic. It is another world, a transcendent dimension (of spirit) that Witt claims to have seen (made manifest when his mother died, facing her death with calm, and possibly in the vision of authentic existence he appears fascinated by, and imagines he observes during his idyll in the Melanesian community), not just a divinized, immanentist conception of the natural world. This raises an issue that will return throughout various philosophical receptions of Malick's work: that of the immanent versus transcendent conceptions of existence or reality manifested in his films.

These metaphysical reflections on truth, mortality and humanity, reflected in the dispute between Welsh and Witt, are, for Critchley, what makes Malick's film a philosophical work. The key to the film and to Malick's work generally, he suggests, is *calm*: the calm acceptance of death, of this-worldly mortality, a calmness present not only as a narrative theme but also as a cinematic aesthetic. Malick's male protagonists, as Critchley observes, 'seem to foresee their appointment with death and endeavour to make sure they arrive on time' (2005: 142–143). Witt is one such character recklessly putting himself in situations of extreme danger, fascinated by the intimacy of death, but with an anticipation of it that brings not fear but calm. Early in the film, Witt describes his initially fearful response to his mother's death as follows: 'I was afraid to touch the death that I seen in her. I couldn't find anything beautiful or uplifting about her going back to God. I heard people talk about immortality, but I ain't never seen it.' Witt then wonders how it will be when he dies, what it would be like 'to know that this breath now was the last one you was ever gonna draw'. And it is here that he finds his answer about the relation between immortality and mortality: 'I just hope I can meet it the same way she did, with the same … calm. Because that's where it's hidden, the immortality that I hadn't seen.'

As Silverman points out, however, this scene actually presents *Witt's mother's* sense of calm, rather than Witt's own recollection of his mother's death. For Witt recalls the *fear* he felt in seeing his mother 'going to meet God'. Yet it is her moment of calm before death that gives Witt a clue as to how to experience his own authentic being-toward-death (Silverman 2003: 328). Whatever the case, the thought Malick presents here, Critchley remarks, is that immortality can only be understood as this calm before death, the moment of eternal life that can only be imagined as inhabiting the instant of one's own death.[9] It is not difficult to link this insight to what Heidegger describes as authentic being-toward-death, as Silverman does in her reading of *The Thin Red Line* as a meditation on the Heideggerian Nothing. Indeed, Critchley himself points to the parallels with Heidegger's being-toward-death, the *Angst* that can be experienced as a kind of

Ruhe, as peace or calm; yet to do so, he maintains, is to risk slipping on one of those Heideggerian hermeneutic banana skins mentioned earlier.

Can we avoid such hermeneutic slips? I doubt that we can, at least not in the sense that hermeneutics, as a theory accounting for practices of interpretation and understanding, describes the necessarily contextual character of all interpretation. It also stresses the fact that we always bring various pre-judgements – assumed ideas, concepts or pre-given frameworks of understanding – to the interpretation and understanding of any particular text or cultural phenomenon. Given what we know of Malick, but also the existential tenor of the film, it is not surprising that the Heideggerian context of *The Thin Red Line* resonates with many viewers, whether we embrace or eschew it, providing a horizon of thought and meaning that is impossible to bracket completely. Not only has Heidegger left an indelible mark on modern philosophical thinking, his work is clearly a contextual feature of the reception of Malick as a filmmaker, even if we reject the role of Heidegger's philosophy in our interpretations of Malick films. Indeed, the voiceover reflections on death, mortality, finitude and our relationship with Being in *The Thin Red Line* gain at least some of their philosophical resonance from their distinctly Heideggerian tenor, even if we can also identify other philosophical influences (e.g. Emerson or Kierkegaard). In this respect, Critchley's strictly 'immanent' reading of *The Thin Red Line* risks foreclosing one of the horizons of thought that nourishes much of the film's metaphysical vision.[10]

This difficulty of avoiding Heidegger becomes clear in Critchley's concluding reflections on the ethical significance of *The Thin Red Line*. Here the theme in question is being open to the presencing of nature, just letting things be, what we might describe, though Critchley does not, as an attitude of 'releasement' in both an ethical and aesthetic sense. Witt's calm in the face of mortality is framed by the massive presence of nature, dwarfing the human drama of war, of physical violence and historical conflict. This beautiful indifference of nature, as Critchley observes, might be viewed as a kind of *fatum* for Malick, 'an ineluctable power, a warring force that both frames human war but is utterly indifferent to human purposes and intentions' (2005: 146). This indifference to human concerns, which differs from the enchanted nature of animism, follows from Malick's broadly naturalistic conception of nature: 'Things are not enchanted in Malick's universe, they simply *are*, and we are things too' (Critchley 2005: 146). Things simply are, luminous and shining, remote from our purposes and strivings, being just as they are, 'in all the intricate evasions of "as"' (Critchley 2005: 147). Malick's camera thus takes on a neutral perspective, calmly revealing their presence not *for* us but *despite* us.

From this point of view Malick is more akin to a poet like Wallace Stevens than to a thinker like Heidegger, although Critchley also leaves open the nature of this relationship. In the end it is a poet who frames Critchley's reading of *The Thin Red Line*, which opens with Stevens' 'The Death of a Soldier' and closes, aptly, with a quotation from 'The Palm at the End of the Mind' – lines resonating with the final image of a coconut shoot emerging from out of the sandy shallows. As with the later Heidegger, we defer to the poet rather than the philosopher when it comes to that mode of poetic revealing which exceeds the philosophical framing of the film, or indeed the framework of philosophical discourse itself. Yet Critchley does this in a discourse on the film that has recourse to philosophical reflection, even if it avoids mentioning Heidegger, thus escaping the embarrassment of slipping on Heideggerian hermeneutics.

For all that, I was left with the impression that Critchley was describing, in all but name, an experience (existential 'calm' in the face of mortality) akin to Heidegger's releasement (*Gelassenheit*). Despite taking care to avoid invoking a philosophical meta-text, Critchley meditates on the way things presence, their luminous appearance, their revealing of a world that we do not master or control; an experience that reveals the mystery of finitude and the calm embrace of time, death and the mystery of Being ('the glory'). Hermeneutic banana skin or not, it seems difficult to avoid talk about Malick's cinematic 'letting be' without invoking, at least implicitly, the Heideggerian thought of *Gelassenheit*. Critchley's film-philosophical reading of *The Thin Red Line* appears rather 'Heideggerian' after all.

The question of a 'Heideggerian cinema' thus presents itself once again. Whereas Furstenau and MacEvoy's approach risked subsuming the film within a 'Heideggerian' framework, Critchley's eschewal of any such framework avoids the question of the relationship between Heidegger and cinema altogether – a relationship that becomes, with Malick, genuinely thought-provoking.

The Thin Red Line's 'Vernacular Metaphysics'

One of the common complaints about film-philosophers is that they ignore cinematic aesthetics and visual style and focus exclusively on narrative content and thematic meaning. Of course, many philosophical film theorists *do* focus on narrative elements, but it is difficult to talk about film without describing *how* a film presents its story. Visual style and aesthetic features are the ways in which film narrative communicates meaning, so any philosophically oriented engagement with cinema must pay attention to 'the how' as well as 'the what' within any given film. This continues to be a lively debate in the case of Malick and becomes explicit in discussions of *The Thin Red Line*. For this is a genre film (war movie) with a very distinctive cinematic style, confounding genre expectations and including aesthetic features at odds with conventional narrative film technique. Challenging the cliché that film-philosophy is indifferent to aesthetics, Robert Pippin's discussion of the film (2013) impressed me by taking up this challenge. It obliquely raises the question of the relationship between the philosophical significance of the war movie and the distinctive cinematic features of *The Thin Red Line* (the role of voiceover, the ambiguous relationship between image and sound, the subversion of genre expectations). This question of style remained linked, in my mind, with the following question: Whether we should describe a film such as *The Thin Red Line* as philosophical, or even 'Heideggerian', whatever this should turn out to mean.

Pippin's approach to the film situates it in relation to the war movie genre, albeit as a highly idiosyncratic and anomalous case. As with all war movies, such films pose and work through a central question:

> How ordinary citizens of commercial republics can both come to participate in acts of extreme violence and come to understand in some way what they are doing, come to confront, much more vividly than they do in ordinary life, that they will kill other human beings and that they may die. (Pippin 2013: 251)

As Pippin observes, *The Thin Red Line* is a war movie that disrupts and subverts so many genre conventions – notably through the confusing use of voiceover and insistence on meditative images of nature – that we are left disoriented and confused, unable to find any meaningful answer to the traditional thematic question that the war movie explores. This implies, he maintains, that the conventional responses to the war movie question are no longer credible, no longer available, which he describes as one of the main points made by the film (2013: 249). By focusing on the film's compositional elements that disorient and confuse viewers, while also evoking a 'vernacular metaphysics'

that would somehow orient the characters within a larger world order
or cosmic whole, the film invites philosophical engagement while
refusing to answer the larger questions it poses.

  Pippin's approach struck me as intriguing because it broaches
the philosophical significance of the film as subverting conventions
of the war movie genre, while also reflecting on the metaphysical
significance of Malick's signature images of nature, organic life and
light. At the same time, despite offering philosophical reflections on
Malick's images as revealing the non-discursive presencing of beings,
Pippin (like Critchley) avoids any specific mention of Heidegger,
existentialism, phenomenology and the like. Instead, he underlines the
broader Hegelian or Nietzschean concern with normative questions
of modernity – how to establish and sustain shared norms of meaning
and value within social and cultural spheres in which traditional
or metaphysically grounded systems of evaluation and sources of
meaning no longer hold – while at the same time avoiding explicitly
philosophical claims made on the film's behalf. This struck me as a
complex and difficult position to articulate, one that nevertheless
seemed encouraged by a philosophical encounter with the film. Like
Critchley, the risk of hermeneutic banana peels looms large in a film-
philosophical approach, which means that the theorist or critic has
to find a way to navigate between formal aesthetic analysis and the
broader cultural-historical (or indeed philosophical) meaning of the
film – a problem that became more acute with each new Malick work.
A film like *The Thin Red Line* invites one to speculate on its apparently
philosophical meaning, whereas its style makes it difficult to articulate
what that meaning might be.

  The film's (unanswered) question comes to the fore in its two central
relationships, namely that between Private Witt and Sergeant Welsh
and that between Lieutenant Colonel Tall (Nick Nolte) and Captain
Staros (Elias Koteas). As Pippin notes, all characters in the film are

presented in sketchy, attenuated form, appearing only briefly in some cases, with little background or context. Where background details or personal recollection do appear (such as Bell's recollections of his wife or Witt's memory of his mother's dying moments), we are shown little that contributes to a standard psychological character profile (Pippin 2013: 251). As for main characters such as Witt and Welsh, they are presented as displaying contrary, even contradictory traits. Witt professes his love for his comrades in 'C for Charlie' company, yet the film opens with him having gone AWOL on a Melanesian island. Welsh declares that war is corrupt, that 'it's all about property' and that the best a man can do is look after himself; yet we see him selflessly risk his life to administer morphine to a dying soldier and protect a malingerer too scared to go out into battle (Pippin 2013). Welsh does so, moreover, in a manner that eschews any attempts at recognition of his heroism (the offer of a nomination for a Silver Star), the mere suggestion of which makes him angry and even more contemptuous of the 'lie' of war ('it's all about property').

In short, the men appear, at first blush, to embody familiar war-movie stock types but soon reveal themselves as far more opaque, ambiguous and contradictory than we might expect. The effect of this de-individualization of character, coupled with an emphasis on their pain, loneliness and isolation, is to block one of the main features of the war movie genre: the intense solidarity among soldiers that would explain their self-sacrificing behaviour (Pippin 2013: 252). Instead, we see soldiers looking frightened, anxious, unable to communicate, confused, depressed, cynical and resigned. Heroism is deflated as an ideal and solidarity undermined. The usual moral justifications offered for necessary violence and heroic self-sacrifice (commitment to defending family, nation and community, obeying orders for the sake of strategic advantage, unwavering devotion to a cause or one's fellow soldiers) are questioned or subverted. And where they do arise, the film emphasizes the moral ambiguity and psychological complexity of any such evaluation of the soldier's actions on the battlefield.

This is true of *The Thin Red Line*'s most dramatic sequence, which carries considerable narrative weight in the film: the assault upon Hill 210 and Captain Staros' refusal to obey Lt. Colonel Tall's order that he launch a full frontal attack against the Japanese soldiers holding a hidden bunker further up the hill. Pippin describes this sequence as the closest the film gets to fulfilling war-movie genre conventions, setting up the expectation that we will sympathize morally with the humanistic Captain Staros, who refuses to sacrifice his men for the sake of Colonel Tall's egomaniacal careerist ambitions (Pippin 2013: 261). Indeed, for Pippin, the sequence sets up the expectation that Staros' refusal of Tall's order – in effect a mutiny on the battlefield – will be shown to have been right, both morally and strategically. It is supposed to be morally right, in saving the lives of the soldiers under his command, who otherwise would have met with senseless deaths; and strategically right, in proposing an alternative flanking manoeuvre that will turn out to be successful in taking the hilltop position.

Instead, according to Pippin, 'despite our expectations and identification with Staros the humanist, the colonel turns out in the end to have been right', namely 'that a direct assault, conducted with full commitment, could succeed' (2013: 262, 263). But it turns out there is no direct assault, from what I can gather, at least not in the way that Tall originally ordered. Rather, Tall heads up to the soldiers' position on the hillside to size up the situation for himself, which has now calmed down, and then takes over the operation, including the decision whether or not to attack at this point. The delay caused by Staros' refusal of Tall's order for a direct assault, which results in a brief cessation of hostilities, buys time for an alternative plan to be devised, one that will prove successful (and which avoids the casualties that would have ensued had Staros followed Tall's earlier order to press on and attack directly). Tall orders that a small number of volunteers led by his favourite recruit, Private Gaff (John Cusack), risk themselves and go to 'see what's up there' on the hill. Gaff does so with his comrades, in a suspenseful, immersive sequence, and reports back that there are five snipers in a hidden bunker on an unguarded ledge – the source of the fire that had crippled the initial assault.

Tall now changes tack: his new plan is to attack the ledge in the morning using a small group of volunteers, which Gaff again volunteers to lead, and to take out the bunker; once that is accomplished the main body of soldiers can then advance up the ridge and attack the main camp atop Hill 210. That plan is executed the next day, in a nail-biting sequence of close-quarter stalking, confrontation and desperate fighting, with the Japanese soldiers either killed or taken prisoner, and Gaff received as the hero of the flanking assault ('flanking from the right', as Staros initially requested). From the standoff between Tall and Staros, Staros' request to try a flanking manoeuvre, to Gaff's indirect assault on the ledge taking out the bunker, a complex strategy eventually emerged under Tall's command that was made possible by Staros' refusal, delaying the fighting, which allowed an alternative strategy to emerge, including the final move successfully led by Gaff.

I take from this complex sequence of events a number of important points: that the conflict between Tall and Staros is more complex than a simple reversal of genre convention that depicts Staros as sympathetic but weak and Tall as ruthless but right (as Pippin construes it). Tall is surprised and enraged by Staros' refusal (given the latter's apparently 'weak' appearance or manner of conduct) but chooses to defer the confrontation by heading up the hill himself. Despite being portrayed as weak and 'humanistic', Staros shows strength of character in his refusal to obey Tall, holding his ground even when Tall questions Staros' judgement now that the crisis has abated. Despite being depicted at times as an 'egomaniacal' careerist, hell-bent on achieving his goal no matter what the cost (in lives), Tall shows an ability to compromise and deal pragmatically with the situation at hand (despite his fury) by taking input from others while preserving his authority (Staros' refusal, Gaff's initiative).

After the successful assault and the dramatic capturing of the Japanese position on atop of Hill 210, however, Tall still needs to punish Staros for his insubordination. He relieves Staros of his command and sends him home to do legal duties, but does promise to award him the Silver Star and the Purple Heart, as though to acknowledge that Staros prevented what would have been a fatal failure of the mission (Tall's original order for a direct assault). That Staros is not presented as having been 'wrong' or Tall as unequivocally 'right' (as Pippin claims) is shown in a moving, poignant scene between Staros and his soldiers as Staros packs his belongings before being sent home. They thank him for refusing the direct assault and organizing the flanking strategy[11]; Staros is touched, calls them his sons, but then masks his emotions by saying he will be relieved to be gone.

Although Pippin is right to stress the subversion of war genre conventions, *The Thin Red Line* does not entirely subvert all of our genre expectations. I would suggest that this sequence *does* engage the viewer to sympathize morally with Staros, while also recognizing the strategic will, purpose and pragmatic skill of Tall, the bravery and initiative of Gaff and the difficulty of defining the shared agency of events during battle. Indeed, the development and denouement of this dramatic sequence only underlines the difficulty of attributing the complexity of a collective action – like the assault on Hill 210 – to the will, decisions or agency of one particular individual (be it Tall or Staros).

As Pippin observes, however, the most confusing feature of *The Thin Red Line*, which nonetheless invites philosophical interpretation, is the manner in which voiceover functions in the film. Not only do these impressionistic, poetic voiceovers function as internal monologues that do not really correspond to the narrative action or character situation, they sometimes seem to reflect a shared, rather than individualized, form of experience. Moreover, the voiceovers are difficult to assign to particular characters and do not always correspond with the character appearing (or whose perspective appears) on screen, inviting misattribution in ways that have caught out spectators and critics alike (see Millington 2010).

The opening voiceover, for example, is unattributed, and unless one has an extremely fine ear, it is impossible to know, as Pippin observes, that it belongs to 'one Private Edward B. Train [John Dee Smith]' (Pippin 2013: 257). It will be his voice (and not Witt's) that speaks the film's most famous voiceover lines about 'the meaning of war, killing, death, and the place of such violence in nature, and which will voice the last reflection we hear ("All things shining")' (Pippin 2013: 257). Indeed, the scenes following the voiceover, depicting Witt canoeing towards the Melanesian island, describing his mother's facing death with calm, naturally invite the assumption that the voiceover we initially hear belongs to him, clearly the most charismatic of the soldiers, which is certainly how I understood the film. Train, by contrast, appears in only a couple of scenes, early on as a scared young recruit saying to Welsh 'the only thing that's permanent is, is dying and the Lord', and 'this war ain't gonna be the end of me or you neither'. And at the end of the film, we see him mouthing platitudes about having become older thanks to the war but not old (Pippin 2013: 258). So why is Train, by any measure, a minor, unremarkable character, a 'simple country boy' whom Pippin doubts could 'have such an inner life', given such prominence with his meditative voiceovers and metaphysical insights?

Pippin's response is to emphasize the seemingly deliberate strategies of deception in Malick's film: non-coincidence of voiceover and image, use of one character's voiceover while presenting visual depictions of another character's experience and so on. The voiceovers are not only often difficult to attribute, or belong to characters barely shown on screen; they also offer contrasting perspectives on the experience of war. Pippin identifies four 'positions' such voiceovers articulated throughout the film: 'Train's Manichean reflections, Witt's concern with death and facing it calmly, Welsh's cynicism, and Bell's romantic idealism' (Pippin 2013: 261). This is an important insight: the individual qualities of each voiceover, each with its particular philosophical outlook, offer a distinctive perspective on the experience of war. Although it is not difficult to identify Welsh's voiceover, or Bell's romantic ruminations, it is only Train and Witt whose voiceovers are apt to be confused or conflated in ways that seem invited by the film.

Indeed, as Pippin observes, it is almost impossible not to attribute to Witt the initial voiceover expressing 'Manichean insights' ('what is this war at the heart of nature?'). And this is also true of the final prayer-like apostrophe of the film, which sums up for many viewers the broader philosophical significance of what we have seen:

> Where is it that we were together? Who were you that I lived with? Walked with? The brother. The friend. Darkness from light. Strife from love. Are they the workings of one mind? The features of the same face? Oh, my soul, let me be in you now. Look out through my eyes. Look at the things you made. All things shining.

The fact that Train delivers this apostrophe in his voice, having appeared briefly on screen summing up his experiences using homely truisms and banal commonplaces, again gives one pause. Most commentators have assumed, quite understandably, that this voiceover features the voice of the now-dead Witt; others attribute it to no one in particular but treat it rather as an expression of a collective voice ('workings of the one mind'). Some critics have argued (notably Millington) that Malick scholars have been confused or remiss in not recognizing that it was Train whose voiceovers garnered most attention; but this assumes that it is relatively obvious which character is to be assigned to which voiceover, when such attribution is, of course, what the film undermines. I suggest that the subtle (and misleading) use of Train's voiceovers in these defining moments is not a careless slip or error on Malick's part. It points, rather, to something beyond the aesthetic and ethical dimensions of the film: a hint towards the religious, something overlooked by commentators focused on whether *The Thin Red Line* is or is not a case of 'Heideggerian cinema'.

Although Pippin notes, for example, that it is Train in the opening voiceover, he does not offer any conjectures as to why the film features Train's Manichean voiceover (of the 'contending powers' in nature) presented contiguously with Witt's existential anecdote about his mother's calm in the face of death. Although it is not accidental that commentators have attributed the 'Manichean' voiceovers to Witt, it is curious that few have speculated as to why the film deliberately invites this kind of confusion.[12] Either Malick is an incompetent filmmaker or there are aesthetic, philosophical or moral reasons why this confusion seems intentional. Pippin suggests that Malick might have deliberately confounded narrative film genre conventions as a way of disorienting the viewer, who becomes 'lost' and thus cannot rely on the conventional assumptions (and platitudes) of the war movie genre (fraternal bonding as a motivation for self-sacrifice, the instrumentalization of soldiers by commanders or politicians and so on). The stark contrast, however, between what we see of Train (an ordinary young soldier sustained by faith) and what we hear ('Manichean' reflections on nature, violence, good and evil) invites further reflection. My suggestion is that Malick is not only confounding genre conventions but making a point about faith: it does not always manifest itself through overt speech or action, but can be a defining element of becoming an authentic self. Train is an ordinary moral 'everyman' who seems far from heroic or 'philosophical' but whose inner life reveals a thoughtful and poetic expression of spiritual experience. Train becomes a de-individualized mouthpiece for a shared experience, even though such experiences are usually only grasped individually. This kind of existential reflection, with an implicit religious dimension, can be grounded in a shared experience of what he calls 'the glory' – a moment of transcendence in facing death calmly, one that resists direct verbal articulation.

To his credit, Pippin links the contemplative character of the various voiceovers to stylistic features of the film. In particular, Pippin refers to Malick's 'meditative' images of nature – studies of plants, animals, birds, trees, sun, water and light – interpolated into the narrative sequences but unconnected to character perspective or plot development. The attention that such images both express and solicit suggests a reflexive dimension to what they depict. As Pippin remarks,

> It is not merely the objects we see when framed this way but rather, given the lingering attention of the camera, if one can put it this way, the *objects in the light of such attention*, photographed as if *seen* in a mode of interrogative attention. (2013: 269)

Given the detachment of these depicted objects from any background framing or context of action, the viewer is left to ponder 'some other dimension of meaningfulness (or some different sort of question about life) to emerge visually' (Pippin 2013: 269). What Pippin alludes to here resonates with Critchley's and Cavell's remarks about Malick's images expressing, in a reflexive manner, the sheer presencing of things, while drawing attention to the cinematic revelation of this very presencing. Indeed, in a manner I would describe as 'Heideggerian', Pippin declares that in these contemplative images of nature, light and life,

> we see not the mere beings ... but see them in the light of the question of what it is for them to be at all, especially to be alive, a presence that cannot be rightly captured as a discursive theme but only in a kind of intimation or disclosure available to a visual art. (2013: 270)

In other words, Malick's images disclose *the being of these beings*, their distinctive manner of presencing, showing them in light of what Heidegger called 'the question of Being' as such, a question that resists discursive articulation but which can be made manifest, I suggest, via the disclosive potential of cinematic (and other visual) art (see Sinnerbrink 2006). This disclosive potential of cinema, which Pippin relates to the 'revelatory' aesthetic tradition of (Continental) philosophy (Hegel, Schiller, Schelling, Schlegel, Schopenhauer, Nietzsche, Heidegger and Merleau-Ponty), reveals the being of these beings (animal, plant, water and so on) in their contrastive presence with 'nonbeing or death'. In a decidedly Heideggerian manner, Pippin describes how this 'intuitive and prediscursive' disclosure, the 'thin red line' between life and death, also announces 'its own unavailability for any determinate thinking, as if something is also being withheld or hidden from such discursive intelligibility, from what the voice-overs alone could make sense of' (2013: 271).

This is an acute rendering, I suggest, of precisely what Heidegger called the 'mystery of Being', the self-withdrawal of Being in the disclosure of beings with their own particular way of being as revealed within a meaningful, temporalizing, world context. Not only that, what Pippin calls the 'ontological attention' Malick's images direct towards the being of beings, revealing themselves in light of the self-withdrawal of Being, is expressed principally through the play of light (and darkness). We see objects or things revealed, Pippin claims, '*in their being illuminated* by this basic ontological question, prompted by their being at all' (2013: 271) – a question expressed in the 'interrogative attention' such images direct at things in their mute presencing. This revelation of things through contemplative images (expressing an interrogative, that is, *questioning* character) raises the question of 'the meaning of their living presence', an aesthetically revealed question – revealed through images – contrasted with the discursive form of questioning that we hear articulated in the film's voiceovers.

The challenge of Malick's cinema, Pippin concludes, is to bring together this pre-discursive aesthetic disclosure of the being of beings and the discursive questioning of the whole within which these beings are at all intelligible. It seems that *The Thin Red Line* can, and perhaps should, be viewed as Heideggerian cinema after all.

I found Pippin's account of Malick's film to be both persuasive and questionable. Not only is the Heideggerian 'disclosive' role of Malick's images rendered explicit, Pippin also raises the possibility of a religious questioning that is immediately qualified or withdrawn (or whose status is left ambiguous). As he remarks, the revelatory images and meditative apostrophes together comprise a 'kind of prayer' or religious orientation towards the mysterious revealing-concealing whole within which such experiences can at all become manifest. At the same time, this possibility of a transcendent dimension of experience is promptly reduced to the sphere of immanence (nature and history).

The ambiguity of Pippin's account of the film becomes apparent in his concluding reflections: he raises the 'metaphysical' question of the whole within which such questioning experience (aesthetic and discursive) becomes possible but then denies that there is any transcendent dimension to this whole or our experience of it. His analysis of the philosophical significance of the aesthetic features of *The Thin Red Line* is couched in implicitly Heideggerian terms, emphasizing the revelatory disclosure of the being of beings through contemplative cinematic images, but he does not frame this interpretation as Heideggerian or as metaphysical and remains ambiguous as to whether it has any further religious-theological significance. This is despite his referring to the 'natural theodicy' raised by the film, the moral or theological significance or 'goodness' of the being of beings and the whole within which they are revealed. At the point where the film leaves open the conjecture that God is (negatively) invoked, whether via prayer-like voiceover or epiphanic cinematography, Pippin reverts to the (modernist) trope of cinematic reflexivity, confining the philosophical meaning of the film to what cinema, as a medium, can show us (or imply by withholding from us). It is thus cinema (rather than God or some other transcendent source) that becomes the subject or addressee of Train's final prayer, thus collapsing its metaphysical and theological significance to the modernist self-reflexivity of Malick's film as the expression of a (god-like) cinematic auteur.

The Thin Red Line as existential ethics

For all the philosophical insights and aesthetic attentiveness in Pippin's reading, it is telling that he at once raised and foreclosed the question of theology or religious experience more generally in Malick's work. This is probably the most sophisticated example of what was to become a recognizable pattern in philosophical engagements with Malick's films (especially with *The Tree of Life*). Although there seemed to me good grounds to persist with the questioning of *The Thin Red Line* as an instance of Heideggerian cinema, this questioning began to show up the limits of confining Malick's work (following *The Thin Red Line*) within a Heideggerian way of thinking. I had previously argued, in a qualified way, how the film's ambiguous 'Heideggerianism' involves its cinematic poetics: the capacity of Malick's cinema, as an artform expressing the technologically mediated disclosure of worlds, to reveal or 'bring forth' the 'being of beings' and 'worlding of world' via audiovisual images (Sinnerbrink 2006). Malick's cinema has the capacity, I maintained, to resensitize us through a *cinematic poesis* towards the sheer presencing of things, while at the same time disclosing different, often conflicting, aspects of our shared historical worlds (Sinnerbrink 2014). Although this captured something important about Malick's work, it did not really address *why* his films seemed concerned to afford us this aesthetically mediated, highly ambiguous experience of transcendence.

I found Pippin's idea of a vernacular metaphysics expressed in the film to be persuasive and compelling, but it seemed to me more apt to describe the film as exploring phenomenologically rich facets of an existentialist ethics. I would now reframe my earlier account of *The Thin Red Line*, acknowledging the Heideggerian resonances of the film, while remaining cautious concerning any strong reliance on Heidegger as a philosophical key to the film. Rather, the ethical significance of *The Thin Red Line* resides in its phenomenologically rich presentations of different attitudes to mortality and its mood-oriented explorations of modes of dwelling: a cinematically revealed existential ethics of acknowledging finitude, contemplating nature/being and an aesthetic valorization of existential mindfulness ('calm') as expressing an ethical mode of being-in-the-world – even in the midst of violent and chaotic world-collapse (the experience of warfare).

The strongly 'existentialist' tenor of the film, however, which most commentators associate with Heidegger, also suggested to me an underlying religious dimension that remains largely submerged throughout the film (despite references to Manicheanism, Staros' prayer asking God to protect his men and the moral problem of nihilism that many characters, for example Welsh, grapple with as a result of their experiences of battle). Train, it turns out, is the character who has the most metaphysically resonant voiceovers, yet all we see of him is a scared young uneducated Southerner, whose religious conviction is all that sustains him in confronting the horrors of battle ('there's just dyin' and the Lord'). It is not accidental that this simple believer is the source of the most famous voiceovers in the film. But what does this signify?

On the one hand, it suggests that the voiceovers express, using a stylized 'language of thought' mode, the feelings, reflections or ruminations of a character, sometimes in a mode that they would be unlikely (or unable) to articulate in everyday speech. On the other, it also suggests that the 'metaphysical' reflections (on one big soul and all things shining), with their Heideggerian and Emersonian resonances, also carry religious or theological overtones that are important for the film. Such an approach still engages with the question of 'Heideggerian' cinema but is also compatible with a variety of transcendental (Emerson) and existentialist approaches to ethical ways of being. This existentialist dimension to the film – consonant with its absence of reflection on the historical, social or political dimensions of war – also points to religious (and not just atheistic) forms of existential reflection. As I was to discover, these assumptions concerning the idea of 'film as philosophy', and of Malick as practitioner of 'Heideggerian cinema', were to be challenged and dramatically transformed with his next film, *The New World*, which added a new dimension to my thinking through the possibilities of film-philosophy.

3

Philosophy Learns from Film: The New World

The 'world', on [Heidegger's] definition, is not the 'totality of things'
but that in terms of which we understand them, that which gives
them measure and purpose and validity in our schemes.

MALICK (1969: XIV–XV)

The critical reception of *The Thin Red Line* established Malick as a 'philosophical' auteur, so expectations were high for his next film, *The New World* (2005). I was keen to see the film, having turned my attention to the problem of film and philosophy, resolving to make this my primary focus in the future and publishing an article on 'cinematic ideas' in Lynch's *Mulholland Drive* (2001) that same year. Enthusiasm for philosophical engagement with cinema was gathering momentum, and scholarly engagement with Malick was beginning to appear. This was evident in the publication of two volumes of essays on his (at that point, slim) oeuvre (*Badlands, Days of Heaven* and *The Thin Red Line*): James Morrison and Thomas Schur's *The Films of Terrence Malick* (2003) and Hannah Patterson's *The Cinema of*

Terrence Malick: Poetic Visions of America (2003). The idea of Malick's cinema as philosophical or even 'Heideggerian' cinema loomed large after *The Thin Red Line*, but it was intriguing to speculate how this might work with *The New World*, an historical costume drama and romance film revisiting the Pocahontas myth.

Unsurprisingly, the critical reception of the film, certainly among Malick scholars, proved to be mixed. As Simon Critchley remarked of *The New World*: 'Very sadly, I have come to the view that the less said about the latter the better' (2009: 27).[1] Indeed, despite widespread praise for his previous films, the general critical response to *The New World* was disappointing. To be sure, Malick's work has always attracted an ambivalent mixture of critical admiration and mixed box-office success (Flanagan 2007: 138–139). As Lloyd Michaels observed, however: 'More discouraging than the predictable complaints about slow pace, pretentious imagery, incoherent voiceovers, empty dialogue, and wooden performances was the mocking tone that informed several reviews' (Michaels 2009: 84).[2] My own response was a mixture of wonder and perplexity, emotional intensity and intellectual curiosity. I was fascinated and moved by the film but did not think it was particularly 'Heideggerian', despite it being clearly focused on the question of worlds, their meaning, making and transformation through conflictual historical encounter. I also had the sense that Malick was developing a new style, was moving away from *The Thin Red Line*'s explicitly existential concerns and that the idea of a philosophical cinema could not be confined within the horizon of a particular way of thinking. Indeed, the aesthetic experience of a film like this one required giving due attention to the non-conceptual, non-verbal ways in which film could show, reveal and disclose. This film could teach one about film, showing how it conveys meaning that resists verbal articulation but can also provoke thought.

Nonetheless, I was still intrigued by the question of Malick's cinema as a way of exploring philosophical or, more particularly, ethical experience via aesthetic means. Writing two years after its release, Adrian Martin remarked that *The New World* 'still feels like a new film, a young film', one that we can respond to as yet only in a fragmentary and preparatory way (2007: 218). I had a similar response and did not write about the film for some years, eventually including a chapter on it in my book, *New Philosophies of Film* (2011a: 177–193). Despite presenting it as a 'case study' in cinematic thinking, I nonetheless had the sense that this film was moving away from the parameters of the 'film as philosophy' debate and exploring something new, indeed the possibility of beginning anew. Perhaps this was fitting for a film that took the encounter between Old and New Worlds as its subject, that aims to make us experience the world – not only cinematic worlds but a sense of the world renewed – in a different way, as *naive*, in the original sense of natural or innocent (the 'innocence of becoming', as Nietzsche put it).

How, then, to approach this enigmatic and untimely work? *The New World* presents a strikingly poetic evocation of one of America's founding myths, the story of Pocahontas and Captain John Smith. Following nineteenth-century tradition, Malick renders the latter as a romantic tale of thwarted love, misguided ambition and spiritual reconciliation, but unlike tradition, the film lingers on the ambiguous dimensions of intercultural conflict, explores diverging attitudes towards nature between Old and New Worlds and shifts the narrative focus towards the usually neglected marriage between Pocahontas/Rebecca and tobacco grower John Rolfe. Despite its apparent shift into the genre of historical epic, it resonated with Malick's other generically idiosyncratic works – *Badlands, Days of Heaven* and *The Thin Red Line* – by presenting an aesthetic meditation on our relationship with

nature, our experience of mortality and the nature of love. Indeed, if
The New World can be understood as historical, spanning the founding
of Jamestown in Virginia in 1607 to Pocahontas' death at Gravesend,
England, in 1617, it is history in the form of mythic poetry (akin to
how *The Thin Red Line* presents the historical Battle of Guadalcanal in
a manner evoking Homer's *Iliad*).[3]

What of the critical reception of the film? For my part, I
approached *The New World* as a work of cinematic *romanticism*:
one that attempts to transform the familiar Pocahontas legend by
presenting the historical encounter between Old and New Worlds in
the register of poetic myth rather than historical fact (Sinnerbrink
2011b).[4] In the words of Pocahontas/Rebecca, *The New World* seeks to
'sing the story of our land'; it is a 'song of the earth' in a romantic key,
evoking not only Heidegger and Nietzsche but Emerson and Cavell.
The film's central romantic narrative – the love triangle between
Pocahontas/Rebecca, John Smith and John Rolfe – has an important
allegorical meaning in at least two registers. The first is the possibility
of a successful 'marriage' or cultural exchange between Old and New
Worlds; and the second, the possibility of achieving reconciliation
with nature – our own mortal nature as well as the nature upon which
we depend – that would sustain any such intercultural reconciliation.

What is puzzling about the film, however, is the manner in which it
attempts to present a seemingly 'impossible' experience, one that fuses
mythic history, subjective reflection and a metaphysical perspective
in which nature itself 'speaks'. This audacious undertaking prompted
Malick's critics to disavow *The New World*'s romantic 'naivety': a
naivety, or openness to the new, expressing the film's fundamental
mood, one at odds with the earlier philosophical reception of *The
Thin Red Line*. Yet this very question of 'the new', the experience of
newness and the possibility of renewing myth, exploring the encounter
between worlds, still seemed philosophically important. Indeed, *The*

New World struck me as an attempt to perform a cinematic version of the kind of 'aesthetic mythology' called for by the early German romantics in response to the crisis of reason and meaning afflicting the modern world (see Critchley 1997: 99–114). In this sense, *The New World* could be viewed philosophically, exploring cinema's potential to enact alternative forms of world-disclosure, aesthetically revealing new ways of being, or dwelling, within a world-context and relationship with nature under pressure from a destructive rationalism, reductive instrumentalism and imperialist violence. *The New World* captures the threshold or origin of an historical myth – the myth of America – one that needs retrieving and rethinking precisely because of the historical disasters of colonialism, the exploitation, historical conflict and destruction of nature *and* culture that we have witnessed in its wake.

The Pocahontas legend

Before turning to the film itself, it is worth saying a few words about the Pocahontas legend that it both adopts and adapts. We know that Malick had entertained for some time the idea of filming the Pocahontas story, having written the script back in the 1970s (Michaels 2009: 78). He returned to the idea for the film only after abandoning a project on the life of Che Guevera.[5] *The New World* also repeats and develops themes and sequences that can be found in *The Thin Red Line* (the sometimes traumatic encounter between worlds, our relationship with nature and the philosophy of love) as well as in *Days of Heaven* (contrasting ways of cultivating and inhabiting the land; the love triangle between Bill, Abby and the farmer). The tale itself is one of the favourite myths of the founding of America, having been the subject of numerous novels, plays and a number of previous film versions.[6] Since 1994 there have been three animated versions, including two Disney animations that emphasized the romantic relationship between Pocahontas and John Smith, introducing a rather cloying strain of New Age spiritualism and sentimental multiculturalism.[7] As many critics have noted, the romantic version of the legend, highlighting the historically dubious possibility of a romantic involvement between Pocahontas and John Smith, is an invention of the nineteenth century. Why does Malick give it such prominence in his decidedly romantic rendering of the tale?

To answer this question we should first consider the 'John Smith' version of the Pocahontas story, which has become a mainstay of American cultural mythology. As Edward Buscombe notes, through innumerable retellings, Smith's notoriously unreliable version of the story 'has acquired mythological elements shared with other stories of encounters between Europeans and Indians, to such an extent that the original "facts" (if they are certain enough to be worthy of the name) have been distorted and obscured' (Buscombe 2008: 35). The basic historical elements of the tale are as follows.[8]

In 1616, explorer and adventurer Captain John Smith, one of the early colonists in Jamestown, Virginia, recounted in a letter how some ten years previously a young teenage girl called Pocahontas, daughter of Powhatan, chief of the Algonquian Indians, intervened to save his life after he was captured and taken to Powhatan's residence at Werowocomoco, twelve miles from Jamestown.[9] Smith describes how after a feast with the chief, he was forced to lie down across two large stones, with natives poised above him ready to beat him to death with clubs, until Pocahontas intervened and his life was spared. In all probability, Smith was subjected to a traditional ritual involving a symbolic death and rebirth that would initiate him into the community, and Pocahontas was most likely performing her prescribed role in intervening and sparing his life (the stylized presentation of this legendary event in Malick's film suggests precisely this kind of 'symbolic' death and rebirth ritual).[10] Over the following year, the lively Pocahontas (a nickname in Algonquin meaning 'wanton one' or 'playful one') develops friendly relations with the colonists, reportedly visiting the colony to trade food and furs or to play games with the local boys (her cartwheels are mentioned). Although she greatly admires Captain Smith and frequently talks with him, there is no suggestion of any romantic relationship between them. In 1609 Smith is forced to return to England (due to serious injuries sustained from a gunpowder explosion), where he remains for the rest of his life. Upon her next visit to Jamestown, Pocahontas is told that Smith has been killed.

In 1613 Pocahontas is kidnapped and held for ransom by an enterprising Jamestown resident, Captain Samuel Argall. She is returned to Powhatan in 1613 in exchange for part of the ransom and some English prisoners and arms in his possession. She moves to another settlement, Henrico, where she begins her education in the Christian faith and then meets and starts a relationship with tobacco planter John Rolfe. After a raid on Powhatan's territory by Sir Thomas Dale (leader of Henrico) and his men, bent on extracting the remaining ransom from Powhatan, the Algonquians attack and the Englishmen respond by burning houses and villages and killing a number of natives. Pocahontas is eventually released; she explains that she has been treated well while in captivity and that she wants to marry John Rolfe. Powhatan consents and the Englishmen withdraw; the marriage between Pocahontas, now baptised as Rebecca, and Rolfe (in July, 1614) signalled a welcome end to hostilities between the colonists and the natives. Rolfe, a deeply religious man, explains his reasons for marrying a 'heathen' as being for the good of the plantation, the good of the colony and for the greater Glory of God (a line quoted directly during an important scene in the film).

Sir Thomas Dale leads an important expedition back to England in 1616 to secure financial support for the Virginia Company and brings along a dozen Algonquian Indians, including Pocahontas/ Rebecca, to ensure maximum publicity for the cause. Accompanied by her husband and child, Pocahontas arrived in England as the 'Indian Princess', and her arrival is the subject of great interest (one of the few contemporary portraits of Pocahontas shows her in Tudor dress). She is received at the court of King James I and introduced to the royal family and to the best of London society. While in London, she learns that Captain Smith is in fact alive and has a meeting with him. At first too emotional to speak, Pocahontas/Rebecca later addresses him as 'father', a term to which Smith objects but upon which she insists. In March 1617, Rolfe and his wife planned to return to Virginia, but Rebecca/Pocahontas fell gravely ill at the commencement of their return journey. She reminds Rolfe, distraught at the prospect of her impending death, that 'all things must die', and that 'it was enough that their child should live' (lines also quoted in the film). She succumbed to her illness and was buried in a churchyard at Gravesend, England. She was twenty-two years old.

Against interpretation: Neer on *The New World*

The Pocahontas legend, in all its variants, is well known; less clear is why Malick was drawn to it as the subject matter of his film. Given the enthusiasm that greeted *The Thin Red Line, The New World* pressed further the question of how to approach Malick's films philosophically while doing justice to their aesthetic character. In what ways could a costume drama recasting the historically dubious Pocahontas myth be 'philosophical'? Was it still related to Heidegger or the idea of a 'Heideggerian cinema'? What sort of relationship could there be between a film like *The New World* and philosophy? These were some of the questions that continued to exercise me over the coming years.

As remarked, one of the most common criticisms directed at film-philosophers is what Wartenberg (2007) calls the 'imposition objection'. In their rush to understand cinema (or certain kinds of film) as philosophical, philosophers either impose an inappropriate 'theoretical' framework in their interpretation of films or, more generally, fail to attend to these films *as films:* focusing on narrative, thematic and plot elements, while ignoring their visual style and cinematic qualities.[11] This criticism becomes acute with Malick's work, where it is precisely the conjunction of a distinctive visual style, confounding of narrative conventions and intimations of philosophical meaning that make 'philosophical' interpretation of his work both tempting and risky. The best example of this critique, modelling a cinematic way of responding to the film, is Richard Neer's extended critical commentary 'Terrence Malick's New World' (2011).[12] Here was a definitive critique of the 'film as philosophy' approach, one that argued that *The New World* was neither philosophical nor romantic, so I was naturally keen to consider what alternative he offered for a proper aesthetic engagement with the film.

Neer prefaces his discussion with a quotation from one of Malick's rare interviews: 'I don't feel that one can film philosophy' – a statement that, as I noted earlier, raises as many questions as it seems to answer. This quotation provides the authorial warrant for Neer's critique of the 'film as philosophy' approach. As he notes, Malick has become a paradigmatic figure in the 'burgeoning post-Theory philosophical criticism' of contemporary cinema; he has been canonized as a bona fide philosophical filmmaker in *The Routledge Companion to Philosophy and Film* (2009), with *The Thin Red Line* honoured with a volume of essays (edited by David Davies) in the Routledge 'Philosophers on Film' series (Neer 2011: 1–2). For these reasons, *The New World* provides an ideal test case for criticizing the philosophical/thematic approach to the film and for demonstrating the virtues of a descriptive aesthetic approach (which Neer insists is not simply 'formalist'). Such an approach describes how the film looks and sounds – pointing out the importance of mise-en-scene, shot composition, lighting, camera movement, audio and music, in short the cinematic techniques deployed in composing the film – rather than focusing on what it narrates as a story or means from a philosophical point of view. We could describe this as an anti-reductionist, or aesthetic expansionist approach to the film, substituting 'thick' aesthetic description of the audiovisual qualities of the work and close consideration of cinematic technique for the more familiar critical discourse on putative themes, narrative events, plot and dialogue and overarching 'philosophical' meaning.

Neer challenges not only the 'film as philosophy' approach but also the aesthetic 'mysticism' approach, with its edifying pronouncements concerning the ineffable meanings Malick's films are supposed to invoke (2011: 2–3). He organizes his analysis of the film's audiovisual style and techniques, moreover, not only against Malick's background as a philosopher but also against his decision to quit academic philosopher in order to pursue film. For Neer, this biographical fact about Malick – as an erstwhile philosopher who then 'quit the field' – can only mean one thing: Malick thought that film could do things that professional philosophy could not, hence that 'any attempt to recoup his work for the academy risks nothing short of travesty' (2011: 2). The academy refers here to 'professional philosophy', and the 'travesty' is violating Malick's own abandonment of philosophy for film, precisely because it appears he deemed the former incompatible with the latter.

It is worth commenting on Neer's claims at this point. First, the question of Malick's abandonment of philosophy is important but does not necessarily determine whether his films are philosophically significant or not. For one thing, we do not really know why Malick abandoned philosophy as a career. Apart from a few brief comments in interviews (where Malick states that he didn't feel he quite cut it as a philosophy teacher and that he didn't feel that one could film philosophy), we have little evidence to help us interpret Malick's decision to quit academic philosophy. It is also worth noting that Malick's thesis topic – on the concept of world in Kierkegaard, Heidegger and Wittgenstein – had been dismissed by his Oxford supervisor Gilbert Ryle as 'not philosophical' enough, which looks like a typical dismissal of a so-called European 'Continental' philosophical topic by a philosopher from the analytic tradition.[13] It is likely that professional philosophy, as practised in the United States and United Kingdom during the 1960s, did not offer a congenial home for Malick, whose interests were focused on existentialism and phenomenology (Kierkegaard, Heidegger) as well as pragmatism, ordinary language philosophy and the problem of scepticism (Wittgenstein but also Cavell). It is not obvious that his decision to leave academic philosophy rules out the idea that the kind of existential philosophy Malick was interested in – and certainly the problem of 'world' – could not be pursued through other means, in this case, film. Nor does it rule out the idea that film and philosophy do share a kinship that is worthy of thoughtful engagement (which inspired Cavell, Malick's mentor, in his philosophical writings on film) or that this potential affinity could be pursued by filmmakers as much as philosophers (the influence of philosophy on certain European auteurs is well known). At the very least, Malick's background as a philosopher and a filmmaker poses a question to us, rather than presenting an 'obvious' biographical fact requiring no further interpretation.

In any event, Neer's central critical point is a sound one, namely that film-philosophers should avoid aesthetic reductionism: that is, focusing on plot, dialogue and the 'literary' elements of a film at the expense of its distinctive cinematic qualities (2011: 3). As Neer remarks, the 'emerging philosophical criticism' does have something valuable to offer in the wake of the collapse of 'High Theory', but it cannot realize its potential 'if it simply quarries movies for exemplary narratives susceptible of moral evaluation, or for illustrations of arguments elaborated in canonical texts – still less, if it conflates movies with screenplays' (Neer 2011: 3). Instead, we should consider the 'look and sound of his films', rather than focusing on their philosophical aspects.

This is sound advice for anyone working on film, certainly for philosophers interested in writing on cinema. Interestingly, however, Neer invokes Malick the *philosopher* (rather than the filmmaker) to get his 'anti-philosophical' response to *The New World* underway. He quotes a passage from the 'Translator's Introduction' to Heidegger's *The Essence of Reasons*, where Malick defends a 'holistic', rather than an argumentative, approach to understanding Heidegger. Referring to understanding Heidegger's 'purposes' as a phenomenologist, his recourse to confusing neologisms and non-standard use of language, Malick writes:

> They are not strictly arguments or descriptions, one suspects, but are designed to make such procedures, and the proper application of them, possible. They assume that we have learned where to look for their relevances ... and that, insofar as we have, we necessarily share his purposes and need not depend on his arguments. (Malick 1969: xvii–xviii; quoted in Neer 2011: 3)

Malick's holistic orientation towards Heidegger's thinking is attuned to the 'relevances' of Heidegger's exploration of the 'question of

Being' and investigations of the 'worldhood of the world' (rather than conceptual definitions and explicit arguments defending a theoretical position). Acknowledging that Malick is referring to Heidegger, Neer takes this remark as offering a 'non-reductive' link between Malick the philosopher and Malick the filmmaker (2011: 3–4). Indeed, Malick's remark can be taken as offering 'guidance for the eyes': a heuristic guide to what Malick's films look like and, presumably, why they look the way they do. The dialectic here is a complex one: Malick the *philosopher*, commenting on how to understand Heidegger's thought, offers a guide to Malick the *filmmaker*; and although these films' 'relevances' stand independently of any philosophical interpretation, Malick's philosophical insights on Heidegger can guide us towards a keener appreciation of his films. It seems film and philosophy can be (non-reductively) related after all, with philosophy playing the role of heuristic 'companion' to (rather than theoretical master of) Malick's works – a view with which I concur (see Sinnerbrink 2011a: 137 ff).

One of the strengths of Neer's analysis is his focus on technique, 'something that philosophical commentaries tend assiduously to avoid' (2011: 4). As he points out, together with cinematographer Emmanuel Lubezki, Malick strove to combine three elements in shooting *The New World*: 'a widescreen format, natural lighting, and deep focus', a combination that posed certain technical challenges (widescreen tends to diminish depth of focus, as does the wide aperture required for low-light shooting) (Neer 2011: 4–5). The use of special lenses helped manage some of these difficulties, especially the effort to keep foreground, middle distance and background in focus simultaneously. To help energize these long, wide shots, Malick's team tended to favour 'long camera movements (handheld or with a Steadicam) and long movements of actors toward or away from a stationary camera' (Neer 2011: 5). Overexposing the film was one solution to Malick's insistence on shooting in natural light (very few 'magic hour' shots in *The New World*, unlike his previous films), a move that tended to separate human figures from their background, but that also gave the sky a blanched, whitish hue throughout much of the film. The colour palette was carefully managed, focusing on earthy browns, greens and greys, avoiding any standout primary colours (unlike some of the shots in *Badlands*, for example) that would direct the viewer's attention.

The overall effect of these techniques was to place human figures relationally within an encompassing 'world' marked by a 'dark earth' contrasted with a 'white heaven' – one of the most distinctive but also 'unsettling' features of *The New World* (Neer 2011: 5). Coupled with the decentred composition used in many shots (depicting figures in 'eccentric' or non-symmetrical relations with the frame), the mise-en-scene also featured 'internal relations' among figures standing or moving in the frame, emphasizing their dramatic and spatial relations with each other but also with their background setting. This visually ordered 'disjunctive relation of figures to their surroundings' – internally related bodies arranged against a dark/white horizon or relational world context – is 'the paramount visual fact, the enabling condition of everything that transpires' in the film (Neer 2011: 6).

The challenge, as Neer notes, is to explain how the cinematic techniques Malick deploys relate to the dramatic action that we see on screen (2011: 7). Although Neer gives a brief summary of the basic plot elements, his concern is not with the narrative per se – a mythic recasting of the Pocahontas/John Smith/John Rolfe story – but with the manner in which Malick's film is concerned to lay out the cinematic, as well as historical and representational, conditions of its audiovisual rendering of this myth. This is evident in Neer's impressive descriptive analysis of the film's opening ten minutes, encompassing the opening credits sequence, poetic prologue, Wagnerian overture, reflections on the cinematic medium and reflections on the social contract myth. Taken together, these elements provide the conditions for the elaboration of *The New World*'s dual articulation of the relation between the 'narrative of discovery on the one hand, and the declaration of the film's own possibilities on the other' (Neer 2011: 13). The former recounts 'the attainment of new truths about entities in the world' (such as Virginia and London), while the latter 'reveals the truth of the medium', the 'truth about the (filmic) world itself – about what has to be in place even to speak of a diegesis, a diegetic world, narrative time, and so on' (Neer 2011: 13).

What Neer argues for, in short, is a 'modernist' understanding of *The New World*, not as philosophical meditation on Heidegger's conception of world or an ineffable exploration of romanticist longing, but as a self-reflexive engagement with the cinematic and historical conditions of possibility for creating a cinematic world – one that is apt for staging and deflating of the myth of world creation. Untutored viewers and misguided film-philosophers might naively assume that the film's narrative is its central focus, the object of hermeneutic interpretation or the matter for aesthetic understanding. The enlightened cinematic critic, however, knows that the Pocahontas myth offers, rather, an occasion for modernist self-reflection on the film's own cinematic, representational and historical conditions of possibility. Neer's 'modernist' account of the film thus offers a sceptical deflationary response to both the philosophical and the romantic search for knowledge and meaning.

Let us consider Neer's dual account of 'world' (cinematic and historical-cultural) as articulated in *The New World*. It is instructive to follow the dialectic between theoretical and aesthetic claims emerging in his complex reading of the film. Neer both refers to, then disavows, Heidegger's thought, as mediated by Malick the philosopher, and then applies these insights to Malick the filmmaker, whose work is supposed to disabuse us of the desire to impose philosophical meaning onto the film. Take, for example, Malick's gloss on Heidegger's conception of world:

> The 'world', on his [Heidegger's] definition, is not the 'totality of things' [Wittgenstein's definition from the *Tractatus* – R.S.] but that in terms of which we understand them, that which gives them measure and purpose and validity in our schemes. What leads Heidegger to offer the definition is not obvious, but it may well be related to explaining why we must, and no less how we can, share certain notions about the measure and purpose and validity of things. And presumably it is important to have that explanation because sometimes we do not, or do not seem to, share such notions. (Malick 1969: xiv–xv; quoted in Neer 2011: 13)

Neer cites Malick on Heidegger's conception of world, which shares much with the later Wittgenstein's 'form of life', not as a philosophical interpretation of the film but as a heuristic 'guide to the eyes': one that might allow us to see, rather than interpret, the film as displaying a sense of world in a manner recalling Malick/Heidegger, without being reducible to the latter. As Neer observes, this is a fine hermeneutic line to walk, for the danger of reductionism looms large. He insists, however, that the film is not to be interpreted as a 'gloss on the Heideggerian conception of worldhood'; rather, 'Malick's own distinction' between the world as a place and the world as 'the constitution of a human form of life' may help us clarify 'the relation of narrative thematics to cinematic technique in the film' (Neer 2011: 14). Malick's cinematic style, for Neer, can be described as a way of relating these two senses of world – cinematic and philosophical – to each other: the narrative sense of characters discovering new worlds (like Virginia or England) and the more 'philosophical' sense (my term) of these characters discovering (or overlooking) 'their own "worldiness"' in encounters with new forms of life and the formation of new affective attachments' (Neer 2011: 14). Malick's relational style, for Neer, shows how a world comes to be constituted: not only the historical conditions of this genesis of world but the 'ethical and political stakes of the enterprise' (2011: 14). Indeed the film's narrative is 'itself an exploration of the grounds of world-making both onscreen and off', a claim that requires the sort of attention to audiovisual style and cinematic technique that neither philosophy nor 'ineffability' can provide (Neer 2011: 14).

The New World as film-philosophy?

I found fascinating Neer's championing of both aesthetic and modernist dimensions of *The New World*, with its dual presentation of world and worldliness (drawing on Malick's insights on Heidegger). Most striking for me was its proximity to what Mulhall identified as one of the main ways in which film can do philosophy. In his book *On Film*, Mulhall specifies three senses in which film can be said to 'philosophize' (2002: 3–6). The first is akin to the *philosophy of film*, where a film explores issues that theorists might consider (like 'the nature of the medium'). The second is *film as philosophizing*, where films explore recognized philosophical ideas, themes or problems (like human identity and embodiment). The third is *film in the condition of philosophy*, where films reflect upon their own conditions of possibility or the presuppositions of their own practice (the dialectic of 'originality and inheritance', for example, inherent to cinematic sequels). These are overlapping perspectives and the distinctions between them are not always sharp, but they provide an illuminating conception of the different ways in which we might define 'film as philosophy'.

Neer's argument that *The New World* is not a romantic rendering of the Pocahontas myth but a complex reflection on the conditions of world-building (both cinematic and historical) is a perfect example of Muhall's idea of 'film in the condition of philosophy'. It would also contribute to the first sense of film as philosophizing, namely drawing attention to the nature of the medium, and to the second sense, in that it explores cinematically, as Neer observes, questions like, 'What is a world?', 'Can we create a new world?' and 'How do we navigate the encounter between worlds'?

To substantiate this claim, let us turn to Neer's account of the dual cinematic and historical reflection on the conditions of world creation and world encounter. Although sceptical of 'thematic' readings, Neer focuses on Malick's 'relational thematic' (images composed so as to emphasize relationality or to 'relate relationships'), which he takes to organize both 'the mise-en-scene and the dramatic action' (Neer 2011: 16). Examples he mentions include the opening underwater shots showing native figures watching the arriving British ships, a shot 'in which water dramatizes the camera lens', and shots using wide-angled lenses that create a distorting curvature effect, such as when a soldier walks into the frame 'and seems to ricochet off the edge of the screen' (Neer 2011: 16). As has been frequently remarked, Malick's films abound in shots featuring frames and frameworks, both literally and figuratively: shots through windows and doors, of cropped figures in tall grass, and a continual recurrence of architectural frameworks, for example, 'cages, stocks, and half-built dwellings', all of which 'emphasize framing as an ongoing structural principle of the habitable world' (Neer 2011: 16). Frequent close-up shots of hands clasping (seen already in *The Thin Red Line*) also literalize 'the principle of relationality' (Neer 2011: 16). Such images are not merely 'symbolic', but also concretely organize the shots in which they appear, creating formal patterns that 'segment and regularize the shots in question' and thus can be described as structuring 'the world as it appears on screen' (Neer 2011: 17). Activities of framing and constructing, of mapping space and measuring time, of dividing up the world and representing it in different ways, for both the English and the Powhatan in their different dwellings and communities, feature conspicuously in the film.

Neer draws from this analysis that Malick's mise-en-scene 'relates relations' both literally and thematically, that is, via shot composition and by depicting activities of framing and constructing respectively (2011: 17). Both the English and the Powhatan 'find ways to enframe and articulate their worlds', the film showing us different modes of dwelling and world that the characters inhabit (Neer 2011: 19). At the same time, Neer remarks that this is not a psychological but an anti-psychological cinema, one that 'de-psychologizes' its characters by eschewing inner psychology in favour of expressive action. It does so by means of two strategies that will become more prominent in Malick's subsequent films: blocking or attenuating 'traditional means of focalizing the camera's gaze as POV' and by the distantiating or alienating effect of incorporating allusions to historical, literary and theoretical texts in the characters' speeches and monologues (Neer 2011: 19–23). As Pippin (2013) observes concerning *The Thin Red Line*, Malick's work both strives to solicit genre expectations and then subverts or blocks these, creating a sense of confusion or disorientation that, in my view, is conducive to thought and reflection rather than simply aesthetic immersion.

For Neer, however, the effect of this blocking of conventional narrative engagement serves to de-subjectivize, hence de-romanticize, the film (2011: 23). Moreover, Neer rejects 'romanticist' readings of the film (which I shall defend below), proposing instead a modernist position that also sounds remarkably close to the Heideggerian 'film as philosophy' approaches he is at pains to critique. Instead of 'reaffirming romantic subjectivity', Neer argues that:

The New World shows the condition of being in a world, understood
as the open field of assignment relations that comprise a human
form of life. (Neer 2011: 23)

Summarizing his impressive analysis of aesthetic strategies and
cinematic techniques, Neer links these to Malick's concern to show
the medium-specific 'worldhood' that conditions the composition of
cinematic worlds:

In its 'dogmatic' technique, its shot composition and framing and
focus, in its editing and mise-en-scene and music and soundtrack,
in the words the characters utter, the actions they perform and the
sentiments they harbour, the film shows worldhood as an essential
condition of the filmed narrative, determined historically and
technically by the resources of the medium in the broadest sense.
(Neer 2011: 23)

Like Critchley and Pippin, Neer disavows philosophy, in particular
Heidegger, as a way of accounting for the film's cinematic qualities. At
the same time, he draws on philosophical themes ('worldhood', 'form
of life') that are distinctively Heideggerian (and Wittgensteinian) in
order to account for why the film has the aesthetic style and narrative
presentation that it does. What Neer describes, for example, as
the condition of 'being in a world, understood as the open field of
assignment relations' is an apt gloss of Heidegger's existential analytic
of 'being-in-the-world' in Division I of *Being and Time* (Heidegger
2010), while his reference to Wittgenstein's 'form of life' (Wittgenstein
1953), also used to address the clash or conflict between worlds,
is unmistakable. Moreover, the film's concern with worldhood
as a condition of cinematic worlds is a striking instance of film as
philosophizing, which also broaches the question of what makes
possible the encounter between worlds, and the related question of
whether a new world is possible.

As Neer observes, through the dramatic action focusing on 'a collision of different worlds', the film poses and explores the following question: 'What would a new world be like, how if at all can one form of life, one world, be attuned to another'? (2011: 23). This is a genuinely philosophical, indeed ethical, question that the film itself elaborates and develops in multifarious ways: Neer's approach, despite itself, starts to sound very much like the 'film as philosophy' thesis he criticizes.

It is clear that Neer is aware of the intricate entanglements between film and philosophy that are revealed in the relationship between Malick's relational style and thematic focus on worlds. Indeed, he cites Cavell's question, alluding to Emerson, as to whether 'the idea of a new world [is] intelligible to mere philosophy?' (quoted in 2011: 23). Both Emerson and Cavell emphasize the need to rejuvenate our language in order for the possibility of thinking a 'radically new world, a radically new order of understanding' to be possible. Yet this desire for a new world, for what Emerson, and following him Cavell, described as a necessarily unattainable world – 'this new yet unapproachable America I have found in the West' – is one that cinema is better placed than 'mere philosophy' to reveal or elaborate.

Neer then describes the film in philosophical terms that suggest not only how film can 'do philosophy' but in some ways surpass it: '*The New World* casts this matter in and through the question of its own newness, its own transcendentalization of "the narrative of exploration and discovery"' (Neer 2011: 24). This 'transcendentalization' refers not only to a cinematic reflection and articulation of the conditions enabling the composition and development of a cinematic world but also to the question of how cinema might be able to depict and narrate the clash between worlds. The dynamic relationship between worlds is articulated across three dimensions: the 'borrowing' of language that characters speak and through which they reflect, the 'anti-psychologistic' priority given to language over psychology and expression and the manner in which the film reflects upon its own conditions and inheritances as a genre picture (Neer 2011: 24). Again, one could not ask for a more emphatic (Cavellian and Mulhallian) expression of the idea of film as philosophy – or film in the condition of philosophy – than Neer's articulation of how *The New World* relates cinematic technique and narrative thematics (i.e. relationality and worldhood) in a self-reflective manner.

Pocahontas with Wagner

The film's most audacious move, which Neer analyses persuasively, is to align the Pocahontas myth with Wagner's Ring cycle. As Neer explains, from the opening sequence depicting three Powhatan girls (or three 'Rhinemaidens') swimming underwater to the E flat drone of Wagner's *Vorspiel* to Das Rheingold; Smith playing Siegfried to Pocahontas' Brunnhilde and Powhatan's Wotan; Pocahontas 'saving' the hero Smith, much like the Valkyrie, by hurling herself between him and her father; and later, Smith, again like Siegfried, renouncing his love of Pocahontas/Brunnhilde 'for the lure of adventure to the Rhine, or in his case the Northwest Passage' (2011: 24). Like Brunnhilde, Rebecca/Pocahontas believes her hero is dead and so marries 'the unheroic and less-than-forthright Gunther, that is, Rolfe' and then 'travels to the royal court of the Gibichungs', which is to say London, to meet with the royals. There she encounters Smith/ Siegfried again 'but refuses to be swayed by his protestations and dies soon after' (Neer 2011: 24).

This persuasive interpretation raises the question as to why Malick would have so closely paralleled the Pocahontas myth and Wagner's Ring. This is a pressing question considering the historically compromised character of this Wagnerian/American myth of nation, with its catastrophic consequences both in regard to the rise of German nationalism and for 'the genocide of the native population' (Neer 2011: 25). Neer, however, takes the film to be presenting a cautionary tale, a deflationary critique, rather than an endorsement of either myth. For Neer, the probing of American nationhood in *The New World* and the German nationalism of the Ring are both paralleled and distinguished; the possibility of a false newness, moreover, is raised and then rejected (Rebecca's rejection of Smith's claim to be a 'new man') (Neer 2011: 25). The invocation of Wagner and of America as myths concerning 'the location of the new' serves to raise the question of the myth of nation, to render questionable the very idea of a 'new beginning' or desire for a 'new world' (Neer 2011: 25). From this point of view, as Neer remarks, it is significant that *The New World* departs from Wagner in important ways: it does not end 'with Valhalla going up in flames a la Götterdammerung'; nor does Brunnhilde die in a spectacular apotheosis, 'riding into the pyre' (2011: 25). Rather, Pocahontas dies in bed, beside her weeping husband, leaving him and her son to return to America without her. In short, far from being a risky paean to romanticism, *The New World*, Neer maintains, offers a deflationary critique of any such 'myth of the new', and of the (Eurocentric) desire to found and know a 'new world'. To realize this, however, requires, so Neer argues, a 'conversion of the gaze' that is the task of the film's stunning final sequence.

Conversion of the gaze

The film concludes with a sequence narrating the death of Rebecca/ Pocahontas, which shows her playing with her son in an English garden; they play hide and seek, peering around hedges, running after each other, laughing and pretending to hide. After a time, the mother disappears, and the son is left alone, wondering where she has gone. At this point, Wagner's prelude begins once again, signalling a new beginning, or rather 'a new iteration of an old beginning' (Neer 2011: 28). For Neer, the parallel established here between game and movie – the camera like a participant playing hide and seek along with mother and child – signals the thematization of all the visual elements (camera movements, framings, arrangement of figures and relations) that have established this cinematic world and its constitutive limits (the mother's death being paralleled with the limits of the film world). Its affective charge is due, he claims, to the establishment of a relationship between the idea of a game, the constitutive limits of any film world and the existential limit of death, a revelation presented in a mood that is joyful – even if expressed through 'some of the most compromised music in the Western canon, and one of the most compromised myths in American history' (Neer 2011: 29). This mood, as I discuss below, undermines much of what Neer claims of the film, namely, his rejection of its romanticism and of its 'naivety' (the myth of the new).

The point, Neer concludes, is that the film leaves us with nothing to decipher, no 'meaning' to extract, no philosophical or narrative resolution to project, no questions to answer (whether these concern the narrative, the question of colonialism or the relationship between *The New World* and Heidegger's *Vom Wesen des Grundes*) (2011: 29). Instead, an aesthetic mood of joy and audiovisual parallel between game and cinematic expression defuses all such questioning, deflates the very desire to know, hence to master, what 'Virginia' is or what the film itself 'means' – 'all are set aside' Neer claims, 'in the eupathic play of mother and child in which the New World returns transfigured' (2011: 29). Dialogue, human presence and the very desire for a 'new world', all disappear in epiphanic images of water, trees, sky and 'forest murmurs' (Neer 2011: 29).

We should note that, despite his rejection of philosophical and romanticist readings, not only does the film-philosophical 'transcendentalization' of *The New World*'s enabling conditions figure in Neer's interpretation, so too does the 'ineffable' moment of epiphanic transfiguration of the world that resists linguistic articulation. Indeed, the point of this final sequence, and of the film as a whole, Neer claims, is to dissipate the very questions that seemed to be animating the drama we have witnessed, collapsing 'the intelligibility of a New World' such that it is no longer a question, 'because the myth of newness – perhaps the American myth – has been renounced' (2011: 29). The film demonstrates, he concludes, the emptiness of the 'myth of the new', of 'everyday yearnings to know the ineffable – political, erotic, operatic, cinematic, philosophical – that is taken to lie on the far side of things' (Neer 2011: 30). In staging, then deflating, such myths, the film shows both their attraction and their danger, not only for the characters within the film but for viewers (or film-philosophers) similarly seduced by such myths of the new, seeking answers to questions like whether the film bears any relationship to philosophy. Indeed, according to Neer, such 'interpretative pseudo-problems instantiate the very affliction that the film works to treat, proposing a relation of knowledge that is simply inapt' (2011: 30).

In a manner recalling Wittgensteinian scepticism, which undermines the desire for metaphysics by dissolving the 'pseudo-problems' of philosophy, Neer interprets *The New World* as performing an analogous 'therapeutic' critique: showing the illusory character of our desire for the new and the 'inapt' nature of our epistemic attitude towards the 'questions' the film seems to pose. Rather, for Neer, the film presents, and reflects upon, the constitution of a (cinematic) world that establishes, as Malick put it, 'measure and purpose and validity in our schemes', without inviting us to speculate or seek knowledge, but rather to see and to feel. This 'conversion of the gaze', for Neer, is meant to deflate the desire to

know 'new' worlds, returning us to where we are with a renewed vision.
It invites us to see the relevances of this (and our) world, and hence to
'abandon both Romantic yearning and philosophical profundity' in
an aesthetic vision of a no-longer-human world (the film's concluding
shots of elemental nature). Neer thus interprets *The New World* as a
deflationary aesthetic critique of the myth of the new, a critique of the
possibility of a transformative encounter between worlds, that the film's
cinematic world-building, mythic reorientation and 'questioning' of
worlds seemed to promise.

A film *and* philosophy approach

For all the brilliance of Neer's account of the film, I found his attempt
to both allow and disavow philosophical engagement with *The New
World* to be fascinating yet problematic. Moreover, his claim that the
end of the film urges a renunciation of the 'myth of the new' struck
me as implausible, mainly because it seemed at odds with the aesthetic
mood of the concluding sequence (which, as Neer notes, is one of joy,
or perhaps sublimity). For all his emphasis on the 'look and sound'
of the film, insisting on the primacy of description, Neer adverts to
a 'philosophical' account of the film's thematizing the technical and
historical conditions of its own cinematic world-building, arguing for
a cinematic reflection on the medium that recalls the idea of 'film in
the condition of philosophy'.

Should we then abandon the myth of 'film as philosophy'?
Personally, I would not be so hasty. As I noted earlier, the critique
of the 'film as philosophy' approach as reductionist, as susceptible to
the 'imposition objection' (imposing philosophical 'meaning' onto a
film at the expense of its cinematic features), can itself be reductive in
certain cases. Hermeneutic engagement with a film, as a complex work

of art, requires description, contextualization, analysis, interpretation, reflection and understanding of a work, and in some cases this might involve recourse to philosophical ideas, concepts or theories which can serve as heuristic devices in establishing and developing aesthetic criticism and interpretative plausibility. This is the case, I would suggest, with Neer's discussion, which has recourse not only to Malick on Heidegger but ideas from Emerson and Cavell. Despite his anti-hermeneutic approach (recalling Susan Sontag's famous essay, 'Against Interpretation') Neer has recourse to philosophical tropes in his aesthetically grounded response to the film, offering a fascinating, if inadvertent, 'film-philosophical' meditation on the notion of world (cinematic and extra-cinematic). The question of Malick as filmmaker *and* philosopher thus remains a live one, for one of the things the aesthetic experience of his films may invite, among others, is philosophical interpretation.

Rejuvenating or rejecting 'the myth of the new'

Neer goes to great lengths to argue that *The New World* stages a deflationary critique, enacting a 'conversion of the gaze' that shows us, via the dissolution of our desire to know, the illusory character of the 'myth of the new'. I drew quite a different conclusion from *The New World*'s aesthetic of sublimity, particularly in its concluding sequence: an audacious transfiguration of the 'myth of the new', with the tragic tempering effect of historical perspective, one that also reveals our shared dependence on nature as the basis for any possible reconciliation between worlds, whether old or new. To be sure, there are many ways one can interpret Malick's films, whether philosophically or aesthetically, and it is clear that *The New World* was for some a disappointing or frustrating film. Indeed, many critics expressed a critical ambivalence concerning the film's romantic 'naivety': its evocation of an ideologically tainted myth (celebrating the colonial 'encounter' between Old and New Worlds) and its deployment of anachronistic cultural and aesthetic tropes (of nature, love and mortality).[14] It is this romanticism – or Malick's *romantic naivety*, the film's 'naive' celebration of nature and risky handling of colonial contact – that troubled a number of critics and scholars alike. As Morrison remarks, if Malick 'were indeed rehearsing North America's myths of origin merely as occasions of neo-Romantic exercises in transcendentalism, or sporadic bouts of an accustomed lyricism, complete with Edenic pastorals and noble savages', then the film would surely deserve to be dismissed for its 'terminal naivety' (2007: 199).

The problem with romantic naivety can be put in the form of a dilemma. On the one hand, *The New World* confronts us, in strikingly realistic fashion, with the dramatic cultural and historical conflict between Old and New Worlds. On the other, it immerses us aesthetically in the 'timeless' space of historical myth – opening up a space (and time) of awe and wonder, via the transfiguring power of cinematic poetry, in which nature itself is allowed to speak. Is the film unwittingly naive or *knowingly* so? And why is the film's alleged 'romantic naivety' so problematic? Either *The New World* is a lyrical, poetic work that lapses into *unknowing* naivety, celebrating what was in fact a tragic historical contact between colonists and natives; or else it is a sophisticated apologia for colonialism, one that *knowingly* elaborates an aesthetically rich but ideologically dubious version of this troubled history. Given these alternatives, it is not surprising that critics tended to opt for the first alternative – *The New World* is compromised by its *unknowing* romantic naivety – without clarifying why this should be resisted. This critical ambivalence points to a difficulty: the film's simultaneous screening of an historical event and an experience of myth, a poetic presentation of subjective experience and a metaphysical attempt to give voice to nature itself (what Neer describes as the transfiguration of the world).

Far from being 'naive', *The New World* struck me as offering a *knowing* kind of romanticism: a concerted attempt to immerse us in the imagined experience of this mythic moment of contact between Old and New Worlds, and to transfigure this tainted myth of intercultural encounter through the aesthetic power of cinematic poetry. The film generates an immersive experience of 'The New World' – inviting an attitude of openness to 'the New' as such – that would transfigure our perception of its history and open up the possibility of renewing its original promise. In short, my suggestion is that the audacity (but also questionability) of Malick's romanticism is to rejuvenate the Pocahontas myth not only to retrieve the possibility of reconciliation between cultures, but also to suggest the possibility of a 'New World' in which our dependence upon *nature* is acknowledged as the basis for any enduring intercultural or historical reconciliation.

From mythic history to cinematic poetry

How to retell this romantic tale of the encounter between worlds, of the possibility of experiencing new world or one's own world anew, in a sceptical and spiritless age? Critics have generally tried to resist *The New World*'s romantic naivety (through irony or scepticism) or restricted it to autobiography (see Sinnerbrink 2009). Here I would like to propose an alternative interpretation of this romantic naivety and a response to the critical ambivalence it provokes.

Let us consider again the film's remarkable opening sequence: an image of quiet movement across the surface of water, as though we were in a boat or canoe, with a voiceover (who will turn out to be Pocahontas) reciting lines from a poem or proem: 'Come, Spirit. Help us sing the story of our land. You are our mother, we your field of corn. We rise from out of the soul of you.'[15] Her voice recites this verse against the prominent background sounds of birdsong, crickets and water. We then cut to image of what will prove to be Pocahontas, shot from below, arms raised heavenward, giving thanks to the sky. This sequence is followed by the credits proper set against a background of animated maps of the Virginia region festooned with animals, birds and waterways, but also marked by ships, dwellings and battles.

Compare this with the opening sequence of *The Thin Red Line*, which begins with images of a crocodile sliding under the water, vast jungle trees and treetops illuminated by sunlight, and a Southern male voiceover asking: 'What is this war in the heart of nature?' *The Thin Red Line* similarly includes images of children swimming underwater illuminated against the water's surface reflecting the sky, followed by an image of Private Witt serenely paddling his canoe on the water's surface, greeting the local fishermen, a beautiful new world that serves as idyllic backdrop for the violent encounter between worlds that is soon to follow. Sub-aquatic images have featured regularly in Malick's films, for example, Bill's death scene in *Days of Heaven* (1978), which shows, from below the water's surface, as it were the reverse sequence, from life to death: Richard Gere's face crashing into the water after having been fatally shot in the back.[16] Crucial scenes from *The New World* will also feature water or a return to water, Pocahontas/Rebecca praying to her Mother/Spirit, or at the end of the film, standing, fully clothed, joyously smiling, having been immersed in water at the moment her spirit is released in death, or the concluding images of water running over rocks before the final sublime shot of treetops swaying in the wind.

The opening image of *The New World*, accompanied by gradually swelling horns announcing Wagner's famous 'Rheingold' prelude, features naked figures swimming amidst fish and against the sunlit surface of the water.[17] We glimpse, momentarily, a beautiful young woman, her face seen from an underwater perspective, her hand gently touching the water's surface. The extended cut of the film dwells on the figure of young girls, one in particular, swimming gracefully beneath the surface, with a voiceover, possibly hers, that continues: 'Dear Mother, you fill the land with your beauty. You reach to the end of the world. How shall I seek you? You, the great river that never runs dry.' We cut to an image of strong young men, seen again from beneath the water's surface, pointing intently off into the distance. The next shot reveals three ships, imposing and grand, entering the harbour and announcing the central contrast of the film: between the New World, which is also a mythic world immersed in nature, and the Old World, which is an historical world of the colonial settlers who have come to establish the first permanent colony on these shores (an inter-title announces that we are about to enter Western history: *Virginia, 1607*). The images of the ships' occupants, commanders, sailors and the like show a mixture of responses, from wariness and caution to amazement and wonder.

A porthole image – a frame within the film frame – shows the ships sailing into harbour from yet another perspective beneath the surface of things. From a darkened background we see a handsome face emerge, a prisoner in chains peering out towards the world, then gazing skyward, hands outstretched, echoing the image of Pocahontas worshipping in the prologue; his purpose here, however, is not to worship but rather to catch the water dripping down on his face from the grill up on deck. The images of Pocahontas and Smith, however, are already linked and twinned; the contrasts between freedom and constraint, community and exile, New and Old Worlds, already deftly set into motion.

The film cuts back to the excited figures on shore, running from their village to a higher vantage point from which they can better see the strange apparition. Our attention is drawn to one character in particular (an unnamed Pocahontas), whose perspective and response frame that of her people and of the film itself, gazing in amazement as the ships sail closer to shore. The film cuts back to the handsome prisoner on the ship, peering again through a porthole, an image that neatly frames another of longboats heading towards the shore, as he smiles in joyful anticipation. These two are destined to meet, their worlds to collide, their fates to entwine; yet this is an encounter whose outcome cannot, as yet, be anticipated, nor one in which our background knowledge of the legend or subsequent history of Pocahontas and John Smith is supposed to figure in our response. It is a moment preparing for an encounter between worlds, between myth and history, an encounter that the film signals shall be presented in a manner that is naive, mythic and poetic rather than documentary, historical or political. Let us add an encounter between worlds that raises the question of marriage, a question presented in a *romantic* key, as the Wagnerian prelude, the first of three appearances of this same prelude in the film, vividly attests.

The second time the Wagner prelude appears is to signal the blossoming of love between Pocahontas and John Smith, their nuptials already hinted or prefigured in the opening sequence of the film.[18] Another voiceover by Pocahontas begins, again evoking or questioning her Mother/Spirit: 'Mother, where do you live? In the sky? The clouds? The sea?' We see images of the interior of a hut, filled with smoke and statues (one of the many varieties of interior dwellings to be found in *The New World*, as well as in *The Thin Red Line*) and of Pocahontas worshipping the sky. An image of the roof of the hut, open to the sky but framed by a small window-like opening, releasing smoke, rhymes with but also inverts the earlier image of Smith's vision of the window-like opening above the hold of the ship, a grilled prison cell opening into which water would drip down to his face. 'Give me a sign', says Pocahontas, 'We rise. We rise'. Like smoke from a fire or clouds from the sea, the spirit rises into the firmament; love takes flight, spanning immeasurable distances. In the extended version of the film, we see an image of Pocahontas' actual mother (played by Irene Bedard), face painted white and reciting a ritual incantation, followed by lyrical and poignant images of Pocahontas and John Smith, their wordless, expressive love beginning to flower, with all the exhilaration, joy and fear that involves: 'Afraid of myself. A god he seems to me.'[19] Her growing self-understanding is figured in a moving vignette showing Pocahontas regarding her image in a broken shard of mirror, laughing delightedly at her image. 'What else is life but being near you', the voice asks, as they read a book together, Smith showing her pictures of that wonder of the Old World, the city of London. Pocahontas' growing recognition of her love for Smith, and for the potential transgression this might entail, is signalled in her reflections on how they appear to others in her community and the knowledge that this blossoming love is nonetheless fated not to last: 'Do they suspect? Oh, to be given to you. You to me.'

The voiceover here and throughout this sequence is punctuated by images of trees, water and birds soaring; a rapturous fusion of nature, spirit and becoming: 'Two no more. One. One, I am. I am', as images of water appear once again along with treetops reaching for the sky, images of Pocahontas and Smith together. The E flat major drone of the Wagner prelude has swelled to its fullest intensity by this point, as we cut to an image of a Powhatan native calling to one of the pair, at which point Smith now begins to speak, narrating how he was suddenly freed by the king and told he would be sent back to his own people, in order to tell them that they could stay until the spring, after which 'they were to go back from where they came'. Against images of Pocahontas taking pleasure in the scent of drying tobacco leaves and giving thanks to the sky, Smith is returned to fortress-like Jamestown, bearing food and gifts for the coming winter. The music fades and finally stops as he is lead into the grey, muddy and depressing fort, the Wagnerian prelude replaced by the sound of barking dogs and a desolate wind.

The Wagnerian prelude has shifted here from an anthem announcing the theme of encounter between Old and New Worlds, and the linked fates of Pocahontas and Smith, to the accompaniment and expression of their burgeoning love, their realization of the limits and impossibility of this love. It communicates Smith's return from the other world, his idyllic sojourn with Pocahontas and life within the Powhatan community – 'there's only this, nothing else is real' – to the stark reality of his other life as soon-to-be commander of a derelict and dying colony. Wagner's romantic theme, which first announced the encounter between Old and New Worlds, has shifted into an anthem for a vibrant but impossible love; the irreconcilable clash between worlds that demands that both Smith and Pocahontas sacrifice their love for the sake of community and tradition, conquest and colonization.

Indeed, it is precisely this theme of *marriage* as expressing the possibility of reconciliation between Old and New Worlds, but also of the discovery – or recollection – of a different way of inhabiting the earth, that holds various parts or elements of *The New World* together. Marriage – or better, remarriage, as is the case with Pocahontas/Rebecca – unites aesthetically the allegorical dimensions of the Pocahontas myth. The 'natural' marriage between Pocahontas and Smith is superseded by the 'cultural' marriage between Rebecca and Rolfe. Indeed, it is only with Rolfe (farmer and cultivator), rather than Smith (leader and adventurer), that the nuptials between naturalized culture and cultivated nature – Pocahontas/Rebecca synthesizing her hybrid 'New World' identity between her Powhatan origins and Virginian settlement – can be realized, however fleetingly.

This romantic myth of 'impossible' marriage is what enables Malick to hold open, in a space of poetic wonder, the possibility of a world other than either the Old or the New. This would be a genuinely 'New World' – experienced through Malick's immersive cinema – grounded upon a renewed relationship with the earth, without which the possibility of mutual recognition between worlds degenerates into conflict and domination. This *knowingly* romanticist gesture – proposing an aesthetic mythology in order to heal the breach of reason and feeling, nature and culture – captures the heart of Malick's supposed 'naivety'. *The New World* is a knowingly mythic recasting of the Pocahontas/Rebecca story as a poetic meditation on what marriage between cultures, but also between human culture and nature, might mean.

In praise of cinematic romanticism

Let us consider the extraordinary concluding sequence of the film, following Rebecca's poignant parting from Smith in the English gardens and her emotional reconciliation with Rolfe ('my husband', she whispers). With the film's third recitation of the *Rheingold* prelude, its original mythical meaning in Wagner's opera has now been effectively reversed. As we have seen, we hear it the first time at the beginning of the film, accompanied by underwater images of fish and native figures swimming, followed by images of the arrival of the colonists' ships, much to the amazement of the 'naturals' watching from shore. The second time the prelude plays is during Smith's idyllic sojourn with the Powhatan, depicting the flowering of love between Pocahontas and Smith and Smith's profound transformation during his sojourn with her people.

When we hear the *Rheingold* prelude a third time, however, its significance has been subtly transfigured: it is no longer an anthem to wonder and possibility opened up by the nascent encounter between worlds; it is also broadened beyond the lyrical expression of love and utopian community that Smith experiences with Pocahontas and the Powhatan. These two rather polarized renditions of Wagner's piece are transfigured in this third rendering, which gives sublime musical expression to Pocahontas/Rebecca's acceptance of death, affirmation of life and reconciling of Old and New Worlds in a no-longer-human world. This swelling, intensifying musical crescendo, accompanying shots featuring the retreat and disappearance of human figures in favour of water, light and trees, suggests nothing less than the self-expression of nature that is momentarily allowed to 'sing', to bear witness to Pocahontas/Rebecca's spiritual reconciliation and her return to (mother) earth. Wagner's prelude is transfigured through aesthetic repetition in a manner that mirrors Pocahontas/Rebecca's own experience of transformation, which is presented, finally, as of a piece with the becoming of nature and time itself.

In this final sequence, the music signals a process of reconciliation, of homecoming, Rebecca/Pocahontas' discovery of who she is and her reconciliation with life and death ('Mother, now I know where you live', she declares, answering the question she first posed at the beginning of the film). The sequence is shown first from the perspective of her child, playing hide and seek with his mother in the English gardens and then looking for her once she disappears (after her moment of recognition, her answering of the question that has guided her throughout). We then cut to Pocahontas/Rebecca's unexpected death at Gravesend, just as she and her family were to return home to Virginia. The moving images of her deathbed parting from Rolfe ('All must die,' she says, 'yet 'tis enough that our child should live') are narrated from a letter Rolfe has written to his son that is to be read by him in the future.

Images of death, recognizable from other Malick films, punctuate the scene: windows, criss-crossed with grills, opening towards the sky; an empty bed; a powerful native spirit figure departing the room in a bounding rush (one of the most sublime images of death in recent cinema). We see a montage of images of Pocahontas/Rebecca's departure from this life; her joyous worship of earth, sky and water; her cartwheels; her sublime celebration of, and return to, the creaturely life of nature. After its final crescendo, accompanied by images of ships departing from the shore, of Rebecca's cruciform gravestone rhyming with that of the ship's masts, seen from below, silhouetted against the evening sky, the music finally ceases – beyond death – with the film's final images of rushing water and towering treetops swaying in the wind. With the music giving way to birdsong, rushing water and forest sounds, the film is fleetingly transformed into a sublime 'song of the earth', one in which nature itself 'poetizes' in a breathtaking moment of mythic possibility.

The three renderings of Wagner's Rheingold prelude mark a profound transformation between the early, middle and concluding parts of the film. These musically and visually rapturous sequences announce the encounter between worlds, celebrating the couple whose idyllic love and shared destinies mark both the utopian possibility and historical tragedy of this encounter, of this marriage between worlds, a marriage founded on finding the right relationship with the earth. Malick's visual symphony combined with Wagner's overture reveals the transformation of the (Western) desire for conquest and domination, transfigured through love, the overcoming of opposition and the need to acknowledge a deeper (spiritual) unity with nature as the basis for a reconciliation between worlds. It discloses the sublimity of nature understood as elemental earth, that which underlies and supports any form of historical human community. Acknowledging this unity with nature is what makes possible – were one inclined to put it in the form of a thesis – the kind of plural co-existence or marriage between worlds, which *The New World* evokes though mythic history and cinematic poetry.

Yet for all that, I would admit, in agreement with Neer, that there is something unsettling about *The New World*'s aesthetic mythologizing. In his remarkable fusion of mythic history, subjective reflection and the self-expression of nature, Malick attempts no less than presenting the experience of an 'impossible' cinematic point of view. On the one hand, the film immerses us, with careful verisimilitude, in the imagined *experience* of the historical encounter between colonists and natives. On the other, it immerses us within a mythic rendering of this event, within the ahistorical space of myth. Both perspectives are then contrasted or momentarily integrated with the sublime presence of nature in all its elemental splendour. *The New World* thus exemplifies what Cavell describes as the defining myth of film: 'that nature survives our treatment of it and its loss of enchantment for us, and that community remains possible even when the authority of society is denied us' (Cavell 1979: 214). Nature is both the deeper ground of cultural reconciliation, and the hidden source of a utopian community that could found a new world; but this experience of nature remains a poetic evocation, a moment of aesthetic sublimity fleetingly celebrated on film. Malick's exhilarating but unstable 'song of the earth' is thus an enthralling combination of historical detail and aesthetic mythology, intimate subjectivity and 'inhuman' nature. The audacity of *The New World*'s romanticism is to allow, through cinematic poetry, nature to reveal or disclose itself as a 'subject', as the elemental ground of this mythopoetic history. This is a perspective that requires all of Malick's cinematic art to be rendered meaningfully, something we might affectively experience, or that might provoke thought – if we are open to this possibility.

Viewed from our historical perspective, this romanticism is knowingly *untimely*, in Nietzsche's sense: acting against the prejudices of the age in favour of a time to come. Malick's romantic naivety is a refusal of the 'worldliness' that would presume to know the meaning of the historical and cultural conflict between worlds, or indeed between human worlds and the earth upon which they depend (not to mention their ontological and cinematic conditions of possibility). This is signalled explicitly in the extended director's cut of *The New World*, which is prefaced by a quotation from Captain John Smith warning that those who think they have experienced Virginia 'do not understand or know what Virginia is'. Malick's romantic naivety remains true to Smith's warning against the arrogance of historical worldliness – and Smith should know, having renounced nature and love in favour of history and conquest, but in the process having 'sailed past' his true Indies, as Pocahontas/Rebecca remarks. Indeed, *we* still do not know, as Heidegger once observed, what worlds are; let alone how to understand the birth of worlds or how to foster their flourishing in a manner consonant with the acknowledgement of human plurality and the difficult reckoning with our finitude.

This is a risky aesthetic undertaking, for it conflicts with our contemporary scepticism towards 'the New'. Malick rejuvenates this possibility of experiencing the New – an American sublimity, we might say – through the poetic power of myth. We can experience this mythic history, however, only aesthetically, through cinematic poetry, and only fleetingly. In the film's final rhapsodic sequence, the fusion of musical and visual sublimity give way to the sound of water running over rocks, of insects and bird song and of wind whistling through the treetops. Malick's 'song of the earth' is thus an aesthetic challenge to our historical scepticism, which always treats romantic naivety – our openness to the experience of new worlds – as untenable and unworldly.

***

Malick's cinematic meditation on worlds – their encounter, conflict and possible reconciliation – not only offers an aesthetic experience of sublimity but also resonates with phenomenological attempts to think the idea of world. Although Neer's corrective to the thematic and narrative-focused readings of the film is salutary, it is also telling that his focus on cinematic technique – Malick's focus on widescreen, depth of focus and natural light – reveals a cinematic presentation of worlds that has cultural-historical, mythopoetic, aesthetic and philosophical meaning. The point is not to shun or dismiss philosophical engagement with a film as inevitably betraying its aesthetic qualities or cinematic features. Rather, it is precisely the complex aesthetic experience afforded by Malick's film that prompts many critics – including Neer – to reach for philosophical themes, concepts or ideas (such as Malick on Heidegger's conception of world) to articulate the significance of this experiential encounter. To emphasize narrative thematic elements or spectator response at the expense of cinematic technique is clearly inadequate; but focusing on cinematic technique and close description while refraining from interpreting why these techniques are deployed to tell a story in certain ways fails to take account of our whole experience of the film. This, for me, is the ultimate lesson of *The New World*: a film that made me reconsider the complexities of the film-philosophy relationship precisely because of its aesthetic revelation of worlds, both cinematic and historical, both old and new.

4

Cinema as Ethics: The Tree of Life

Restoring our belief in the world – this is the power of modern cinema (when it stops being bad). Whether we are Christians or atheists, in our universal schizophrenia, we need reasons to believe in this world.

DELEUZE (1989: 172)

When *The Tree of Life* was released in 2011, expectations were high that Malick was returning to form, with reports of a period 1950s familial drama set in Waco, Texas, coupled with contemporary scenes shot in downtown Austin. There were also rumours that footage from his obscure and ambitious project *Q*, a visually spectacular documentary project on the origins and development of the universe, had somehow made their way into the film. I read the movie press stories avidly, tracking the images released during shooting, and the speculations of critics that the scheduled premiere of the film at Cannes would reveal either a masterpiece or an incomprehensible 'difficult' work. The 2011 Sydney Film Festival, usually held in June, and often screening a few choice Cannes picks, scheduled *The Tree of Life* at the magnificent State Theatre, an eclectic late 1920s former movie palace in Sydney and one of my favourite venues for watching movies. True to form, *The Tree of Life* had received both high praise and sarcastic dismissals at Cannes, with reported cheers and boos during its screening. Nonetheless it had managed to win the Palme d'Or that year. As Robert de Niro tried to explain, 'it had the size, the importance, the intention, or whatever you want to call it, that seemed to fit the prize'. When the film screened at the Sydney Film Festival, the State Theatre was packed, and I found myself seated between two female moviegoers who seemed to epitomize the polarized response to the film. The woman on my left was clearly enraptured, breathlessly captivated by the magnificent images on screen, whereas the woman on my right fidgeted, groaned and guffawed, exclaiming impatiently when the film was done, 'Thank god that's over!' Their responses distracted me even though the film was enthralling. *The Tree of Life*'s 'whatever you want to call it' was again polarizing audiences. For me the film was an overwhelming emotional aesthetic encounter that left me in an awestruck, reverential state of mind.

Whereas *The Thin Red Line*, in my experience, had posed the question of film and philosophy, or indeed film *as* philosophy, *The New World* had shown that the question of film's relationship with philosophy was more complex than first appears. Like other theorists (particularly Mulhall and Wartenberg), I thought that film and philosophy shared a complex relationship that could, in some cases, be understood as film contributing to philosophical thinking by cinematic means. I agreed with Mulhall, Neer and others, however, that this relationship does not mean that philosophy should subsume cinema under a theoretical framework, nor that philosophical criticism should focus on the 'literary' aspects of a movie at the expense of its cinematic techniques and medium-specific qualities. *The Tree of Life*, moreover, made this question more perplexing by throwing into question the very notion of 'philosophy' that we might bring to such a film. It also pushed further

Malick's experimentations with narrative form, his emphasis on audiovisual style (the interplay of moving image, voiceover, movement, music and sound) and figuration of religious as well as metaphysical and existential themes in a manner that defied conventional aesthetic or theoretical categories as applied to narrative film. *The Tree of Life* thereby prompted me to rethink how philosophy could be transformed or communicated experientially. It offered an encounter suggesting how philosophical thinking could be elaborated aesthetically through cinematic art. It also made the question of belief – indeed of faith – something we should consider in relation to the aesthetic experience of the film, and hence bring to our understanding of its moral-ethical, or more broadly metaphysical, significance.

I have returned to writing on this film on numerous occasions (see Sinnerbrink 2012, 2016a, b, 2018), each time finding something different to focus on, further nuances to explore, different perspectives to elaborate, all while maintaining my conviction that the film was both aesthetically complex and philosophically suggestive. The fact that I kept retuning to this film, never quite getting the measure of it, should have suggested that it was pointing to something I needed to understand better. On the one hand, my sense was that the question of film and philosophy would have to be recast to focus more on *ethics* in relation to aesthetics, but on the other, more obliquely and insistently, I had the intuition that exploring this question in Malick meant that I would have to consider more closely the relationship between religion, film and philosophy. The latter point became clearer to me in subsequent years, through my engagement with Malick's 'weightless' or 'love and faith' trilogy (see Chapter 5); but the roots of this shift, intuited rather than comprehended, were already present in my responses to *The Tree of Life*.

So what did my encounter with the film teach me in the case of *The Tree of Life*? As both a religious work of art and a meditation on belief, it was not surprising that *The Tree of Life* was both praised and criticized. A question I wanted to explore, given both its critical acclaim and popular dismissal, was why the film generated such polarized responses. My impression was that these conflicting responses, both rapturous and rancorous, turned on the question of *belief*. A number of questions imposed themselves at this point. Can film depict belief, spiritual experience and love in a manner that transcends moral and cultural scepticism? Is belief in cinema still possible? Can it give us, to use Deleuze's phrase, 'reasons to believe in this world'? Was the aesthetic experience afforded by this particular film still something 'philosophical'?

With its fusion of moral, historical, metaphysical and spiritual visions, my conjecture was that *The Tree of Life*, with its aesthetic riches, aimed to cultivate belief – a sense of trust, care or love – in this world. This did not involve 'belief' in the epistemological sense of the world as an object of knowledge but in the lived existential sense of an ethical stance towards our shared worldly existence as meaningful and valuable. At the same time, the film sought to reveal by aesthetic means, a sense of transcendence – call it grace in the midst of nature or existential care amidst the everyday – that remained rooted in the 'immanence' of everyday existence. In this regard, it seemed to me that Malick's film echoed André Bazin's desire to show how cinema was an idealist and technological miracle: a medium of aesthetic revelation capable of evoking personal, historical, even cosmic memory. Malick's wager was that cinema, as a poetic machinery for the creation of revelatory images, could give us 'reasons to believe in this world' – an aesthetic affirmation of existence, despite our pervasive moral and cultural scepticism.

Like many commentators, I had come to see Malick's films as structured through contrasts – light and dark, subjectivity and cosmos, nature and world, good and evil – that were expressed both cinematically, through audiovisual style, and thematically, through the fragmentary poetic elaboration of narrative vignettes. Malick's signature style – flowing, mobile camera movements; the use of natural light; non-scripted performances aiming at authenticity and spontaneity; a fragmentary, episodic, audiovisually driven narrative; the interpolation of abstract image sequences; the use of intimate, reflective, prayer-like voiceovers; borrowed dialogue referencing literary, philosophical and religious sources; an artful sequencing of music to set mood and allude to aesthetic, cultural and theological themes – reached full flower with *The Tree of Life*.

Style, however, is visual form in the service of narrative meaning, even in a film as abstract, fragmentary and poetic as *The Tree of Life*. The key to the film, it seemed to me, lay in the complex dialectic between 'the way of nature' and 'the way of grace' that unfolds throughout the work. These two paths through life compose a dynamic relationship articulated at a number of levels, from the personal to the metaphysical, expressed cinematically in the contrasts between movement and stillness, action and reflection, light and darkness and so on. This dialectic between nature and grace – which comprises a complex 'unity of opposites' – links the young Jack's (Hunter McCracken) attempts to reconcile his father's (Brad Pitt) egoistic self-interest with his mother's (Jessica Chastain) love and mercy. It relates the sublimity of nature in its elemental power, the blind striving of life struggling to exist, with a transcendent dimension of spirit that unites us with the cosmos as a whole.

Another way of putting this is to say that the film expresses what Thomas Nagel calls the 'religious temperament' (2010): a concern with the meaning of human existence in relation to the cosmic whole of nature. For Nagel, the religious temperament animates ancient philosophy, yet is curiously absent in a lot of modern thought, particularly mainstream analytic philosophy. It can be described as the attempt to respond, through metaphysical or existential reflection, to the 'human yearning for cosmic reconciliation'; it concerns the desire, strongly articulated in Plato, 'to achieve the kind of understanding that would connect him (and therefore every human being) to the whole of reality intelligibly and, if possible, satisfyingly' (Nagel 2010). The religious temperament, which can be shared by religious thinkers, artists and philosophers (including atheists), involves acknowledging and responding to the 'cosmic question': namely, 'How can one bring into one's individual life a recognition of one's relation to the universe as whole, whatever that relation is?' (Nagel 2010: 3–5). From this point of view, *The Tree of Life* appears as a film explicitly expressing the religious temperament, one that is at once philosophical, religious and mythic. It is a film that attempts to respond to the cosmic question through art, to retrieve and renew a sense of belief in the medium of cinema and its power of aesthetic revelation.

In thinking about the film's religious mood, I was reminded of one of Bazin's remarks on Robert Bresson's *Diary of a Country Priest* (1951), which resonates beautifully with Malick's numinous 'hymn to life'. It too, in Bazin's words, is 'a new form of drama, one that is specifically religious, or better yet, theological: a phenomenology of salvation and grace' (Bazin 2009: 150). *The Tree of Life*'s mythic evocation of cosmic, historical and personal memory, its phenomenological presentation of contingency and the radiance of nature, the epiphanies of the everyday and its commitment to the transformative power of cinematic experience, all suggested powerful resonances with Bazin. From this perspective, we could rethink the relationship between film and philosophy in an expanded manner in order to include the religious temperament. This would enable us to acknowledge Malick's existential and metaphysical explorations, through a reconfiguring of narrative style, of the cosmic question through cinema.

'Our picture is a cosmic epic, a hymn to life'[1]

As remarked, it was not surprising that *The Tree of Life* polarized critics. Apart from Malick's distinctive style (to which I return below), this was due to its remarkable coalescence of genres and its complex, symphonic structure, combining at least three dimensions: an evocative (and partly autobiographical) family melodrama/coming-of-age/memory film set in 1950s and 1960s Texas (as well as in the present), featuring Hollywood stars Brad Pitt, Sean Penn and Jessica Chastain; a sublime 'creation' interlude on the origins of the universe and evolution of life on earth, combining Kubrick-style cosmic meditation with awe-inspiring nature documentary (which was later released as an independent work, *Voyage of Time*, 2016); and a romantic-religious hymn celebrating existence, acknowledging grace in the face of suffering, and the life-affirming, transcendent power of spiritualized love. Such a film clearly challenged philosophically oriented critics. As remarked earlier, *The Thin Red Line* (1998), with its Heideggerian meditations on Being and the worldliness of the world, and its Emersonian evocations of 'one big soul' and 'all things shining', attracted much philosophical attention.[2] Far less enthusiastic was the reception for *The New World*, Malick's mythic love story and historical costume drama, with its romantic-elegiac explorations of the nascent encounter between cultural-historical worlds and poetic meditations on our historical dwelling in nature.[3] *The New World*'s cinematic exploration of the idea of 'world' still exercised critics, even those (such as Neer) sceptical of the idea of film as philosophy. *The Tree of Life*, however, presented greater challenges to the idea of 'film as philosophy', or to the idea of Malick as filmmaker and philosopher, an artist evoking aesthetic experience through films that invite philosophical reflection. As Kent Jones remarked, Malick's 'intense interest in origins – of violence, of the universe itself' – made his films 'anomalous in modern culture' (2011: 26). Indeed, Jones was not alone in detecting what he described as 'a strain of embarrassment in some of the more hostile reactions to *The Tree of Life*' (2011: 24).

One explanation for this hostility, apart from the predictable complaints about Malick's style, would be the anxiety generated by the film's spiritual-religious dimensions, a pattern that has become marked with Malick's most recent films.[4] Repeating the reception history of Malick's four other films, critical responses to *The Tree of Life* were polarized between rapturous celebration and sarcastic ridicule. Noted critic Roger Ebert, for example, praised Malick's work as 'a film of vast ambition and deep humility, attempting no less than to encompass all of existence and view it through the prism of a few infinitesimal lives' (2011). Amy Taubin, by contrast, complained that 'the film's attempt to represent the presence of the Creator in all living things from the Big Bang to the End of Time relies on an aesthetically insufferable pile-on of maudlin voiceover combined with a glut of classical religious music' (2011: 57). Taubin's complaints concerning Malick's use of voiceovers (used far less than in *The Thin Red Line*) and rich musical repertoire[5] is representative of a common strain of critical rejection. What separates the perspectives of Ebert and Taubin, I suggest, is less a dispute over the film's aesthetic qualities than one over its status as a religious work of art, which is a topic that leaves many film theorists ambivalent or embarrassed.[6]

While acknowledging the link between Malick and Neoplatonist philosophers such as Johannes Scotus Eriugena – his theophanic metaphysics of light as the expression of divine life, 'all things are lights' – Kent Jones dismisses the description of *The Tree of Life* as a 'religious' film in the sense of one adhering to Christian doctrine. It is more a crossover, he observes, between 'Eriugena's vision of life of earth and pre-orthodox Buddhism', a work fixated not on the afterlife but 'on the "glory" of *this* life' (Jones 2011: 26). A film can be religious of course without adhering to Christian or any other particular doctrine; and there is no good reason to hold that acknowledging the film's religiosity is incompatible with a critical appreciation of its aesthetic qualities. Indeed, it is precisely *The Tree of Life*'s 'Christianity', or its religiosity more broadly construed, that accounts, I suggest, for much the film's highly polarized reception, the curious mixture of aesthetic acknowledgement (of the film's cinematography, for example) and critical rejection (of its metaphysical pretentions, artistic overreach or religious orientation).

We might describe the critical response to the film as falling into two camps: those interpreting the film from (and as bound by) a secular perspective (in which the question of religion is not thematic or else is treated critically) and those interpreting it from (and as expressing) something closer to a postsecular perspective (in which the question of religion is made explicitly thematic or even endorsed by the film). One of the most telling aspects of this clash between secular and postsecular approaches concerns the differing interpretative strategies that critics have deployed in order to deal with (or else avoid) the film's Christianity/religiosity. There are four that a survey of the film's critical reception reveals: (1) uncritical affirmation of the film because of its religious content (the Christian interpretation of the film),[7] (2) uncritical rejection of the film for essentially the same reason (the anti-religious response),[8] (3) disavowal of the film's religious content in favour of its aesthetic merits (the 'aestheticist' reading) and (4) acknowledgement of the film's aesthetic merits and transformation of its religious content into generic or 'post-secular' forms of spirituality (the 'revisionist' approach).[9] One common pattern was to downplay the religiosity and praise the film's aesthetic virtues; a contrasting alternative was to criticize the film's alleged aesthetic vices as a way of rejecting its religiosity. The difficulty, however, is that these two aspects are inextricably entwined (e.g. the use of voiceover in the film). *The Tree of Life*'s religious/theological dimensions therefore pose a problem, not only for evaluating aesthetic responses to the film but for understanding the relationship between film, philosophy and religion more generally.

David Sterritt (2011), for example, praises the film as a 'stunning achievement', an ambitious, personal film evoking 'a sense of divine wonder by artfully juxtaposing an autobiographical *Bildungsroman* with sublime artefacts chosen from the visual, verbal, musical, gestural, and architectural treasures' gleaned from the long history of Judeo-Christian thought. Nonetheless, he criticizes what he takes to be Malick's theological position: the film's shift from philosophy to theodicy, 'arguing for God's goodness despite the evidence of a fallen, iniquitous world', which thereby removes, he claims, the human dimension of pain, struggle and suffering (Sterritt 2011: 57). There is much to be said about this question of theology, since the film contrasts precisely the human dimension of pain, struggle and suffering – the grief afflicting not only the mother who loses R.L. but also Jack, whose struggle to reunite with his brother in spirit defines the trajectory of the film – with an aesthetically transfigured experience of nature, the world and of individual human beings in their irreplaceable singularity. The latter contributes an answer to the former: the aesthetically mediated experience of joy, wonder and transcendence in relation to the world is itself a response to the question of theodicy posed by the film (why do we suffer when God is supposed to be benevolent and love creation?) and the broader 'cosmic question' (what is the significance of my individual existence in relation to the cosmos as a whole?). The aesthetic, the moral and the theological are inextricably entwined in *The Tree of Life*, despite critics' various attempts to separate, sequester and hierarchize them in different configurations.

There is, moreover, what we could call a hermeneutic antinomy that *The Tree of Life* seems to generate, which Moritz Pfeifer (2011) describes by contrasting religious-idealist and analytic-modernist perspectives on the film. As Pfeifer observes, on the one hand, there is *the idealist*, for whom *The Tree of Life* is an ineffable aesthetic and emotional revelation, showing beauty and reality in ways that evoke spiritual truth. On the other, there is *the analyst*, for whom the film should be analysed and understood as a self-reflexive historical meditation on memory and childhood experience, mediated by cinema and popular cultural imagery (the glass coffin image from Disney's *Snow White*, for example; the 1950s fascination with space, science and the universe; or even, I would add, the wry reference to *Fight Club* in the scene where the Father (Brad Pitt) cajoles his sons to 'hit me!').[10] From this point of view, any spiritual or religious meaning to be gleaned from the film is relativized: either mediated via the perspective of the various characters or else referencing, more or less ironically, other cinematic works (Kubrick's *2001: A Space Odyssey* and Tarkovsky's *Mirror*, for example).[11]

In response to this antinomy, Pfeifer attempts to maintain a duality of idealist and analytic perspectives that breaks down, however, since it is precisely the mediation between the two that slants him towards the analytic perspective. Hence Pfeifer's rather melancholy reading of the film, which, he claims, 'grieves over its own discoveries', and his sceptical conclusion: 'all these images [e.g. Jack's image of his mother in a glass coffin] depict the promise of a sensation immune to change knowing that this sensation, if it shall appear, will not only be different, but also pass away. They are images that discredit themselves in the illustration' (Pfeifer 2011). If there is a conclusion to be drawn from the opposition between idealist and analytic perspectives, it is to show how they are dialectically related and transformed throughout the unfolding of the film.

Alternatively, one can take the film straightforwardly as a religious work of art, an approach favoured by many Christian viewers and critics, some of whom point to Malick's own religious faith as explicit evidence of authorial intention. Indeed, as I read more of these analyses, which began appearing in the years between *The Tree of Life* and the release of *To the Wonder* (2012) and *Knight of Cups* (2015), I was struck by how coherent and illuminating theological interpretations of these later Malick films proved to be (see Plate 2012). Could it be that the philosophical approaches, on the one hand, and the cinematic approaches, on the other, were both missing something vital in these films? Missing something essential not only to engaging with Malick's cinematic art but to comprehending the idea of film as philosophy?

A good example of this religious/theological reading is Christopher Barnett's (2013) discussion of *The Tree of Life* as a theological-religious work of art, drawing on Malick's explicit references to the Book of Job, to Christian theology and the cinematic aesthetics of wind/breath as indirect figurations of spirit/*ruach*/*pneuma*. Exploring the use of wind imagery in Malick's films, Barnett points out that this use of wind or breath as a way of figuring spirit or the presence of spirituality in nature and in the world puts Malick's nature imagery in a long cultural and historical tradition of religious symbolism (2013: 5–10). The explicit focus and emphasis on images of wind or breath in many important sequences within *The Tree of Life* (and other works) supports the idea of Malick's celebrated naturalism and poetics of natural beauty as having a simultaneous spiritual-religious significance within the framework of a Christian theology of spirit understood as *ruach* or *pneuma* (Barnett 2013: 11 ff.). Moreover, the power of Malick's/Lubezki's cinematography, along with his pointed use of explicitly religious music, combines a commitment to aesthetic realism and material expressivity with an exploration of implicit spiritual meaning.

At the same time, Barnett argues, this religious reading can be reconciled with the more familiar Heideggerian approach to Malick's films – like *The Thin Red Line* and *The Tree of Life* – as centred on the late Heidegger's thought of releasement or *Gelassenheit*: the ethical-attentive attitude or comportment of 'letting-be' that allows things to appear in their own manner of Being (2013: 18 ff.). In this way, the film's theological-religious concern to evoke God's divine spiritual presence in everyday reality can be reconciled with its ethical commitment to an attitude of contemplative releasement: the film's distinctively aesthetic expression of care for all manner of beings as set against the background 'mystery' of the revelation and self-withdrawal of Being.

One of the virtues of Barnett's religious-theological reading of the film is that it offers aesthetic evidence for the film's concern with theological and religious expressions of spirituality. It also acknowledges the film's ethical concern with the Heideggerian contemplative attitude of 'letting-be'; the film's implicit criticism of Mr O'Brien's (Brian Pitt's) activist, instrumentalist, pragmatist stance towards the world; and its tacit endorsement of Mrs O'Brien's (Jessica Chastain's) graceful attitude of caring comportment or letting-be ('love everything').

At the same time, however, it neglects to frame this reading against the historical-cultural background of the O'Brien family story – the manner in which this microcosmic, domestic world resonates within the macrocosmic dimension of the origin (and end) of the cosmos – or to explore in more depth the question of cinema in relation to spiritual experience in a postsecularist context. What is the significance of such a story, presented in such an impressionistic, fragmentary manner, within an American cultural context that has experienced its own version of 'the Fall', a cultural loss of hope, meaning and possibility? From this point of view, *The Tree of Life* is not only a prodigious memory film and spiritually inflected familial melodrama but can be understood as a cinematic (and perhaps ideological) allegory of America's 'Fall' into a spiritually vacuous form of technological advancement and materialistic conformism.

It is clear, in any event, that *The Tree of Life* invites a Christian, 'spiritualist' reading, not only because it begins with a quotation from the Book of Job, features a Job sermon lifted directly from Kierkegaard and religious symbolism deriving from the history of Judeo-Christian religious artistic traditions. It is also because the narrative centres on Jack's odyssey from existential despair to spiritual reconciliation – a transcendent reunion with his departed brother ('Find me'), whose tragic death marks the O'Brien family's shared horizon of experience. Such a reading, however, needs to be integrated with the film's 'naturalism', its commitment to a 'compatibilist' account of relationship between religion and science, Christian spirituality and evolutionary biology, both of which are given equal validity in the movie. This is one of the key background problems, I suggest, motivating the movie's cinematic, critical and aesthetic reflection: the (cultural as well as personal) experience of nihilism and how we might respond to it artistically (through cinema). From this point of view, *The Tree of Life* can be understood as an instance of cinematic ethics reflecting a cinema of 'belief' (in this world), one that is capacious enough to encompass religious and spiritual experience, scientific naturalism as well as an existential-ethical transformation.[12]

At the other end of the hermeneutic spectrum are readings of the film that avoid overt acknowledgement of or engagement with the film's Christian-spiritualist dimensions or allusions. Some critics remain resolutely hostile to any Christian interpretation of the film, or towards the film itself for its Christianity, whereas others remain 'agnostic' on *The Tree of Life*'s religiosity, so to speak, acknowledging the religious aspect but then translating or transposing this into a more philosophical, postsecular register. A good example of this 'agnostic' approach is Shawn Loht's (2014) philosophical reading of *The Tree of Life* as offering a cinematic-aesthetic 'argument' for an (environmental) ethics that is compatible with a Heideggerian existential ethos of authentic dwelling. As Loht observes, the film contrasts the 'two ways through life' – a Nietzschean will to mastery and rational control of nature and fate, versus a Christian ethic of universal love and grace open to nature and contingency. Following Heidegger, he suggests the latter offers a more appropriate mode of human dwelling more in keeping with our own nature than the former mode of existence, which remains the dominant social ethos within modernity. The film, for Loht, enacts a cinematic mode of argumentation that seeks to show how a more authentic mode of dwelling, resonating with Heidegger's conception of existential authenticity, remains an ethical possibility worthy of philosophical exploration in what Heidegger called our 'destitute times'. To be sure, his reading emphasizes the manner in which both scientific-evolutionary and religious-spiritual perspectives are presented as (potentially) complementary perspectives on human existence – its origins, development and meaning – in response to the contemporary crisis of environmental devastation and moral-political disorientation. Nonetheless, his approach also avoids the question of religiosity in favour of a more robustly secular Heideggerian approach combined with an eco-aesthetic concern with environmental crisis and the threat this poses to our fragile sense of world.

Although Loht remains neutral on the question of religion – acknowledging its importance for the film without giving it a key role in interpreting its meaning – he privileges the film's philosophical dimensions thanks to a Heideggerian understanding of authenticity.

This is evident in his account of the cinematic argument for the 'way of grace', which the film presents as offering a more existentially and ethically grounded mode of existence in keeping with our human nature (as dwellers, thinkers or what Heidegger describes as 'shepherds of Being'). In this respect, the film's theological-religious perspective is largely subsumed within a Heideggerian environmentalist ethics of dwelling that pays less attention to film's important historical-cultural background.

The latter, I suggest, is mediated through the idealized world of Jack's childhood experiences (1950s America's loss of innocence, the perceived 'Fall' from the 'magical' child-like world of hope and possibility) to the nihilistic wasteland of modernity seemingly devoid of meaning or authenticity (the adult Jack's evident despair, soulless dwelling, unhappy marriage and alienating work). Indeed one of the film's central challenges – articulated more explicitly in Malick's *To the Wonder* (2012) – is the spiritualized rediscovery of the redemptive/transformative power of love as a personal and cultural response to the enervation of moral-social relations between men and women that haunts our fragmented sense of community. We might put this as the film's exploration of the ethical potential of cinematic art, not only as a means of exploring ethical experience but also as a cinematic-cultural response to the problem of nihilism or pervasive cultural-moral scepticism: a spiritual-aesthetic affirmation of existence in response to the attenuation of meaning, value and purpose in modern life.

An alternative approach is to reframe the question of how film and philosophy are related by acknowledging the film's religious dimension while also keeping open the multiplicity of senses – including moral-ethical or philosophical meaning – evoked by its aesthetic sublimity. In particular, this means focusing on the manner in which the film evokes a sense of wonder towards the world or affirmation of existence despite the experiences of pain, struggle and suffering that envelop the O'Brien family. From this point of view, *The Tree of Life* can be viewed as a meditation on belief: from belief in life, nature, love and God to an ethical-existential belief in this-worldly existence (mediated via memory), a belief expressed in and encompassed by the aesthetic power of cinema itself. The question of belief enables us to acknowledge both aesthetic and religious dimensions of the film, thus allowing the apparently conflicting analytic and idealist perspectives – call these nature and grace – to be, if not reconciled, then brought into dynamic relation with each other. It would also enable us to rethink and expand the question of film and philosophy in order to shift it towards moral experience and ethical understanding, showing how existential and metaphysical thinking are solicited as part of the film's 'aesthetic theodicy': its response to the religious question of suffering and the existential ethic of overcoming despair through love.

Belief in cinema: *The Tree of Life* as mythic work

In a brief but rich essay, 'Cinema and Theology' (1997), André Bazin identified three ways, historically speaking, in which film has tackled religious themes. The most common is by retelling the Christ story, the 'stations of the cross' film; then there is hagiography, the melodramatic 'lives of the saints' movie; and finally, one can dramatize the spiritual, psychological and social struggles of the priest, the most exemplary instance of which is Bresson's masterpiece, *Diary of a Country Priest* (1951) (Bazin 1997: 64). Another approach he did not mention, however, concerns films that deal with theology in less explicit ways. One can frame the cosmic question concerning the search for human meaning in relation to the universe as a whole, addressing and expressing the religious temperament by means of a microcosmic narrative (focusing on particular characters or a small group like a family) set against the macrocosmic order or existential background of our place in the universe. Such films will have an allegorical dimension, such that the personal or social drama takes on a deeper meaning when set against this cosmic background or inflected via existential concerns (e.g. Dreyer's *Ordet*, Bergman's *Winter Light* or even Kubrick's *2001: A Space Odyssey*). As S. Brent Plate observes, this search for meaning using a microcosmic narrative situated within a macrocosmic order is one way in which cinema can participate in the religious practice of world re-creation, or what we could call a cinematic cosmology, or more precisely, a cosmogony (a creation of worlds). As Plate remarks, with reference to *The Tree of Life*:

> Cinema is part of the symbol-creating apparatus of culture, yet it also aspires to more: to world-encompassing visions of the nomos and cosmos. Cinema allows us to see in new ways, through new technologies, re-creating the world anew, telescoping the macrocosmic part and far away, and bringing these visions to bear on the microcosmic structures in the here and now. (Plate 2012: 535)

This is certainly relevant to approaching *The Tree of Life*, which could be defined as an ambitious work of cinematic cosmology or cosmogony (world re-creation) that nests the microcosmic moral-theological drama of the O'Brien family, their moral-existential struggle with the Jobian question, 'why do we suffer?' within a sublimely rendered vision of macrocosmic world-creation (and destruction). We can still approach this as a philosophical film but in a more refined sense, both morally and metaphysically: exploring how the question of suffering can be reconciled with belief in the world, a question that is open to existential, moral-ethical, as well as religious-theological interpretations.

The obvious starting point is the film's opening quotation from the Book of Job, which situates the film within a Christian theological tradition: 'Where were you when I laid the foundations of the earth? ... When the morning stars sang together, and all the sons of God shouted for joy?' (Job 38:4,7). The film's title reiterates this theme, referring to the Tree of Life found in the Garden of Eden. The tree of life symbolizes the source of life (eternal life) and the source of healing for divided peoples (cited in the Book of Genesis and in the Book of Revelation).[13] At the same time, the film's title is also a multivalent cultural symbol that spans many world religions, mythological accounts of the origin of life and Darwin's conception of evolutionary development. This coalescence of meanings in the title of the film – combining Christian, mythological and evolutionary senses – is reflected in its synthesis of disparate styles and genres. As remarked, there are three narrative/mythic dimensions of *The Tree of Life*: the familial melodrama, the historical-spiritual Fall or loss of the American Dream and the cosmological creation myth combining spiritualism and naturalism. All three are woven together in the microcosmic story of the O'Brien family set against a cosmic background that situates and contextualizes the religious-existential questions of spiritual redemption from despair and affirming existence in the face of human suffering.[14]

To these three narrative/mythic dimensions correspond four distinctive and overlapping styles of cinematic presentation: (1) fragmentary vignettes featuring mobile flowing camera (Steadicam), intimate voiceover expressing thoughts, reflections, impressions in a confessional or prayer-like manner, accompanied by a musical score complementing and attuning the mood of the sequence; (2) more conventional narrative passages with static shots, rapid cutting, shot-reverse shot sequences, conventional dialogue, motivated action, no music and relatively transparent plot development; (3) more abstract sequences with decontextualized images of lone figures, use of wide shots, distorting lenses, variable camera movements (both mobile and static), combinations of sequence shots and rapid montage, accompanied by notably elliptical and ambiguous voiceovers, often with religious overtones; finally, (4) quasi-documentary/essay style abstract images involving stylized visual effects, animated sequences combined with live action footage of animal, plant and biological life, amidst cosmic as well as 'primordial' landscapes, accompanied by musical scoring with a distinctly religious mood. *The Tree of Life* moves seamlessly between these four modes of cinematic presentation, adapting and combining each style across all four narrative/mythic dimensions of the film.

As becomes evident with closer viewing, each style corresponds to a particular type of cinematic sequence: the first 'subjective' style, for example, corresponds roughly with the subjective dimensions of the familial melodrama and the 'Fall' from innocence sequences. The more conventional narrative style corresponds with the more overtly plot-driven sequences of the familial melodrama. The abstract sequences, in contrast, dominate Jack's journey from existential-spiritual despair to an experience of grace through love; and the abstract documentary style corresponds most obviously with the creation mythology from the birth of the world, development of life, to the vision of its demise at 'end of time'.

The film opens using the fragmentary vignette style (Jack's voiceover or prayer) but combined with abstract imagery (a 'Lumia' image from Thomas Wilfred's work, Opus 161, 1965).[15] It then continues this impressionistic vignette style but shifts to a more recollective register (recalling Mrs O'Brien's childhood and adult memories). The announcement of R.L's death – via a Telegram we never see, and devoid of dialogue as Mrs O'Brien collapses (while jump cuts interrupt the sequence) – suggests an experience of traumatic excess. Similarly, Mr O'Brien is told the news by telephone (he is shown in close-up, then from the back, then framed against an airplane whose engines obliterate all other sound), which creates both a sense of intimacy and emotional involvement that nonetheless retains a certain distance, avoids revealing psychological interiority, hence remains somewhat opaque. The family's grief, by contrast, is shown in a more conventional narrative style, although accompanied by subjective voiceover (Mrs O'Brien questioning providence), and then shifts, after Mrs O'Brien's 'way of nature versus way of grace' voiceover, to the more abstract 'creation mythology' sequence, accompanied by expressive religious music.

All three mythic/narrative dimensions and overlapping cinematic styles communicate within a topology that could be called *mythopoetic* (combining myth and poetry). As far as the narrative is concerned, the first layer (1) is the familial melodrama, which centres on middle-aged architect Jack O'Brien's (Sean Penn) spiritual-existential crisis on the anniversary of his younger brother's death (killed when he was 19). Set during the course of this one day, a despairing O'Brien recollects, via a complex use of flashbacks, the lost life and joy of his childhood, growing up with his two brothers, stern father (Brad Pitt) and serene mother (Jessica Chastain) in Waco, Texas, during the 1950s.[16] From the opening moments ('Brother. Mother. It was they who led me to your door') to the closing voiceover ('Keep us. Guide us. To the end of Time'), it is Jack's journey to 'find' his brother, to reconcile himself to mortality and loss through love (of family, of the world and of God) and Mrs O'Brien's conversion of grief and suffering into affirmation and acceptance ('I give him to you. I give you my son'), which together define the film's otherwise fragmentary narrative and religious-theological trajectory.

(2) The second layer is the historical-spiritual story. The O'Brien family's story depicts – mainly through visual style, mise-en-scène, framing, composition and inspired use of light – a mythic Fall from the romanticized historical 'Eden' of the 1950s Midwest to the spiritually destitute space of contemporary urban America, marked by the imposing, geometrically ordered glass and steel architecture of downtown Houston.

(3) The third layer is the cosmological creation myth, a sublime sequence of creation images interpolated within the familial melodrama and historical 'Fall', which evokes the miraculous emergence of life within a re-enchanted universe; a naturalized cosmos developing with evolutionary vitality and imbued with aesthetic grandeur and spiritual wonder. This third story culminates in an eschatological myth (Jack's transcendent vision of the 'end of time', and experience of spiritual redemption and the overcoming of despair), which brings together the familial melodrama, story of the Fall and the mythic-spiritual quest in an aesthetically transcendent experience of spiritual reconciliation through love.

This mythic tenor of the film is signalled in its opening sequence, which frames what follows as a response to God's challenge to Job, defying him to comprehend the vastness of creation. Could we, as mere mortals, have witnessed the birth of the universe and emergence of life from the primordial darkness? In response, we see a numinous image of coloured light set against a dark background (another 'Lumia' image), accompanied by signature Malick background sounds of susurrating nature (wind, waves and bird cries). This abstract style recurs in related sequences throughout the film, adding the 'cosmic' metaphysical background that will frame the microcosmic familial drama. Taken by some critics as a depiction of God's presence, the image, as Jones remarks (2011: 24–26), highlights Malick's fascination with light, his neoplatonic, theophanic equation between light and life, the metaphysically and aesthetically rendered sense of 'all things shining'.

Such theophanic cinematography also expresses, I would add, the intimate relationship between cinema, nature and the everyday: the luminous 'realism' of Malick's cinema, its Bazinian power to capture an aesthetically transfigured reality through radiant images of place and duration. Almost every outdoor shot in the film, for example, displays the setting sun, in the background yet shining brilliantly through trees, radiating across faces, a benevolent eye illuminating the everyday world. Natural light bathes all, allowing each figure, each living creature, each tree and animal, to appear in their singularity in a luminous and revelatory show of presencing. These are radiant images of expressive mobility, of attending to prescencing as such, images that celebrate the sheer beauty of existence, what Heidegger called the ontological power of beauty – or better, its *ontopoetical* power – to reveal the truth of beings, of 'all things shining'.

Still in 'mythic' mode, the film proper begins with a typically Malickian voiceover, belonging to the adult Jack, pitched as a meditation or confession directed at an unnamed presence: 'Brother, Mother. It was they who led me to your door', accompanied on the soundtrack by a deep rumbling, ocean sounds, and faint bird cries. The line anticipates the image of an empty doorframe in the desert wilderness, a threshold or passageway between worlds, before which we see Jack hesitate at decisive moments in the film. Like Pocahontas/ Rebecca in *The New World*, whose voiceover invocations call for her 'Mother' (her own and mother earth), Jack's voiceover, like that of his own mother, hovers between recollection and meditation, confession and revelation, voice of conscience and silent prayer. Like all Malick's voiceovers, the voice both belongs to a particular character and serves to articulate a communal experience. It narrates a particular character's story, witnessing his or her subjective experience, while also taking on an 'any person whatever' role: that of a mythic narrator witnessing a shared or collective experience transcending the particularities of psychology, place or history.

The mythic use of voiceover continues with the introduction of Jack's mother. Her childhood recollections as a girl sequenced in lyrical images flowing from girlhood encounters with nature to courtship and married life, introducing her family, her husband and sons, images accompanied by a voiceover that invokes the duality of nature and grace that lies at the heart of the film:

> In man's palace there are two ways through life: the Way of Nature and the Way of Grace. You have to choose which one you'll follow. Grace doesn't try to please itself. Accepts being slighted, forgotten, disliked. Accepts insults and injuries. Nature only wants to please itself. Gets others to please it too. Likes to lord it over them. To have its own way. It finds reasons to be unhappy, when all the world is shining around it, and love is smiling through all things.

Interestingly, the poignant musical accompaniment to this opening sequence is 'Funeral Canticle' composed by John Tavener and Mother Tekla, a piece both gently mournful and serenely uplifting. This sequence epitomizes Malick's impressionistic vignette style: briskly cut mobile images – what we could also call a 'paratactic style' linking images in a connective or additive series – capturing representative, contingent moments, memories or impressions, cut together according to mood and movement rather than action or plot development, usually accompanied by voiceover and/or musical scoring. We see a young girl, hands clutching a window ledge, looking joyfully at the scene outside; a field with grass and animals, the girl holding a kid goat, her face only half in frame; images of sun and clouds; a field of sunflowers; the girl contemplating cows, only her moving hand visible in the frame; then shot from below, her hair obscuring her face; or shot from behind, with her father, hugging and holding her, his face also obscured from view. After a black screen, we see images from her married life, life in a small town, a dizzying mobile shot of her swinging on a swing, shadows reorienting our vision, the camera moving in sync with the swing. We see her sons playing together with her outside, and then cut to inside the house, communicating with the outside, introducing the father, who says grace before lunch ('bless these boys'); then the boys playing with their dog and parents, running with their mother in the street, all overlooked by the majestic, sunlit tree in their yard. The images sometimes correspond with the voiceover (the father introduced to us accompanied by Mrs O'Brien's voiceover on 'the way of nature'; or an ironic shot following R.L. from behind, accompanied by the line that 'no one who takes the way of grace ever comes to a bad end'). Sometimes they contrast with it (shots of the family playing joyfully together in the front yard, as Mrs O'Brien's voiceover describes how the 'way of nature' likes to lord it over others and have its own way).

The duality of nature and grace, personified by characters both in communion and in conflict, features in a number of Malick films. It is evident in contrast between Witt and Welsh in *The Thin Red Line*, Smith and Pocahontas in *The New World*, even Kit and Holly in *Badlands*. There is opposition and struggle but also interweaving or entwining of these poles, which are intimately related, mutually transforming but never fully reconciled. This is true in *The Tree of Life*, which situates the dialectic between nature and grace within a religious-mythic frame, while exploring their complex attunement in a dynamic, Heraclitean 'unity of opposites'. Malick both evokes and subtly shifts the religious dimension of this relationship, their initial opposition revealing a more complex dialectic as the film unfolds.

It is clear that *The Tree of Life* articulates the relationship between the way of nature and the way of grace within a Christian theological context. As a number of interpreters point out, Mrs O'Brien's description of the contrast between the two ways through life is reminiscent of medieval mystic Thomas à Kempis's account in *The Imitation of Christ* (Book 3, Chapter 54) (see Rybin 2012: 172).[17] The way of nature is that of self-preservation, the struggle for survival, rational egoism; the way of grace, by contrast, is that of self-transcendence, openness to the world (or God) and selfless or agapic love. The traditional understanding, as in à Kempis, is that we must overcome the way of nature and choose that of grace instead. At first blush, it might appear that the film takes the same view. The contrast between nature and grace, for example, seems mapped directly on to the characters of Mr and Mrs O'Brien, the stern, egoistic, disciplinarian father versus the loving, forgiving, gracious mother; or between young Jack torn between these two conflicting impulses in contrast with the aesthetic sensitivity of his younger brother, the budding guitarist, R.L. (Laramie Eppler).

At the same time, the film also complicates this contrast, showing how grace and nature co-exist, struggling and vying with each other, grace having need of nature but also how nature is imbued with grace (as Mrs O'Brien says, nature torments itself, ignoring the beauty and glory shining through all things). The film does not simply endorse the mother's grace and forgiveness, which Mr O'Brien at one point calls 'naive', against the father's 'fierce will' and desire to 'lord it over others' – his way of preparing his sons for the way of the world. On the contrary, the mother's grace is tested by the loss of her younger son, which she takes as God's personal slight against her. The father struggles with his own suppressed feeling, his sensitivity and vulnerability, his thwarted musical ambitions and aesthetic, even moral pleasure in the transports of music, a poignant reminder of a life path not taken. Neither character is entirely representative either of nature or of grace, even though each clearly decides in favour of one path over the other, the family presumably being the place where both paths encounter and conflict with each other. Like 'this war at the heart of nature' (*The Thin Red Line*), or the struggle between British colonists and Powhatan 'naturals' in *The New World*, the ways of nature and grace in *The Tree of Life* remain locked in a dialectical embrace, each pole depending on the other yet maintaining itself in a relation of dynamic tension with its opposite. Indeed, Jack's story is precisely that of the struggle between these two ways, his lifelong quest to reconcile nature and grace ('Father, mother: always you struggle inside me') – to rediscover the glory that imbues the world and nature with light and love. The sequence ends with the boys climbing the tree, the shot of R.L. followed by a powerful waterfall and an image of what we could well call 'the tree of life'.

As remarked, Mrs O'Brien describes the 'two ways' through life as something the nuns taught her, a spiritual teaching to guide us on life's path. The challenge, however, is to maintain grace and love in the face of senseless suffering and loss. The crucial point in Mrs O'Brien's voiceover thus comes at the end of this sequence, where she concludes her meditation with a recollection prompting an avowal of faith: 'They taught us that no one who loves the way of grace ever comes to a bad end. I will be true to you, whatever comes.' 'Whatever comes', however, is not fortune and happiness but loss and despair, the sudden death of Mrs O'Brien's beloved youngest son, a promising classical guitarist. We jump abruptly forward in time (from the 1950s to the late 1960s), to a newer house, and the arrival of a telegram, which Mrs O'Brien receives in silence, as the musical accompaniment dies down and sharp diegetic sounds (door, envelope, footsteps, birds in the background) fill the airy, gently lit space of the house. She reads the telegram, the traumatic blow of the news signalled by a jump cut, the camera then perched at her side, close over her shoulder; she tries to absorb the news, which is too much to bear; another jump cut, followed by the camera gently pulling back and ascending, a sympathetic witness to her grief, as she rises, nearly stumbles and cries out in pain.[18]

The abrupt and traumatic breach in their lives is emphasized in a brutal cut, from Mrs O'Brien's cry of pain to a close shot of Mr O'Brien, the camera again perched near his shoulder, taking the fateful call, the traumatic news registering on his face, all other sounds obliterated by the engine of a plane waiting on the tarmac. Like Mrs O'Brien's telegram, we hear nothing of the call's content, as the camera pulls towards his face and holds, the shock of the news evident in his pained and speechless expression. The trauma obliterates all familiar coordinates of the world, which collapses around the family. All diegetic sound dies away and a musical accompaniment begins, a deep and foreboding rumbling with the suggestion of a bell tolling (Francisco Lupica's Cosmic Beam Take V, which also features in *The Thin Red Line*). The camera lingers with Mr O'Brien, illuminated by sunlight, turns around him agitatedly, whips forward to show us the plane and ground staff, Mr O'Brien's body, like his wife's, crumpling with grief and shock, as he reels forward in despair before a setting sun.

Another shot of the setting sun, as the camera descends from the crown of a tree towards its base, marks the transition to the next sequence, filmed in more conventional narrative style. Nonetheless, this section also features freely flowing camerawork, improvised long takes and a fragmentary presentation of moments, events and actions, as the O'Briens grieve for their dead son. The musical accompaniment changes to a melancholy, chilling passage from the first movement of Mahler's First Symphony. The mournful tone befits the images of Mrs O'Brien walking aimlessly around her street in despair, the light now dull and flat, Mr O'Brien following behind her, both trying to comfort her and to keep the neighbours at bay, followed by poignant shots of the empty rooms in the house, of R.L.'s paintbrushes and guitar, of

R.L. playing guitar as a child, his absent presence in their world only emphasizing their pain and loss.

The son's death is clearly the event that defines this family odyssey, Mrs O'Brien and Jack both struggling to reconcile their loss with belief in a benevolent God. The grandmother (Fiona Shaw) tries to counsel the mother, advocating a Christian stoicism in the face of pain and suffering: 'The Lord gives and the Lord takes away ... sends flies to wounds he should heal.' We see, in painful close-ups, the raw grief and anger mixed in Mrs O'Brien face, followed by images of an empty treehouse shot from below, a dead tree against a grey sky, with sounds of shrieking in the background. In a significant moment during her grieving, we hear both the prayer she recites, overlaid, in a louder voiceover, by her internal questioning of God, asking plaintively, 'What did you gain?' Mr O'Brien, in closeup, reminisces about R.L., about how hard he was on the boy, 'criticising him for how he turned the pages' during piano practice. We see a rare reverse shot of Mrs O'Brien looking attentive but gazing warily, first down then up at her husband, as she listens to him, in tears, saying how he made his son feel shame, 'my shame' – 'poor, poor boy', he mutters in tears, as the handheld camera moves slowly around him. The closeups give way to a striking, Tarkovsky-like wide shot of an unsteady Mr O'Brien walking alone through a grove of trees, the poignant exchange accompanied by Giya Kancheli's quiet and mournful 'Morning Prayer'. The modulation of mood, from intimate revelations of grief to framing this personal tragedy by the world and nature, primes us for what follows, an affective transposition to the present.

The Lumia image returns, followed by an abstract sequence of blurred motion, coloured lights, suggesting rapid movement and the passage of time; these images mark the transition to the present day, and the story from the perspective of the adult Jack. An abstract sequence of images flits by: traffic in fast motion, a mysterious doorway, an illuminated salt pan shot from low on the ground, the adult Jack in a black suit, shot from below, lost by an empty doorway in the desert, as his voiceover intones, 'In what shape, what disguise, … ?' An abrupt cut to a bedroom reveals the adult Jack awakening suddenly in a disoriented state, his wife beside the bed, looking away, the colour palette of the room and figures all greys and dull greens, with the sound of the ocean in the background. The couple wander silently, alienated and solitary, around their elegant but soulless architect-designed house, the camera moving freely, like a silent witness, throughout the glass-walled, segmented space. Jack lights a candle in a blue glass. 'I see the child I was', we hear in voiceover, accompanied by flashback-recollection images of himself and his brother as children. 'I see my brother, true, kind; he died when he was nineteen.' The close shot of the blue candle glass cuts to skyscrapers seen from below – rhyming with the familiar Malick images of trees shot from below – framed and enclosed by the metallic and glass canopy of Jack's architecturally modern workplace, where he drifts distractedly from task to task in an aimless, disoriented manner.

Waves of grief reach across time, his brother's loss still affecting Jack in his adult life, as he struggles with his despair. The camera closes in on his face, as he stares dejectedly out of the glass walls of the skyscraper: 'World's going to the dogs. People are greedy, just getting worse', he murmurs in voiceover, recalling his character Welsh in *The Thin Red Line*. Ascending a glass lift in his austere modernist work-building, we hear a curious electronic beeping sound in the background (recalling a medical heart monitor, suggesting something like a crisis or near-death experience). He apologizes to his father for their exchange of harsh words about his brother's death, a loss that has marked his whole life: 'I think about him every day and I just shouldn't have said what I did, and I'm sorry. It's just … this day.'

He drifts through the rest of the day, presumably the anniversary of R.L.'s death, sound and image track dissociating throughout the sequence, voices and snatches of conversation drifting in and out of focus, as Jack sees images of light, sky and moving clouds, intercut with office scenes, with ocean sounds once again prominent in the background. The film gradually shifts into the more abstract visual style seen earlier, a shot of a solitary tree, amidst the concrete expanse, his voiceover asking an unknown Other (his brother, his deeper self, God?): 'How did I lose you? Wandered. Forgot you.' An oceanic image of powerful crashing waves seen from below gives way to a shot of Jack in a black suit, washing his face in water, wandering in a spiritual wasteland, with the sound of ocean and wind accompanying his running footsteps, as we shift between his building (the present) and his brother as a child (the past). Although set during the course of one day, yet spanning in memory his childhood in the 1950s, as well as the origin and end of time, Jack is a character in despair, without purpose or authentic selfhood, clearly suffering from Kierkegaard (1968) called the 'sickness unto death'.

A claustrophobically framed mid-shot focuses intently on Jack, who appears almost paralysed, unable to move, his ordinary routine interrupted by images of the past. In despair over his brother, we see an image of the young R.L. shrouded in a curtain, being kissed by a messenger figure and prepared for death, and then in a dramatic long shot, a young boy standing alone on a beach shore: 'Find me', he says.[19] Another close shot of Jack's face, distressed and disoriented by these involuntary images – of his mother, of himself and R.L., of the adult Jack witnessing his mother and father grieving after hearing of their son's death – as we hear him ask, 'How did she bear it?' The traumatic affective power of the past is signalled not only through this series of fragmentary vignettes but in the off-screen sound of his mother's wailing.

The mood shifts again via a cut to an arresting image of the murmuration of a flock of birds against a twilight sky. We hear Mrs O'Brien ask, as though breaking off from prayer, 'Was I false to you?' and see her wandering alone in the forest, in despair, staring tearfully in a grief-stricken state, before the film cuts to black. Another Lumia image appears as she asks: 'Lord. Why? Where were you?' accompanied by the majestic and plaintive strains of Zbigniew Preisner's 'Lacrimosa'. What follows is one of the film's most stunning sequences, what we might call its cosmological creation myth: an extraordinary fusion of abstract imagery, nature footage and cosmic speculation.[20] Many critics have claimed that this sequence is filtered through Jack's consciousness (see Pfeifer 2011), his boyish fascination, typical of the 1950s, with space, dinosaurs, the universe and the like (although it is R.L. that we see reading a book about space travel). It is introduced, however, via Mrs O'Brien's voiceover, the mother recast in the role of Job, questioning God for inflicting so much suffering upon a faithful servant ('Lord. Why? Where were you'). Mrs O'Brien's words echo the quotation from the Book of Job that opens the film ('Where were you when I laid the earth's foundation … '). She asks, both in the form of questioning and praying, 'Did you know? Who are we to you? Answer me', against images of the birth of the earth, volcanic lava flows, ocean waves and rocks breaking, followed by a stunning erupting volcanic cloud. 'We cry to you', she whispers. 'My soul', as the camera glides over newly created landscapes, 'My son', as we cut to images of sky, 'Hear us', and a thundering waterfall. After a brief black screen, and flashes of light, we see the first signs of life emerging amidst images of a primordial Earth.

We might describe this extraordinary sequence, which features the creation of worlds and appearance of life on earth, Malick's cinematic cosmogony: showing Mrs O'Brien (and the viewer) what no mortal could ever see – a cosmological myth of creation, a re-enchanted vision of the universe combining evolutionary naturalism with spiritual sublimity. Malick's images span the abstract images of the cosmological emergence of matter, the evolution of life from the primeval chaos, the appearance of dinosaurs on earth, including a startling 'state of nature' sequence in which a predatory dinosaur displays a moment of animal grace towards an injured herbivore.[21] What to make of this extraordinary image? I take it as a mythic moment of emergent consciousness, of nascent empathy – an evolutionary anticipation of altruism – arising against the instinctive drive of nature as red in tooth and claw. Mrs O'Brien's voiceover returns after this moment of animal grace: 'Light of my life. I search for you', set against images of Jupiter's rings and planetary swirls. 'My hope. My child', she intones, accompanied by a passage from Berlioz's Requiem.[22] This movement of the sequence concludes with the mythic depiction of a meteor hitting the earth, extinguishing the dinosaurs, destroying in the blink of an eye what had taken eons to evolve.

The second movement of this cosmogonical creation sequence, accompanied again by the low bass rumble of Lupica's Cosmic Beam Take 5, features Jack's voiceover against images of churning underwater waves and a frozen earth. He confesses to us, to his brother and perhaps to God: 'You spoke to me through her. You spoke with my through the sky, the trees', as we see the adult Jack again stumbling in the wilderness. 'Before I knew I loved you. Believed in you', a plaintive prayer contrasted with the unsettlingly ironic, theologically charged image of a sea snake coursing across the surface of the water, followed by what we could call Malick's 'tree of life' signature image. Still in prayer mode, he asks: 'When did you first touch my heart?' a question that ushers in a moving montage of images of the courtship of the young Mr and Mrs O'Brien. Accompanied by Ottorino Resphigi's graceful waltz (Siciliana Da Antiche Danze Ed Arie Suite III), it shows us their falling in love, their nuptials, her pregnancy, an extraordinarily lyrical depiction of gestation and birth – a line of child figures, shrouded in white and guided by messengers, one of them abandoning a submerged, flooded bedroom, opening a door and swimming upwards towards the light. This poetic sequence, which embeds the appearance of Jack in the world within a broader cosmogonical myth, linking macrocosmic and microcosmic stories, then subtly shifts into a powerfully engaging, fragmentary, yet fluid rendering of childhood experiences – from the perspectives of infant, toddler, growing child and teenager. Accompanied by Holst's stirring and wondrous Hymn to Dionysus (Op. 32, No. 2, H 116), it is composed in the impressionistic/paratactic vignette style we have seen previously.

What the cosmological myth shows is how nature and grace are not opposed but co-exist within a dynamic unity of opposites (suggesting a pagan pre-Socratic vision combining Heraclitean cosmic fire with Empodocles' divine principles of love (*philia*) and strife (*neikos*) as the basic impulses attracting and separating matter in the universe). It shows how a naturalistic-scientific understanding of the evolution of life in the universe can co-exist with a sense of spiritual transcendence, an experience of the numinous and an acknowledgement of spiritual experience, the transfiguring power of love and faith. And finally, it shows how the lives of an ordinary family are embedded, yet also embraced, by a sublime vision of re-enchanted nature (and spirit) in which human joy and suffering have their place, where the religious problem of suffering finds an aesthetic response – an aesthetic theodicy or what the young Nietzsche called an 'aesthetic affirmation of existence'. The sublimity of the cosmos, from the overwhelmingly vast to the infinitesimally small, echoes the sublimity of mind or spirit – indeed the miracle of the cinema – that can contemplate and reveal such wonders in the form of moving images.

This is nowhere more evident than in the film's concluding sequence, Jack's eschatological vision of spiritual reconciliation through love. Accompanied by Berlioz's 10. Agnus Dei (Requiem, Opus 5, Grande messes des Morts), the sequence opens with images of cosmic fire, the powerful eruption of fiery energy radiating from a star (or the sun) before a tiny planet (perhaps the earth). Jack's voiceover whispers, prayer-like, 'Keep us. Guide us' – as the camera glides miraculously over the surface of the newly formed Earth – 'Till the end of time'. A flash of light against the darkness announces the birth of a New World. An image of an eclipse, a dark globe obscuring the light of the sun, creates a cosmic, God-like, eye. What sounds like Jack's brother, R.L., whispers to us, in voiceover, 'Follow me'.

The cosmic images give way to a more abstract sequence, composed of religious imagery combined with elemental images of water, earth, light and sky. Images follow of candlelight, angelic messenger figures, the young R.L. being escorted (by Mrs O'Brien as a child?), then the young Mrs O'Brien, as a girl, opening a mysterious doorway into the light. The mysterious co-existence of layers of time and the temporal enfoldings of personal and cosmic memory are powerfully suggested in this sequence. Cut to the adult Jack, following his younger self as a boy, through the desert wilderness landscape we have seen previously, the camera running in pursuit of the young Jack clambering over rocks. A jetty leading towards the horizon, an image of two shrouded corpses laid out beneath the sky, a 'Jacob's Ladder' image, shot from below and held for several moments, all announce the explicitly religious nature of the vision Jack appears to have (and that we share). One image, a point-of-view shot from deep within a grave, presided over by one of the angelic messenger figures, slowly beckoning, shows a wizened hand being raised towards messenger in an apparent act of resurrection. Images of hands grasping each other, hands on shoulders and hands giving thanks to the sky underline the theological trope of reconciliation and the evocation of religious mood of forgiveness. More explicitly, a deceased bride, lying on a bedframe, appears resurrected in the following shot, images that make it plain that we are in the presence of Christian theological symbolism and iconography.

Water images, waves churning seen from below the water's surface, now mark the transition to the 'shores of eternity' sequence, probably the film's most controversial and oft-discussed section. As Caruana notes (2018: 82), this is not some fanciful depiction of heaven or the afterlife, as some critics opined, but rather Jack's spiritual vision or felt experience of the meaning of spiritual transcendence and reconciliation through love. The adult Jack shot close and from below, the camera accompanying him, is shown walking along the sandy shores, water gently lapping his feet, surrounded by a multitude of other figures also wandering along the sands. Jack sees R.L., a long shot of him standing on the shores, as seen earlier in the film. Amidst the crowds walking along these shores, we see Jack fall to his knees, a female robed figure approaching him; another figure approaches the kneeling Jack, walking slowly, as we see Jack lean forward, embracing the mysterious figure's feet. Other figures appear, the boy with the burnt neck seen earlier in the film, Jack's middle brother, Steve (Tye Sheridan), Jack encountering his mother, appearing as she was when younger, who embraces him, Jack walking alongside his father, placing his hand on his shoulder, in slower motion, against a luminous sky flecked with birds. We see the young R.L., holding his hand over a flashlight, before an image of Jack and R.L., then Jack carrying R.L. on his shoulder. The mother embraces R.L., clasping his face with an expression of ecstatic love. Jack watches intently as the family is reunited, his mother and father kissing and R.L. smiling at Jack – in a vision spiritualized love, the family embraces and is reconciled at last.

The final phase of the 'shores of eternity' sequence focuses on Jack and the family's reconciliation with the departed R.L. and his mother's acceptance of his loss and sacrificial act of thanksgiving. These sequences are challenging precisely because they are both abstract and subjective; visionary and symbolic while also expressing the felt experiences of despair, loss, love and hope. Malick's images follow each other in a flowing, rhythmic sequence, shaped by mood and musical dynamics rather than narrative sequencing or character perspective. After another evocative shot of churning waves seen from below the water's surface, followed by a submerged doorway (as seen earlier) opening in the water towards the light, we cut to images of darkness on the shores, anonymous wandering people milling together. A girl (the young Mrs O'Brien?) with the blue candle glass, which we saw Jack light early in the film, announces the transition to a depiction of sacrificial reconciliation, the mother finally letting R.L. go in memory and spirit, finally finding peace through love.

The powerful surging waterfall image recurs, as we return to a view of the mother and R.L. embracing. We cut to inside a house before an empty desert salt plain, dazzlingly white, opening the door and letting the young R.L. go, watching him wandering alone upon the brilliant white earth, as the adult Jack touches her shoulder and hair. A dazzling low-angle mobile shot tracks along the mythic salt plain, following Mrs O'Brien's shadow, as she walks towards the horizon, her body illuminated by the setting sun against the mountains. The screen fades to white for what is presumably Mrs O'Brien's own departure through death. We see angelic messenger figures caressing her, Mrs O'Brien's beatific face, shot from below and radiant with light, the camera moving rhythmically around her, as the dance of hands, face and light unfolds – a beatific mood announcing her gratitude for life, her reconciliation with loss, her preparation for death. 'I give him to you', we hear her whisper, intercut by overexposed images of hands bathed in dazzling light, touching, praying and giving thanks: 'I give you my son' – Mrs O'Brien's echo of God's sacrifice of the living Christ is hard to mistake – as her prayer-dance comes to an end.

The final shots return us from Jack's ecstatic vision of transcendence to his transfigured existential relationship with the ordinary, everyday world, in all its mundane grace and beauty. The camera pans slowly from the sky to reveal a field of sunflowers. After an abrupt cut, we see Jack in the lift back at his place of work, descending behind glass walls, accompanied again by that peculiar heartbeat-like electronic pulse; then a shot of a tree framed by architectural grids, as seen during the descent, which finally brings us back to earth. Jack now returns to everyday reality as a man transformed. Shot from below, standing outside his building bewildered and confused, Jack moves around like a man awakening from a deep sleep, unsure of where he is, as we hear the sounds of traffic, voices, the reassuring murmur of everyday life. We cut to a close shot of Jack's face, perplexed at first, agitated and unsure, then more calm, focused, slowly revealing the slightest hint of a smile on his lips – a moment of revelation, a transfiguration of the commonplace. The film now cuts to the glass skyscraper, shot from below and framed against the sky, like one of Malick's signature shots of trees rising towards the heavens, followed by a shot of a bridge (The Golden Gate?), serene against the evening sky, as a bird swoops before us, recalling similar closing shots in *The New World*. *The Tree of Life*'s final shot, however, returns us, in circular fashion, to the very beginning, the film loop eternally upon itself: the Lumia image, accompanied now by the sounds of birds, of winds and of waves in the distance – a world both natural and human transfigured through a spiritualized vision of love.

Appendix: *Voyage of Time: Life's Journey* (2016)

The Tree of Life's concluding moments, with their cosmic background and spiritual transfiguration of the everyday, provide an entry point into Malick's first experiment with documentary. Released in two versions 2016 – a shorter IMAX version (45 minutes) narrated by Brad Pitt and a longer (90-minute) version narrated by Cate Blanchett – Malick's first full-scale documentary is a stunning companion piece to *The Tree of Life*, providing not only a backdrop for this film but for the other three films made during the same post-*Tree of Life* period (*To the Wonder* (2012), *Knight of Cups* (2015) and *Song to Song* (2017)). *Voyage of Time* is the culmination of over forty years of work; Malick had been conceiving this project since the 1970s, compiling footage over many years for an experimental poetic documentary on the origin of the universe and development of life, culminating in human life, on Earth. The idea behind it goes back to a project simply entitled *Q*, which Malick had been working on for decades in between his feature films. Production proceeded in fits and starts, including a lawsuit taken out by project backers Seven Seas against Sycamore Pictures, claiming that Malick had failed to meet his contractual obligations and ceased work on promised projects while making *The Tree of Life* and the 'weightless' trilogy films. Footage from the project was used in the 'creation' sequence of *The Tree of Life* but some shots were also interpolated into the O'Brien family narrative sections and others (churning waves seen from below the water's surface, for example) appeared in subsequent films such as *Knight of Cups*.

Having seen *Voyage of Time* only after Malick's other more recent films, it struck me as a mythopoetic marvel – at once metaphysically ambitious, cinematically sumptuous and spiritually reflective. Viewed retrospectively, it becomes clear that *The Tree of Life* and *Voyage of*

Time share a common vision, aesthetic sensibility and metaphysical orientation – how to evoke a sense of wonder towards nature and pose the cosmic question through cinema, from both naturalistic and spiritualist perspectives, in both metaphysical and religious terms. This audacious project was intended to address both a younger, popular audience (via IMAX technology) as well as a more reflective one (perhaps those open to the work thanks to *The Tree of Life*). In the event, the film was received with a mixture of perplexity, amazement and curiosity. Some critics were unsure what to make of Brad Pitt's naive, declarative, explanatory voiceover compared with Cate Blanchett's more questioning, speculative, spiritual ruminations. Although the images were universally praised for their brilliance and evocative power, the voiceovers and 'abstract' structuring of the piece – combining the symphonic structure of Reggio's *Koyaanisqatsi* (1983), the visual grandeur of Carl Sagan's *Cosmos* and metaphysical ambitions of Kubrick's *2001: A Space Odyssey* – left many viewers perplexed, especially concerning the 'religious' quality of Blanchett's voiceover. Although the obvious link with *The Tree of Life* was duly noted, the film was received, curiously enough, as almost entirely a standalone piece. The further links between *Voyage of Time* and Malick's other late works – all made in the five or so years after *The Tree of Life,* and all likewise drawing on the background 'cosmic question', while exploring metaphysical-spiritual dimensions of love – tended to pass without comment.

Although the film was screened in Melbourne, complete with live orchestral accompaniment, it did not receive a screening in Sydney (I was hoping to see the IMAX version but our enormous IMAX theatre had closed for renovations shortly before the film's Australian release). Although I only managed to see the Cate Blanchett/*Life's Journey* version much later, *Voyage of Time* still left me feeling amazed and overwhelmed, despite an obvious loss of scale on the small screen. The fact that I saw it while completing this manuscript only added to my sense that this companion piece to *The Tree of Life* also had to be understood in relation to Malick's last three films (what I call his 'weightless' trilogy). It confirmed my intuition that Malick was attempting to marry evolutionary naturalism and metaphysical spiritualism, and added weight to my contention that the focus of his later films was exploring metaphysical, religious, and existential meditations on love.

Against a background note of perplexity – what was Malick attempting to say with this visually remarkable work? – reviews converged on noting the ambitious, experimental scope of the project and acknowledging its audiovisual splendour. Voiceover, as ever, was a point of contention, with some critics mocking Brad Pitt's remarks (perhaps not realizing the genre or audience intended), and others puzzled or intrigued by Cate Blanchett's more overtly meditative or prayer-like reflections. Many critics acknowledged the moods of wonder, amazement or gratitude that the work opened up, without reflecting much on the significance of evoking awe and reverence. Two of the best reviews, however, Eric Hynes in *Film Comment* and Richard Brody in *The New Yorker*, acknowledged and discussed all of these elements. Hynes observes that the film 'is simultaneously more ambitious than any previous science or nature-oriented documentary – already a grand even macrocosmic genre – and yet atypically humble and unstable' (Hynes 2017). The awe-inspiring physical facts of the universe, as he observes, are presented in a manner undercut by 'subjective perception and irresolute emotion'; and although lacking *The Tree of Life*'s narrative elements, 'it remains a spiritually close sibling' of that film (Hynes 2017). Brody notes the 'breathtaking intensity of its stylistic unity and the immediate, firsthand focus of its philosophical reflections', describing the film as 'a sort of cinematic cosmogony, a lyrical collage that looks at a

broad spectrum of natural phenomena artistically and imaginatively'
(2016). Brody is also one of the few critics to note the link between
the sublime grandeur of nature and the physical and moral suffering
of human beings on our planet, taking these interspersed sequences
of the homeless, impoverished, and distressed as the film's posing of
important moral-aesthetic questions: 'What does the transcendent
beauty of the natural realm have to do with human suffering? Is it
absurd to contemplate that beauty given the woes of the world?'
(Brody 2016). These are questions that any attentive viewing of the
film should reveal, given the stark contrast between the sublime
images of cosmic creation and the 'realist' handheld digital video
footage of social suffering and spiritual disorientation.

For my part, I took the film as both dedicated to conveying the
sublimity of nature and dynamism of life in the universe, and as a
metaphysical-spiritual meditation on the relationship between cosmic
evolution and human suffering. *Voyage of Time*, moreover, appeared
to me to continue the late Malick's experimental bent (despite some of
the footage used going back the 1970s), consolidating the trajectory of
his recent films as exploring non-linear forms of narrative abstraction
combined with abstract forms of poetic metaphysical reflection.
It emphasizes Malick's fascination with the possibilities of cinema
to express both compelling realism and speculative imagination,
to combine a naturalistic conception of the universe with a moral-
metaphysical questioning of our place within it. *Voyage of Time*
reflects, using sound and image, on the significance of the evolution
of life, the emergence of human consciousness, and the role of love in
providing meaning in a world that is both technologically advanced
and socially fragmented, materially rich and spiritually bereft. It is
not just a nature documentary but an experimental cinematic 'prayer
poem' that explores the 'cosmic question', questioning the sufficiency
of science, technology, and material advancement to address our

deeper interpersonal and social, religious and existential, need for meaning and purpose.

There are clear parallels with the 'creation sequence' from *The Tree of Life* but also significant differences. The former is embedded within a familial melodrama, foregrounding the cosmic question theme by situating the O'Brien story within the origin and emergence of life in the universe; the latter is a prayer-like meditation on this same question, addressed to an unspecified other ('Mother') as transcendent source of life, being, and value, offering a way of responding to the evident strife and conflict dividing our shared world. It follows the 'voyage of time' itself from the Big Bang, creation of the cosmos, evolution of life, to the disjointed social and political world of the present. In *The Tree of Life*, the powerfully liturgical musical accompaniment carries the images into the realm of the sublime; in *Voyage of Time*, the musical accompaniment is more restrained, mood-like or atmospheric, and does not overwhelm or ground the images in the same way (there are long sequences featuring either silence or naturalistic ambient sounds, be they water sounds, waves, wind, steam or gas, birds and other creatures, human voices, and so on). The former is an audiovisual meditation on the Jobian question of reconciling human suffering with belief in a benevolent God; the latter is a more questioning, prayer-like reflection on God's simultaneous presence and absence, the attempt to find spiritual solace and moral meaning in both a sublime 'great chain of being' and a human, all-too-human reality riven by conflict and suffering. Both films share Malick's remarkable combination of naturalistic and poetic presentations of Nature and metaphysical-moral speculations on the relationship between life, love, and the universe. Like Mrs O'Brien and Jack O'Brien in *The Tree of Life*, we are shown 'the foundations of the earth, when the morning stars sang together': from the coalescence of matter out of the void and formation of celestial bodies to the evolutionary emergence of life;

from CGI animated renderings of the origins of organic life, aquatic creatures, and prehistoric dinosaurs, to early hominids hunting, painting, and worshipping across a newly created Earth.

As Brody (2016) remarks, the unity of visual style and subject matter in the film is astonishing. *Voyage of Time* maintains a mesmerizing shot rhythm and subtly flowing camera that articulates the temporal movement and evolutionary trajectory of life emerging out of an elemental void. This is achieved via poetically articulated, rhythmic sequences of 'paratactic' shots which, when linked together formally and associatively, compose a remarkably textured and dynamic sense of the physical universe. The camera, so to speak, becomes a monadic instance of self-reflection within the universe itself. It shows what could never have been seen by human eyes, imagining, via cinematically articulated naturalistic images, how the universe itself came to be and how life began its evolutionary journey, culminating in our consciousness of this very process (human beings have invented the technology by means of which this 'self-consciousness' of the universe comes to represent itself through images).

Malick's rhythmic montage of images, each following the other in a smoothly flowing stream, carries our consciousness for ephemeral intervals, like the flow of time itself. The film is beautifully organised according to an audiovisual patterning following both visual form and kinetic dynamics. *Voyage of Time* is composed in a mode of serial repetition, each shot flowing in connected series – 'this, this, this, ... ' – interspersed with periodic black screens. The effect is both cumulative and progressive, paratactic and flowing, making links and connections, marking relations and resonances, patterns and dynamisms, across different but related categories of space and time, life and bodies, from the microscopic to the celestial. Contrasting patterns of matter and movement, light and darkness, void and form, the microcosmic and the macrocosmic are connected across vast changes in scale that are rendered miraculously compatible (cosmic gases, the formation of galaxies, and eclipses of planets visually linked with cellular division, synaptic connections, and an eye's iris and pupil). Cinema itself is the technological miracle enabling our temporal voyage – a cinematic rendering of *Life and Time* that links our limited, finite consciousness, with the sublimity of Nature, the enfoldings of temporality, and dynamism of Life.

Most responses to the work note that it is a documentary – recalling poetic-symphonic, non-linear works such as Reggio's *Koyaanisqatsi* (1983) – but there are also particular narrative film resonances. In addition to *The Tree of Life*, one could mention Kubrick's *2001: A Space Odyssey* (1968) as well as the speculative-imaginative renderings of cosmological phenomena associated with general relativity (such as black holes and event horizons) in films such as Christopher Nolan's *Interstellar* (2014). Unusually for a documentary, however, *Voyage of Time* begins with a prologue, before the opening credits, and starts with a black screen image, an interval of silence broken by Cate Blanchett's measured voiceover: 'Mother. You walked with me then, in the silence, before there was a world, before night and day. Alone in the stillness, when nothing was … '. The titles appear, culminating in the drawn image of celestial spheres with the title 'Voyage of Time' superimposed. From the start, *Voyage of Time* announces itself as a cinematic prayer poem, addressed to 'Mother', and voiced by an unnamed woman, reflecting or meditating but also questioning and pleading, as images showing the marvels of the universe and mysteries of creation appear before us. Her opening lines describing how she 'walked with Mother' before there was a world suggests a mythic dimension to the work beyond merely finite corporeal existence or a strictly evolutionary narrative. It conjures a metaphysical presence or spiritual point of view that is also physically sensuous and humanly expressive, yet also outside or beyond time – both eternal and present at once.

The opening images of sky, cloud and sun, of a heaven and earth revolving in and as time, are coupled with the first of a series of recurring digital image sequences of people, of suffering and strife, destitution and disorientation, of a world in chaos or 'crazy life' (Koyannisqatsi). It frames the cosmogony that follows with images of humanity bereft and lost, suffering and solitary, without a sense of place or purpose, torn by strife and conflict. The voiceover continues, echoing other female voiceovers in other recent Malick films (notably in *The New World* and *The Tree of Life*; but also lines appearing in *Knight of Cups*): 'Mother. Where are you? Where have you gone? Full of trouble. A riddle to myself. Am I not your child?' These questions frame all the remarkable images that follow, the vast cosmic journey that unfolds, which serves both to heighten our sense of wonder and leave us doubting whether such questions could ever be answered. The accompanying 'mundane' digital video image sequences – of poverty and mental illness, of conflict and suffering, contrasted with cultural traditions and religious rituals – will punctuate the extraordinary revelation of 'Life's Journey' throughout the film, anchoring the cosmic wonder and metaphysical speculation in our contemporary world, with all its moral disorientation and social distress. The film is composed according to these contrapuntal lines – poetic, prayer-like voiceover; dazzling images of nature and the sublimity of the universe; handheld digital video sequences of human connection and disconnection – all addressed not only to us but to 'Mother' as the transcendent yet immanent source of life and of meaning. All that we see, hear and experience remains enveloped or embraced by time and universe itself. This is an evocation of awe, wonder and sublimity, however, that is not only about reverence towards nature or marvelling at the cosmos but of finding meaning and purpose, of acknowledging love as what binds us to each other as well as to the universe as a whole.

Voyage of Time unites these extraordinary sequences – the formation of matter out of the void, the emergence of planets and galaxies, the evolution of life and adventure of organisms, the appearance of early human beings and their imagined experience of the world, to our uncertain and strife-torn present – and renders these as a questioning of our own place in the universe, as beings for whom our place or purpose remains uncertain, beings for whom our very existence remains in question. This repeated questioning is at once personal and metaphysical, philosophical and spiritual. This questioning offers a counterpoint to the images we witness unfolding before us, spanning the spheres of self and world, the origin of nature, the nature of love and the end of time. Indeed, the voiceover addresses 'Mother' as many things – as 'Life-giver and light-bringer', as 'abyss of light', as 'giver of good', as 'all-beholding, blazing, shining through all Time' – suggesting a divine source in nature that is at the same time expressive of the universe as such – echoes of Spinoza's God as *deus sive natura* – combining both transcendence and immanence, experienced as absent or unknown, yet also manifest in the chaotic plurality of forms of life in nature. Malick's mysterious 'Mother' god – immanent-transcendent, pantheistic yet absent, source of love and purpose, splendidly manifest in creation, elemental and luminous yet unknown to us and withdrawn into darkness – leaves us with questions and wonder, with thought and doubt, with a loving embrace of our neighbour and a contemplative distance from our world, itself but a finite and fleeting episode in the voyage of time.

***

Like Bazin, Malick shares a conviction in the mythopoetic power of cinema to reveal reality anew, to transfigure the everyday, to illuminate the world and nature with a revelatory power that inspires belief – images with the power, to use Deleuze's phrase, of giving us 'reasons to believe in this world'. The sublime realism of Malick's *Voyage of Time* and the creation sequence from *The Tree of Life* combine cosmological speculation, evolutionary naturalism and spiritual sublimity, attempting to convey the grace in nature and the nature underlying grace. They show us how the microcosmic dramas of individual lives are enveloped by a metaphysically and spiritually sublime sense of the macrocosmic whole. Taken together, both films offer a re-enchanted mythic vision of the living cosmos of which human beings, with their pain and suffering, hope and joy, are a tiny yet significant part.

The Tree of Life suggests an explicitly Christian theological rendering of the spiritually transfiguring power of love: love as an expression of the divine, as the spiritually transcendent power to overcome the pain of loss and the suffering of misfortune – a cinematic rendering of God's reply to Job. Although resonant with other religious traditions and symbols, *The Tree of Life* finally could be described as a Christian aesthetic theodicy, directed both to Jack and to us, however sceptical we might be concerning God, love or transcendence. In *Voyage of Time*, however, this emphasis on transcendence finds its counterpoint in a celebration of immanence. It is not a specifically Christian monotheistic God, nor a pagan deity, but something closer to a mystical pantheistic – or rather, a *panentheistic* – vision of the divinity of nature pervading all its marvellous plurality of forms, yet also somehow transcending and extending beyond time and space (see Culp 2017).[23] It celebrates, in the form of a cinematic prayer poem, the wonder of life appearing randomly in the universe, the evolutionary drama of life developing on earth and the sublime miracle of human consciousness. At the same time, given Malick's attention to the possibilities of cinema, it celebrates our technological capacity to represent and render reality and experience, not to mention the universe itself, through extraordinary images of gravity and grace. The voyage of time and drama of life's journey is also a cinematic odyssey.

5

Discourses on Love: Malick's 'Weightless' Trilogy

To love people is the only thing worth living for, and without this love you are not really living.

KIERKEGAARD (2009: 375)

Throughout this book, I have been concerned to narrate my involvement in film-philosophy via my encounter with Malick's work, reflecting on how my aesthetic experience of his films transformed my approach to the film-philosophy relationship. From an aesthetic appreciation of *Badlands* (1973) and *Days of Heaven* (1978) to exploring the existential ruminations of *The Thin Red Line* (1998), I found myself preoccupied with how Malick's work raises the question of a 'Heideggerian cinema' in ways that invite, but also check, further philosophical reflection. With his middle to later work, this question has expanded to embrace the question of ethics or morality and cinema. This shift encompasses an exploration of cinematic worlds and the clash between different modes of human dwelling in *The New World* (2005) and the potential of cinematic responses to the 'cosmic question' concerning existential meaning, moral purpose and religious experience in *The Tree of Life* (2011).

Although Malick's films have been both celebrated and criticized for their philosophical and existential qualities and concerns (see Davies 2009; Tucker and Kendall 2011), his more recent work expands the idea of 'film as philosophy' so as to encompass spiritual-religious experience and metaphysical-theological themes.[1] As Caruana remarks (2018: 71), it is Kierkegaard (rather than Heidegger or Wittgenstein) who emerges as the key thinker for the later Malick, one who has been all but neglected in the existing critical literature.[2] In conjunction with this religious and theological turn, Malick's concern with the philosophy of love – what it means, what it demands and what it makes possible – becomes a key focus in his later films. Indeed, what I shall call his 'weightless' trilogy – *To the Wonder* (2012), *Knight of Cups* (2015) and *Song to Song* (2017) – explores the limits, possibilities and confusions attending different conceptions of love (drawing on Plato and Kierkegaard), from the romantic and ethical to the spiritual and religious.[3] It also expresses cinematic responses to the moral-cultural problem of nihilism that shapes much of Malick's oeuvre (see Sinnerbrink 2016a: 89–103).

These films present the subjective experiences of characters, or what I call cinematic 'figures', who seek fulfilment in erotic-romantic love, the hedonistic pursuit of pleasure and experiential novelty. In their groundless, 'weightless', aesthetic (sensuous) pursuits, however, they fail to achieve what Kierkegaard called the task of becoming a self: integrating finite and infinite dimensions of one's subjectivity, via recognition of one's dependence on an infinite being, failing which one remains in a state of existential despair (see Kierkegaard 1968: 141). These thematic concerns, moreover, are articulated and expressed through a cinematic style that has become a distinctive, recognizable and controversial feature of his work. These later films push to the limit Malick's experimentation with narrative abstraction, impressionistic voiceover, allegorical presentation and the poetic evocation of mood through image montage, camera movement and non-linear narration. They challenge not only philosophical film theorists, struggling to acknowledge the emphasis on religious-theological themes, but also film theorists sceptical of Malick's repeated use of certain cinematic tropes, and abandonment of conventional modes of narrative engagement.

What to make, then, of these provocative works? We can start by reflecting on the relationship between cinematic form and thematic content: Why does Malick adopt such an attenuated narrative form, such an impressionistic, fragmentary style, such an improvised mode of shooting, conjuring the narrative mostly during post-production? The clue, it seemed to me, lay in these film's treatment of groundless or 'weightless' subjects in search of fulfilment through romantic/erotic love and creative self-expression. Indeed, all of these experimental cinematic strategies are apt for the exploration of the phenomenon of love in an age of sceptical disbelief. One way of putting it is to say that Malick's 'weightless' trilogy offers a Christian existentialist version of Antonioni's humanistic 'eros is sick' trilogy (*L'avventura* 1959, *La notte* 1960 and *L'eclisse* 1962) mediated via a Kierkegaardian-style critique of the present age (a diagnosis of empty subjectivity and cultural distraction rooted in existential-spiritual despair).[4] They offer a cinematic exploration of the misguided elevation of romantic/sexual love to the highest source of personal, moral and social meaning in the modern world. Echoing the late Godard, notably *Hail Mary* (*Je vous salue Marie*) (1985) and *Nouvelle Vague* (1990),[5] while framing these narratives via philosophical fable and moral-religious allegory, Malick's trilogy challenges familiar narrative conventions and cinematic modes of presentation. His late films undermine narrative expectations concerning the formation of the couple by means of a subjective, impressionistic, revelatory poetic style attuned to the moral-spiritual dimensions of love as much as its sensual-emotional aspects.

Malick's later films present a phenomenologically rich exploration of different kinds of love, from the erotic-romantic, familial-communal, to the spiritual-religious. This exploration is manifested through his later film's distinctive style, which serves to present the 'weightless' (groundless, shifting and distracted) subjectivity defining much of our contemporary moral-cultural experience. These ephemeral figures (rather than solid characters) reflect a condition of contingent desiring coupled with ethical disorientation; they seek but fail to find happiness through sensuous pleasure, experiential novelty and the detached pursuit of erotic-romantic love. Malick's 'weightless' trilogy, I suggest, thereby recapitulates both a Platonic and a Kierkegaardian movement of ascent from aesthetic, ethical, to religious experiences of love. They emphasize the transcendence at the heart of erotic-romantic love, and the anticipation of *agape* or divine love (of God for humankind, and of humankind for God), as a cinematic response to the moral scepticism and psychological narcissism of our age.

Mood in Malick's later films

As many critics have noted, Malick's later work – from *The Tree of Life* up to *Song to Song* – has become increasingly abstract, poetic and experimental (see Kendrick 2017). These films deal only marginally with the familiar 'structures of sympathy' (Smith 1995) defining emotional engagement in conventional narrative cinema (perceptual recognition of character identity, perspectival alignment with character perspectives, moral-aesthetic allegiance with character qualities, traits or values). Rather, Malick's films explore a more attenuated, diffuse, impressionistic mode of engagement. Character recognition is de-emphasized, and movie actors are presented as allegorical 'types'. Emotional engagement with characters is replaced by diffuse personages that lack firm, identifiable qualities. Such figures are psychologically opaque with attenuated personal identities; they express themselves via gestures and movements accompanied by fragmentary, impressionistic voiceovers, which suggest existential and religious forms of sensibility. Audience expectations of arresting dramatic performances by Hollywood stars – such as Ben Affleck and Rachel McAdams, Christian Bale and Cate Blanchett, Ryan Gosling, Michael Fassbender and Rooney Mara – are disappointed. Such actors appear more like Bressonian 'models' than Hollywood performers, reciting few spoken lines, improvising scenes with little structure and avoiding the character arcs typical of mainstream narrative films.[6]

Little wonder, then, that Malick's most recent films have been received in a sceptical, dismissive manner. The favourable critical consensus over *The Tree of Life* (after an initially sceptical response) gave way to perplexity, disappointment, even hostility with each subsequent Malick film.[7] Rather than a symptom of Malick's creative exhaustion, I claim that these three films develop an experimental aesthetic strategy that offers novel narrative presentations of subjectivity and an ethical as well as theological exploration of varieties of loving experience.[8] This critical portrait is presented via an aesthetically immersive phenomenology of contemporary subjectivity, using cinematic style to express, and critically reflect on, the moods of distraction, boredom, and melancholy pervading contemporary moral-cultural experience.

So how do such moods work in Malick's cinema? Moods can evoke ethical experience through film in three related ways (see Plantinga 2012; Sinnerbrink 2012, 2016b). The first is the 'subjective-phenomenological' aspect of mood (showing what something is like, how it feels to experience X, presenting a distinctive experiential perspective on Y), which typically unfolds as part of a dramatic narrative scenario expressing either the perspective of a character or the worldview articulated by a film. The second is the 'moral-psychological' aspect of mood (how it affects our moral sympathies and antipathies again towards characters, situations or ideas, how it affects or orients moral judgements, how it exercises or stymies moral imagination, potentially shifts ethical attitudes and moral convictions or how it alters our disposition towards action).[9] The third is the 'ontological-aesthetic' dimension of mood (how it contributes to the composition of a meaningful cinematic world, draws our attention to certain features of that world, making things salient, affectively charged or matter to us). This third ethical dimension of mood contributes to how a cinematic world is composed and communicated: moods that reveal a world and dispose the viewer to notice, attend to or be moved by both the singular details and sheer existence of this world.

Malick's films, for example, present cinematic worlds imbued with certain moods, which invite reflection on themes such as the radiant splendour of nature, the contingency of human identity, the mundane presence of transcendent beauty and revelatory moments of moral grace, the moral-metaphysical and sensual-emotional aspects of love. Making something beautiful or arresting makes it meaningful, shaping how much we care about and thus respond to things (and to people) within the world. Mood can make the world – including salient elements and complex aspects of it – matter to us in ways that might ordinarily remain implicit or 'backgrounded', or put differently, indifferently present or unremarked by our perceptual attention. The selection of elements and manner of composition of a cinematic world thus takes on implicit ethical significance as shaping our responses to narrative film.

All three aspects of mood are relevant to Malick's films but in ways quite unlike conventional narrative film. The subjective aspect of Malick's 'weightless' trilogy – with its flowing camera movements, fragmentary voice and image sequences and emphasis on light and movement – reveal an impressionistic 'inner' experience that is diffusely distributed across different characters and their varying milieus. The first aspect of mood, the phenomenological description of desire, is highlighted through dynamic camera movement, brilliant light and handheld shots, relating bodies through movement, gesture and framing, and expressing feeling or reflection via subjective, poetic voiceovers. These sequences reveal the world to those in love as bright, expressive and wondrous but also suggest a subjectivity that also remains guarded, generic or 'weightless'.

The second aspect, the moral-psychological dimension of mood, is striking but opaque in these films: sensuous alignment with minimal psychological interiority results in the evocation of affective, mood-like states whose expression in action remains arbitrary or contingent. Characters feel but do not really act; they reflect at times, but do not really communicate; they desire distraction, novelty, experiences but also feel bored, restless and empty. They express themselves through movement and gesture, which are both open and expressive but also guarded and ambiguous. For these reasons it is difficult to engage with such characters, who are both intimately rendered figures and generic allegorical 'types'. It therefore remains difficult to experience the kind of sympathetic emotional engagement typically at work in narrative film.

The third aspect of mood reveals worlds in ways that accentuate their sensuous qualities, phenomenological richness and existential value. The sheer beauty of Malick/Lubezki's images, whether of nature or urban settings, are cases in point, drawing our attention to the everyday and revealing it poetically, as something implicitly meaningful and aesthetically rewarding. These images articulate aspects of experience otherwise obscured or ignored, showing how a 'conversion' of attitudes towards the world reveals it as more experientially rich than we might otherwise expect. Malick's later films evoke this third sense of mood – as revelatory and world-disclosing; as resensitizing our receptivity to the world and others – in ways that invite ethical reflection, or even a conversion of attitudes consistent with an ethic of self-transformation (see Rossouw 2017).

The most productive way of approaching Malick's later films, I would suggest, is as evoking moods – joy, wonder, anxiety, restlessness, boredom, longing – inviting sensuous immersion and meditative contemplation. Such moods can play a significant role in what I am calling 'cinematic ethics': cinema's power to evoke an ethical experience that can prompt aesthetic, moral-psychological, even cultural transformation; the aesthetic 'conversion' of our feelings and perceptions, attitudes and orientations – the transformation of our ways of apprehending the world.[10] In Malick's most recent trilogy, this dimension of cinematic ethics is evoked through varieties of mood and the poetic disclosure of different attitudes towards existence. Indeed, they aim at something like an 'aesthetic theodicy', a cinematic mode suggesting the presence of divinity, or expressions of divine love, in the everyday world, where the latter is revealed as transfigured through aesthetic presentation (see Scott 2017: 172–175); or put differently, as an experientially rich, 'aesthetic justification' of existence (Nietzsche) revealed via cinematic means.[11] Whether these films achieve such aims raises a further question: namely, the efficacy of Malick's invitation to 'convert' from the aesthetic to the religious sphere of existence, and whether cinema can communicate religious experience as such.

A Kierkegaardian cinema?

Malick's approach in these late films follows a trajectory that he has been developing since *The Tree of Life*. They offer a cinematic exploration of Platonic and Kierkegaardian discourses on love as articulating a movement from the sensuous, bodily sphere of the aesthetic (erotic love), through the ethical sphere (familial, communal or fraternal love) to the religious (agape or divine love).[12] The latter sphere, expressing the infinite, in turn grounds and envelops the other two spheres, expressing the finite individually and socially, thereby contributing to what Kierkegaard described as the task of achieving a self (reconciling finite and infinite dimensions of the self through the love of God).[13] From this Kierkegaardian perspective, we are sick with (or of) love, confusing erotic with agapic and kenotic love, demanding of the former that it substitute for the latter. Indeed, the problem presented by erotic love is the attempt to make a finite object (the beloved) the subject of an infinite passion: this miscorrelation between infinite passion and finite object expresses a miscorrelation within the self, which results in a condition of existential despair (the failure to reconcile infinite and finite dimensions of selfhood in relation to the eternal) – Kierkegaard's sickness unto death.[14]

How does this become manifest in the 'weightless' trilogy? All three films offer versions of the 'immediate sphere of the erotic', coupled with explorations of both the ethical and the religious spheres of love.[15] For Kierkegaard, three spheres of existence defining stages on life's way (aesthetic, ethical and religious) confront us with an existential choice, the famous Either/Or: either choosing to remain within the sensuous sphere of a self-affirming, hedonistic aesthetic existence; or choosing to choose the higher sphere of ethical existence, a commitment to morality, communal ethical life and living according to the world's objective norms (rather than the aesthete's ironic distance from or sceptical disdain for shared moral values).

Yet the tension, even contradiction, between these two spheres of existence remains: the danger of nihilistic, subjective groundlessness in the aesthetic sphere (of which the romantics were accused); or losing one's individuality in the rigid devotion to moral duty and commitment to 'objective' norms and values (the problem of how to become an authentic Christian within an inauthentic institutionalized Christendom). According to Kierkegaard, the only way to resolve this tension, and its states of despair, is through genuine religion, which can only be suggested from within the spheres of the aesthetic and the ethical (this is what we find in Malick's 'weightless' trilogy, which hints at the religious sphere while remaining grounded in the aesthetic sphere in its dialectical relationship with the ethical).

This movement of transcendence and self-knowledge through love is expressed through an experimental narrative poetics that strips back character to the level of allegorical 'types'. It replaces directed character action with expressive, non-teleological forms of gesture and diminishes psychological motivation and explicit emotional engagement in favour of the implicit expression of mood, existential reflection and spiritual orientation. In this sense, Malick's cinematic style is expressive of a Kierkegaardian existentialist meditation on faith and love, depicting characters caught within a self-defeating dialectic of desire: a movement towards (metaphysical or divine) self-transcendence coupled with a pull towards sensuous immanence. Far from being a joyless jeremiad, Malick's trilogy offers a captivating exploration of Kierkegaard's sphere of the aesthetic: one that valorizes possibility, is experientially fragmented, distracted, and at once ironic and curious.[16]

Father Quintana's Kierkegaardian sermons on love, contrasting love as a feeling and love as a duty, stand as an epigraph for the trilogy:

Love is not only a feeling, love is a duty. You *shall* love, whether you like it or not. You say your love has died? Maybe it is waiting to be converted to something higher.

How is this meditation on love manifest in the 'weightless' trilogy, which focuses on, but refuses to fulfil, the desired 'formation of the couple' defining narrative cinema? A number of features of Malick's late style are significant here. The first is an evident fascination with movement: the dynamic, flowing camera, questing restlessly through the lived space of the characters, roaming freely across nature and landscape at will, relativizing particular subjective perspectives via a revelatory disclosure of the world. Life itself in its contingency, its dynamic expressivity, its revelatory glory, animates all of Malick's cinematic works. This roving camera becomes a kind of witness in its own right, one whose trajectories are organized via the axes of verticality (transcendence) and horizonality (immanence), presenting finite and 'infinite' movements as expressive of a dynamic sense of world.

Second, there is the impressionistic presentation of sound and image, where voiceover does not always match image, and which often 'floats' between characters and thus remains difficult to attribute. Main characters – Ben Affleck, Javier Bardem, and Olga Kurylenko in *To the Wonder*, Christian Bale in *Knight of Cups*, Ryan Gosling, Rooney Mara and Michael Fassbender in *Song to Song* – have little explicit dialogue and minimal verbal expression. Scenes featuring multiple characters will sometimes background spoken dialogue in favour of inner meditation, deliberately mismatching image and sound to evoke their detached and distracted subjectivity. This is a cinematic style expressive of characters failing to achieve authentic selfhood or lives grounded in the (finite and infinite) experience of love.

Third, this combination of mobile point of view and ambiguous character presentation shifts the narrative perspective away from familiar emotional engagement and towards a poetic expression of moods. This emphasis on mood is the third recognizable feature of the Malick's late style. The rendering of individual characters, cast using highly respected Hollywood actors, creates an expectation of pleasurable engagement or possibilities for identification that remain unfulfilled. Malick's characters, rather, are akin to diffuse Humean selves – loosely connected bundles of impressions lacking a clear agential centre or identity over time. They float through the world as ungrounded entities, whose feelings, impressions and moods reveal a world that is itself floating, lacking substance, while also being revealed, at times, as beautiful, even wondrous. This symphonic fusion of music, image and movement, sometimes harmonious, sometimes dissonant, captures moments of contingency amidst a world that reveals itself, when transfigured by love, as expressive of grace and beauty.

Malick's 'weightless' (Love and Faith) trilogy

Malick's three most recent films form a trilogy of thematically related and stylistically similar works (see Rewin 2017; Hammer 2017).[17] Drawing on elements already present in *The Tree of Life* (contemporary settings, flowing camera movements, impressionistic voiceover, fragmentary presentation of subjective experience, non-linear narrative sequencing), *To the Wonder* (2012), *Knight of Cups* (2015) and *Song to Song* (2017) all explore contemporary experiences of love, especially romantic love, through an experimental style of cinematic presentation that is also strongly allegorical. All of Malick's narrative films are, or feature, love stories, where these are not confined to the more conventional cinematic focus on romantic love but encompass the less commonly depicted forms of familial, communal and spiritual-religious forms of love.

In narrative terms, the films are all remarkably simple. We have a romantic couple, an American man and a French-Ukrainian woman in Paris, whose relationship withers and cannot be sustained after they move to the American Midwest, coupled with a priest in crisis searching for a source to replenish his faith, striving to find salvation through love and works amidst the poor and the afflicted (*To the Wonder*). We follow a hedonistic Hollywood screenwriter, whose pursuit of erotic experiential novelty, as a means of finding but also losing himself, reflecting the seductive movie dream-world to which he belongs, remains detached from the possibility of a deeper sense of love (the 'Pearl' of his thwarted quest) that would enable him to transcend his existential malaise (*Knight of Cups*). Finally, we witness a creative young woman, a musician living life from moment to moment, searching for meaning through love and music, forming a loving but precarious relationship with another drifting musician; both of them are tempted by a worldly, Mephistophelian seducer (a record producer), who forms a three-way relationship with the musicians, then forms another relationship with a different woman that ends tragically. The musicians struggle to find creative and romantic satisfaction in a world of cultural distraction and experiential novelty. Both couples experiment with living life contingently in a cycle of repetition lacking aim or purpose; one couple ends up destroyed by it, the other abandons this hedonistic but empty world, finding fulfilment in starting a new life together in the country (*Song to Song*).

All three films are centred on romantic love but also feature a variety of different modes of loving relationship – familial, parental, artistic, ethical and religious – with a central contrast drawn between exclusive, self-satisfying (erotic) and universal, self-emptying (kenotic or agapic) love. All three feature figures who lack definable identities, are presented with minimal backstory or context, express themselves through gestures rather than directed action, floating through life, and their love relationships, in an improvised, contingent manner.

Indeed, in this respect all three films are allegorical, framing each narrative by way of morality tales, philosophical fables and religious myths. These include the Platonic myths of love in the *Symposium* and the *Phaedrus*; Christian allegories of the kinship between erotic and divine love such as the biblical Song of Songs; Bunyan's everyman morality tale *Pilgrim's Progress*; the 'Hymn of the Pearl', which derives from the Arabic poet Shihab al-Din al-Suhrawardi's allegorical 'Tale of Western [or Occidental] Exile' but also features in the Gnostic Acts of Thomas.[18] We could also include Augustine's *Confessions*, allusions to Dostoevsky and Tolstoy, Percy's *The Moviegoer*, passages cited from Kierkegaard's *Works of Love* and his other philosophical-literary texts such as *Either/Or* and *The Sickness unto Death*. These myths and texts provide allegorical frameworks for Malick's trilogy (although less explicitly so in *Song to Song*), situating these contemporary moral parables within a rich cultural history of philosophical, artistic and religious meditations on love.

As in Malick's other films, literary, artistic, philosophical and religious sources are condensed and synthesized by way of imagery, voiceover, symbolism and quotation. Elemental images of water, desert, wind and sunlight add a mythical and theological significance to signature landscape scenes and 'golden hour' location shots. Characters allude to philosophical and religious figures, such as Della's (Imogen Poots') comment to screenwriter Rick (Christian Bale) in *Knight of Cups*, 'Love, and do what you want – a saint said that', alluding to Augustine, as she chides Rick for being weak, for not wanting love but rather 'a love experience'. *To the Wonder* shows Marina (or her shadow) wistfully contemplating the famous French medieval 'Lady and the Unicorn' tapestries (depicting the sense of sight and the one on love, titled *À mon seul désir*).[19] We hear her remarking to herself: 'What is she dreaming of? How calm she is. In love. Forever at peace' – not only a reference to her own ambiguous desire for love and eternal peace but also a reflexive moment focusing on the act of cinematic contemplation.

Knight of Cups uses the symbolism of the Tarot card deck to shape its allegorical character 'types' and to organize its elliptical narrative 'chapters'. In addition to the Knight of Cups, we have the Moon, the Hanged Man, the Hermit, Judgment, the Tower, the High Priestess, Death, and Freedom (one that, intriguingly, does not appear in either the Major or Minor Arcana).[20] Indeed, one way of describing Rick's quest and journey is that he must find a way for the Knight of Cups to become Kierkegaard's 'Knight of the Faith' (1968: 49 ff.): the authentic individual able to embrace life, whose faith allows him or her to act freely and independently in the world inspired by nothing but 'the absurd', namely the experience of divine love (hence 'Freedom'). All three films combine this mythic/allegorical framework with impressionistic, poetic evocations of subjective experience. This cinematic allegory of love and its discontents is merged with a Kierkegaardian Christian-existentialist critique of the impoverishment of egocentric erotic/romantic love in the absence of a deeper grounding of this desire in divine love.

'You *shall* love, whether you like it or not' (*To the Wonder*)

Like many Malick fans, I had been keenly awaiting the release of *To the Wonder* (2012), less than two years after *The Tree of Life* (2011). I knew it featured two actors who had not previously worked with

Malick (Olga Kurylenko and Ben Affleck), that it was a love story set partly in Paris, partly in Oklahoma, that it had clear religious allusions and was entirely set in the present. After the simultaneously lyrical and epic quality of *The Tree of Life*, I was intrigued to see how this next film would be received. Disappointingly, the film lasted barely a few weeks in our local cinemas, and I managed to see it alone in an almost empty theatre. Reviews were quite harsh, ranging from mildly praising but perplexed to dismissive, scathing or mocking. The refrain that Malick, reclusive genius, was now in decline, making too many movies too quickly (*Knight of Cups* and what was to become *Song to Song* were shot almost back-to-back), began to circulate more widely. I felt a sense of loyalty to the work, finding it understated and more intimate than I had expected, subtly beautiful and moving, with some wonderful visual passages and images, but also abstract, beguiling and obscure in ways that made me want to understand its religious and theological layers. My sense of a continuing elaboration and refinement of Malick's 'late' style was undiminished. So too was my intuition that these late films were pushing further towards a religious *and* philosophical meditation on love. With the subsequent release of *Knight of Cups* and *Song to Song*, it became clear that we were dealing with a trilogy. It was only after repeated viewing – much like the experience of poetry – that I felt I was beginning to understand and appreciate these fascinating and elusive, aesthetically and morally challenging films.

To the Wonder marks an important break in Malick's work by being entirely set in the present and incorporating contemporary media technology as part of its narrative presentation (iPhone and GoPro footage feature in all three films). The narrative itself is simple, archetypical, combining two separate but resonant narrative lines: one on romantic love, the other on divine love, suggesting the necessity, but also difficulty, of reconnecting these forms of love within the modern (secular) world. The film invites us to consider erotic-romantic love from a spiritual perspective and the search for divine love as rooted in existential care and love of the neighbour. The film focuses on a couple in love (sensuous, ethereal ex-dancer Marina (Olga Kurylenko) and quiet, brooding environmental inspector Neil (Ben Affleck)), whose relationship blossoms in Paris and Normandy (their powerfully symbolic visit to the famous medieval abbey of Mont Saint-Michel, known in French as 'La merveille'). The dazzling beauty of Paris, and melancholy wonder evoked by Mont Saint-Michel, then gives way to the flat, suburban monotony of Bartlesville, Oklahoma, whose identical cul-de-sac family homes back on to vast plains and rolling hills. Marina's and Neil's romantic passion is evident early on, but their attempts to cultivate this love so as to combine passion with commitment remain ambiguous and obscure: 'If I left you because you didn't want to marry me,' as Marina remarks, 'it would mean that I didn't love you'. Her desire for a deeper union with Neil remains tempered by her non-committal declarations concerning their relationship ('I don't expect anything; just to go a little of our way together'), and Neil's inability to communicate (he barely speaks any lines in the film).

Despite their hesitations, they leave France for the United States and move back to Neil's hometown of Bartlesville. The film then follows the collapse of Marina and Neil's unstable relationship, a fragile bond based on feeling and circumstance rather than care and commitment. The disintegration of their love prompts Marina to leave Neil and return to Paris with her daughter Tatiana (Tatiana Chillane), who later leaves Marina to live with her biological father. Marina soon finds that she is even more lost and unhappy in Paris than she was with Neil in their isolated family home and eventually contacts him pleading to take her back.

Following Marina's departure, Neil commences a relationship with an old flame, Jane (Rachel McAdams), a shy cattle rancher whose marriage is on the rocks. After a tentative initial encounter, they commence a love affair that blossoms but becomes stalled by Neil's guardedness, his inability to open himself to her. They strive to make the relationship succeed, a liaison marked by the contrast between Jane's passionate declarations of love and Neil's undemonstrative demeanour. Jane even tries to anchor their love in a shared faith, getting Neil to read the Bible with her in the hope, presumably, that this might strengthen their romantic bond.[21] Despite her efforts, their relationship repeats the same pattern of contingent feeling, emotional closure, and moral disorientation that lead to the collapse of Neil's relationship with Marina.

When Marina contacts Neil again, telling him she is unhappy, can't find a job in Paris and wants to return to the United States, he is torn but decides to help her. He breaks off his relationship with Jane and agrees to sponsor Marina's return and to marry her – first in a soulless, depressing civil ceremony, with prisoners as witnesses, then in a church ceremony, which remains emotionally muted and shadowed by doubt. Their plan proves to be ill-judged: Neil remains emotionally closed, possibly still committed to Jane, but unable to love either woman. Marina (along with her daughter) once again finds her new home stifling, her surroundings deadening, lacking the freedom that she craves. Her attitude is embodied by her visiting Italian friend, the free-spirited Anna (Romina Mondello), who exhorts Marina to leave Neil, to become free, experiment with life, treat it like a dream ('in a dream you can't make mistakes') – a figure paralleled in *Knight of Cups* by hedonistic amoralist Tonio (Antonio Banderas) ('there are no principles, only circumstances').

Both Marina and Neil, however, despite their desire for fulfilment, remain captured by a self-affirming form of eros: seeking in romantic/

erotic love a pleasure and excitement that would enliven their being, defining them as individuals, but expecting that the other should supply whatever additional qualities might be lacking in oneself.[22] In the end, both end up disappointed, each resenting the other for being unable to provide both freedom and fidelity, intimacy and excitement, deep union and loss of self. Marina, resigned but resolved, returns to Paris, to an uncertain future, while Neil is left alone in Oklahoma, unsure whether he still loves Marina, Jane or somebody else.

The second narrative line centres on the crisis of faith being experienced by a Latin American Catholic priest, Father Quintana (Javier Bardem), who has some connection with Marina and Neil through the church (Marina confides in him her marriage difficulties, and Neil his having to choose between Marina and Jane). We are introduced to Father Quintana during one of his sermons on the difference between human and divine love, wiping his glasses in a distracted, mechanical manner, his voice subdued, lacking passion and conviction, while conveying what serves as a commentary on erotic-romantic love such as we have seen thus far:

> There is a love, that's like a stream that goes dry when rain no longer feeds it. But there is a love that is like a spring coming up from the earth. The first is human love, the second is divine love and has its source above.[23]

Marina is in the pews, listening to the sermon, and is struck by this distinction. She recognizes the drying up of her love for Neil and seeks solace in the church. She tells Father Quintana how she was married at seventeen and had a child but that her husband starting running after other women and left her; how in the eyes of the church she is still married to that man but desperately wants to be a wife to Neil. The implication is that at one level she desires to have a child with Neil, but at another remains ambivalent and conflicted about what motherhood involves. She enjoys her interaction with children, and clearly loves her daughter, but remains anxious about compromising her freedom and unsure whether she should desire a child.[24] Early in the film, she asks Tatiana in Paris, once Neil invites them to the United States, whether she would like a little sister. Most of the scenes depicting Neil and Marina in love feature moments of playfulness in ways that suggest a certain childlike quality to her, which turns to seriousness, even melancholy, when confronted with the realities of adult life and the emotional challenges of her relationship with Neil. There is a poignant scene at a lunch gathering in Bartlesville, where both Marina and Neil are touched but also left uncomfortable by the deep sense of familial emotional harmony at their host's home. And finally, there is a painful scene at the gynaecologist where Marina, evidently experiencing difficulties with her IUD, is relieved to be told that she does not need a hysterectomy but hesitates when asked by the doctor, 'Would this be a time you might consider children?' 'Someday', she replies, listlessly. The question of motherhood remains a pressing and ambiguous one for Marina, despite the film's obvious fascination with children, infants and family.

Father Quintana, for his part, is unable to offer much conviction to back up his sermon, clearly suffering from his own spiritual crisis of faith and love. His voiceovers, combining reflection, meditation and prayer, reveal his desire to experience divine love coupled with his sense of separation or distance from God. He wants to experience that sense of divine presence that animated his earlier faith but has since been lost; he goes through the motions of Catholic ritual, preaches and ministers to his flock, but lacks passion or conviction – he is in a state of Kierkegaardian despair. His inner struggle mirrors that of another famous cinematic priest, Pastor Tomas Ericsson (Gunner Björnstrand) in Bergman's *Winter Light* (1963). Like Bergman's silence trilogy (with its insistence on the silence of God), Father Quintana is shown in his daily routine, his engagements with marginalized and troubled souls battling poverty, drugs, environmental hazards, disease and destitution (including a pointed occasion when he refuses to answer his door to a distressed woman in need of help).[25] He laments God's absence and asks despairingly for some divine acknowledgement. It is only through his continued efforts to console and comfort the more afflicted, suffering members of his flock that he finds peace and solace, an experience of divine love – of God's presence expressed through the encounter with others – that he had been seeking elsewhere.

In the film's coda, after an arresting shot of Marina entering a darkened airline boarding bridge, fringed with blinding light, we cut to a long shot, from inside of a house looking out to a beautifully designed garden. In the background, through a glass darkly (framed by large, wall-length, glass sliding doors), we see two small children playing outside, a prominent water feature flowing conspicuously in the garden. An unnamed woman and Neil are shown walking around the garden, independently of each other. The whole scene, a static long shot, suggests that Neil has found peace, the love of a wife and family, yet hints that the sense of distance and disconnection underlying Neil's love relationships somehow remains.

This suggestive vignette is followed by enigmatic fantasy or vision, one that recalls comparable spiritual-religious scenes from *The Tree of Life* and *The New World*. We see Marina in a brown dress, lying asleep on the damp earth, awakening with a sense of confusion or uncertainty. She explores the wet, empty fields, tasting water drops poised on twig buds and bounding through the forest. Fragmentary images follow, oneiric or visionary, showing her walking, skipping, dancing; these shots are cut abruptly, capturing momentary intensities rather than continuous actions. We see her framed against an evocative background of natural environs and creaturely life, embracing the slopes and plains, populated by distant cows, with an empty homestead illuminated on the hilltop (it appears we are back in the Midwest). Recalling Pocahontas, she gives thanks to the heavens and turns briefly towards the sky, shot from below and gazing off-screen, as a dazzling golden light briefly illuminates her face. She then disappears from view, reminiscent again, in costume, choreography and mood, of Pocahontas'/Rebecca's return to Mother Earth at the end of *The New World*.[26]

The sequence suggests, perhaps, that Marina does not return to her life in Paris (all we see are some fragmentary images of her wandering alone at night in the rain) but can only find her sense of life by being spiritually reborn. Indeed, Marina's departure 'into the light', and subsequent vision of herself wandering alone, solitary but at peace, finding the blinding light, suggests a death and rebirth. This ambiguous sequence then cuts to a serene long shot of Mont-Saint-Michel, inviting us again to contemplate the climb 'to the wonder' – the (Platonic-Christian) ascent of love (erotic to spiritual) – that we have followed throughout the film.

This abbreviated sketch of the film's basic storylines underlines that it is akin to a moral fable, a metaphysical-religious allegory, rendered in cinematic terms. At the same time, this allegorical dimension is presented in an abstract style, at once subjective, esoteric and poetic. As cinematographer Emmanuel Lubezki remarked, *To the Wonder* is less tied to theatrical convention and more purely cinematic than Malick's previous films (see McNab and Lubezki 2011). As I suggest below, this involves a deliberate destabilizing of narrative expectation and aesthetic convention that expresses the fragmented subjectivity of the film's central figures and their exhilarating but frustrating attempts to find fulfilment through romantic-erotic love. It is a style that mediates between an allegorical morality play and the aesthetic presentation of modern 'weightless' subjectivity that strives for experiential novelty and a sense of identity in a world of cultural distractions. The title of the film itself is suggestive. Although wonder is a mood frequently evoked in relation to Malick, it is tied here to the experience of love, its transfiguration of our sense of being-in-the-world. More concretely, it is figured allegorically thanks to the medieval Abbey of Mont Saint-Michel that formerly served as a site of religious pilgrimage but now serves modern tourism and is known as 'the Wonder of the Western world'. Marina and Neil are introduced in the throes of experiencing romantic-erotic love, which engulfs the lovers, enlivening but also threatening to obliterate them (as Marina, in French voiceover, says, accompanying the opening video footage of the film, 'Newborn. I open my eyes. I melt. Into the eternal night. A spark. I fall into the flame'). They drive out to the famous Abbey, admiring its isolated beauty on the tidal sands, both removed from the mainland and subject to the ebb and flow of the tides. They attempt to walk across the quicksand-like surface, laughing as they almost stumble and fall, suggesting a playful joy but also a fragility and instability to their passion, an uncertain ground to their fluctuating love. They wander through the 'enclosed garden' of the Abbey courtyard, complete with shot of a single rose (the enclosed garden and rose being well-known metaphors not only for the nexus between erotic and spiritual love but also feminine love and devotion, featured, for example, in the Song of Songs and in the medieval French courtly love poem the *Romance of the Rose*).[27] Marina even remarks on how they 'climbed the steps to the wonder', accompanied by a shot of stone steps leading upwards, introducing the metaphors of ascent or transcendence through love that will dominate the film (and which also features heavily in *The Tree of Life*).

This is made explicit in *Knight of Cups*, which includes an allusion to Plato's *Phaedrus* on the desire for transcendence at the heart of

erotic love, an experience of love reminding us of the divine beauty
we experienced in a more purified state of being:

> Once the soul was perfect and had wings and could soar into
> heaven where only creatures with wings can be. But the soul lost
> its wings and fell to earth, ere it took on an earthly body. ... [W]
> hen we see a beautiful woman, or a man, the soul remembers the
> beauty it used to know in heaven and ... the wings begin to sprout
> and that makes the soul want to fly but it cannot yet, it is still too
> weak, so the man keeps staring up at the sky like a young bird that
> has lost all interest in the world.[28]

In Plato's *Phaedrus*, our desire for beauty, when aroused by the
physical beauty of another person, is actually a recollection of the
divine beauty our souls knew before we fell to earth. Erotic love is the
spark that moves us to begin the ascent from the bodily realm of the
senses, via communal love of the community, to the moral-spiritual
realm of philosophical love, concluding with the glimpse of God or
the idea of the Good itself – our ultimate object of love even if we do
not realize this in the midst of erotic passion. This Platonic myth of
love provides an orienting allegorical frame for all three films.[29]

This myth is coupled with the Kierkegaardian discourse on love
as requiring *choice*. As Father Quintana says, quoting Kierkegaard's
Works of Love, we must *choose* to love, choose to love one's neighbour
as oneself, as a duty inspired by divine love – 'You *shall* love, whether
you like it or not' – in order to move through the finite spheres of
the aesthetic and the ethical, which together point to the sphere of
the religious (the infinite) (Kierkegaard 2009: 34–57). This movement
of ascent involves recognition of the beauty revealed in the world
and through others, and a commitment, a leap of faith, towards an
experience of divine love. Such movements – what Kierkegaard would
call 'movements of the infinite', the Knight of the Faith's transfigured

sense of experience and subjective attitude of freedom and grace in response to the world[30] – are manifested through the fluid camera and visual splendour of the images animating the whole of the 'weightless' trilogy.

Malick/Lubezki develop this 'revelatory' cinematic aesthetic to great effect in a series of related figurative movements of ascent and descent: the camera tilting upwards towards the sky and light or depicting bodies falling downwards, for example, into water – a swimming pool – shot from beneath the water's surface (the remarkable underwater GoPro images in *Knight of Cups*, shot in slow motion, of dogs diving into a swimming pool, teeth bared, trying desperately to reach a desired toy, slowly sinking out of reach – one of the most striking images of desire in recent cinema). Or shooting low, with distorting fish-eye lenses, as a character ascends a rocky slope or hillside, climbs stairs or gives thanks, gazing up at the sky, like Marina's vision at the conclusion of *To the Wonder* (shots that also feature prominently in *The Tree of Life* and *Knight of Cups*). These vertical sky-reaching movements stand in contrast to the flowing horizontal earth-hugging movements of the camera as it follows characters walking along streets, across fields or within domestic spaces (*To the Wonder, Knight of Cups*).

These two axes of movement – a vertical axis of spiritual transcendence and a horizontal axis of earthly immanence – provide a rich matrix organizing the horizons and patterns of expressive physical movement within the frame.[31] At the same time, these vertical and horizontal axes imbue camera movements with a dynamic as well as symbolic significance. They reveal different attitudes towards, and ways of inhabiting, our world: ways that encompass both immanent and transcendent dimensions of our engagement with the world, which in turn reflect the finite and infinite dimensions of the self in relation to the other.

'How do I begin?' (*Knight of Cups*)

Knight of Cups continues the exploration of romantic/erotic love and distracted, hedonistic subjectivity. It offers another variation on the seductive lures of Kierkegaard's aesthetic sphere, without really moving beyond it. Its ephemeral, 'weightless' characters experience brief moments of insight concerning the necessity of acknowledging the ethical (familial, communal, social) sphere of value, and only fleeting hints of the religious sphere that would reconcile finite and infinite dimensions of alienated subjectivity through an acknowledgement of divine love. It continues Malick's poetic evocation of world-revealing moods in the service of a quasi-phenomenological presentation of what the world is like for someone within the aesthetic sphere of existence (something like a dispersed, fragmentary, contemporary cinematic recounting of Kierkegaard's 'Diary of a Seducer') (1959: 297–440).

Rick (Christian Bale) is a successful Hollywood screenwriter disaffected with life, disconnected from the world yet fascinated by the desire for some kind of transcendence through erotic experience. Much like Guido (Marcello Mastroiani) in Fellini's *8½*, Rick attempts to transcend his ennui through erotic encounters and episodic immersion in Hollywood Babylon. He is a sleepwalker who has drunk deep from the wells of oblivion but in the process forgotten his vocation, sacrificing art and his authentic self for pleasure and distraction. This is a journey expressive not only of Rick's existential-spiritual malaise but of the cultural milieu of which he is a part – the seductive world of Hollywood (cinema) itself. As becomes clear, the film's loose, episodic structure is organized via the symbolism of the Tarot card pack. As allegorical stages on life's journey, each chapter depicts the various 'guides' (male and female) as Rick embarks on his quest but quickly falls into a spiritual slumber, forgetting the pearl of his quest, and only gradually reawakens, through experiences of love and their failure, to find the orientation and attitude – through a deeper love – to properly begin.[32]

Like *To the Wonder*, *Knight of Cups* combines Malick's fragmentary style with mythic and theological allusions but also draws attention to the manner in which cinematic form (above all, Hollywood) participates in, and audiovisually reflects, the sensuous, seductive presentation of the world that so fascinates Rick. From its opening scene, the film presents itself as a latter-day retelling of Bunyan's *The Pilgrim's Progress*, quoting almost verbatim its opening prologue:

> the Pilgrim's Progress, from this world to that which is to come, delivered under the similitude of a dream; wherein is discovered the manner of his setting out, his dangerous journey, and safe arrival at the desired country …

With its fragmentary, paratactic style, the film itself is presented 'under the similitude of a dream'. The theme of an existential-spiritual slumber, Rick's somnambulistic floating through the world, provides a tenuous thread linking the 'weightless' experiences of sensuous pleasure (the visual motif of bodies suspended, floating, diving or swimming in water, defying gravity through dance, movement or gymnastic display, recurs throughout the film).

The film's title, accompanied by Vaughan Williams' Fantasia on a theme of Thomas Tallis, introduces us to the pilgrim, Rick. He is shown in long shot in a desert landscape with mountains in the background and a dried-up stream in the midground, framed by a setting sun. Much like Jack in *The Tree of Life*, we cut closer to see Rick looking lost, disoriented and confused. The cosmic background of this quest is suggested by intercut images of the aurora borealis, shot from space, a dazzling visual marker of natural wonder – and hint of the earlier 'cosmic question' – framing the spiritual odyssey of this modern pilgrim, a stranger in a strange land. The voiceover/narrator continues to intone, against images of a lost Rick, a highway and further images of the Northern Lights, lines from *The Pilgrim's Progress*: 'As I walk through the wilderness of this world, I lighted on a certain place where was a den, and I laid me down in that place to sleep; and as I slept, I dreamed a dream.' The narrator's recounting of Bunyan's tale, seeing a man far from home, a book in his hands and a burden on his back, gives way to Rick's voiceover, against cosmic images of light and earth, followed by worldly images of driving through a highway tunnel illuminated by blinding light: 'All those years, living the life of someone I didn't even know.' Like Jack in *The Tree of Life*, what Rick has lost remains buried in childhood memories: a sense of freedom and joy, of sensuous enjoyment, physical connection and wonder at the world – impressions shown through handheld GoPro/DV footage of children, shot from their point of view, playing and swinging, a dog chasing a ball at grass height – expressions of playful delight in existence.

At the same time, the film also recounts the story of the Pearl (an Islamic mythic tale but one that resonates with the Gnostic Acts of Thomas), which Rick's father, Joseph (Bryan Dennehy) narrates in a voiceover directed at Rick. The father asks if Rick remembers the story he used to tell to him as a boy: 'about a young prince, a knight, sent by his father, the King of the East', intercut by images of Rick as a boy playing with his sister as a child, followed by playful young Japanese women, in street fashion costume, laughing with the adult Rick in a convertible. The second signature piece in the film now appears, the melancholy minor-key clarinet theme from Wojciech Kilar's 'Exodus'. The father continues, narrating how the man was sent 'West into Egypt, to find a Pearl, a Pearl from the depths of the sea', accompanied by GoPro images of water, waves churning at a beach, shot from underwater, and a dazzling swimming pool. These images give way to an LA Penthouse party, showing Rick with the Japanese women standing by the side of a pool, with his brother (as it turns out), and Hollywood starlet types adorning the scene. 'But when the Prince arrived', the father continues, 'the people poured him a cup that took away his memory', accompanied by handheld close images of a drunken Rick, stumbling over a couch, rolling around with the girls. 'He forgot he was the son of the King, forgot about the Pearl and fell into a deep sleep', as iPhone images of balloons, streamers and fallen angel partygoers in the aftermath of the revelry complete the scene. Like Jack in *The Tree of Life*, Rick is shown staring vacantly out of the apartment windows at the skyscrapers across the way; we see revellers coming back down to earth, sleeping, staring, some in animal (goat) masks, and a melancholy angelic figure gazing out the window.

The father continues: 'The King didn't forget his son. He continued to send word, messengers, guides … ' accompanied by images of Rick in a nightclub setting at night, an empty dance floor with a large multiscreen display in the background. The screens show a mesmerizing video work, now foregrounded in full screen: a jump-cut, black-and-white animation of a young woman – or messenger – playing with cardboard photographed masks – fake eyes shifting position unnervingly across her face, head and body – and body paint, covering her flesh in black, leaving only her eyes visible, gazing directly at us. The film seems to suggest we are concerned here with the play of images, of seductive appearances and the play of identity. Appearances proliferate and deceive in Rick's seductive and stylized world of manipulated image-making, of which this film itself is a part. Malick's reflection on cinema here – specifically on the gaze, the depiction of women, of faces as expressions of identity, of fantasy images of contemporary (gendered) identity – is hard to miss. We are watching not only an allegorical expression of fragmented identity but a self-reflexive display of how images shape our fantasies in our media-saturated, appearance-oriented culture.

Again, much like *To the Wonder*, *Knight of Cups* mediates these allegorical tales via the Platonic myth of love, the transcendent movement from erotic, communal, to spiritual or intellectual love.[33] This third 'Platonic' dimension of the allegories of love is also recited via an unidentified voiceover during important scenes in the film (Rick meeting with Della (Imogen Poots) at an aquarium, gazing upwards towards the gracefully swimming fish, as the voiceover recounts Plato's myth of the transformation of erotic into intellectual love). Both *Knight of Cups* and *Song to Song*, as I discuss below, remain focused on the character's inability to transcend what Kierkegaard called 'the immediate sphere of the erotic': the aesthetic sphere of sensuous pleasure, the pursuit of novelty, stimulation and the interesting, coupled with an ironic distance from the ethical sphere of institutionalized norms and moral values (Kierkegaard 1959: 43 ff.). Rick combines an ironic distance from his work, his lovers, even from his hedonistic pursuit of pleasure, with a sense of estrangement from the world, his deeper self and an ambiguous longing for self-knowledge and existential transformation through love.[34]

Rick's world is a world of weightless subjectivity, a world illuminated by images of light. It expresses a sensibility that seeks to be grounded in the earth, to capture the physical energy of fire and the sensuous fluidity of water. As though to mark the existential grounding of the earth, the film returns repeatedly to landscape and sky images. These are expressions not only of spiritual confusion or existential despair but of aesthetic wonder and a sensuous revealing; they signify our belonging not only to the world but to the mysterious earth as well as the heavens or cosmos that envelop it.

As though to emphasize this unstable grounding of existence, we witness the existential interruption of Rick's world, an abrupt ending to his spiritual slumber, rendered in a remarkable earth tremor sequence. Against a menacing rumbling background, Rick is shown being rudely awoken from his sleep, a handheld camera tracking his agitated movements, windows and furniture shaking, pot plants dropping and sirens going off in the background. Disoriented and confused, he rushes downstairs and heads outside. People and dogs are wandering around; the concrete ground is strewn with fallen pot plants and gushing water taps. The camera whips and scans across the room, a sympathetic witness sharing Rick's disorientation and distress. Helicopters hover overhead – an unsettling recurring image in the film – as the earth trembles. Rick drops to his knees, laying his head on the ground, as though listening for a message from the earth itself.

Back in his apartment, he showers, and we see subjective images of reverie: Rick at the beach with a blond woman, then back in his apartment, on a freeway, the dazzling sun, driving on a highway. His voiceover resumes: 'See the palm trees? They tell you anything is possible. You can be anything, do anything, start over', which anticipates the 'message' that free-spirited pole dancer Karen (Teresa Palmer) gives him later in the film (in a chapter entitled 'The High Priestess').

We see Rick at work, at a writers' or production meeting, looking as bored and lost as Jack in *The Tree of Life*. Rick remains cut off from the fragmentary conversation, lost in his own thoughts, images of the highway and driving to the desert blocking out the mundane world. We cut to a Hollywood studio lot, with miscellaneous actors, a stage set and Rick wandering around, inured to the fantasy world he has helped to create.

His father's voiceover resumes, accompanied again by the William's Fantasia for Thomas Tallis. 'My son', he declares, as hangar doors slowly close, 'you're just like I am. You've yet to figure your life out', he says as we see Rick walking pensively across the rooftop of an apartment building at dusk. 'Can't put the pieces together. Just like me. A pilgrim on this earth, a stranger. Fragments, pieces of a man.' We see Rick back home in his apartment, solitary, desolate, a fan whirring overhead as he watches TV alone. 'Where did I go wrong'? he asks. By way of response, we see images again of the desert, of water in a swimming pool shot from underwater, then a girl jumping in and climbing out of the pool, a remarkably illuminated POV shot on digital video. We cut to the first Tarot Card intertitle, the Moon, which introduces Della's (Imogen Poots') story, the first in the six tales of women – be they guides or messengers – Rick meets in his confused quest, mistaking erotic love and experiential novelty for the Pearl of self-knowledge and transformation through love.

Each relationship in *Knight of Cups* is ephemeral and interrupted, fleeting and inconclusive. Rick's fascination with Della – a commanding, fascinating but enigmatic figure – loses its emotional core when she realizes his distance, his inability to give himself, describing him as 'weak', as desiring a 'love experience' rather than love itself. Their sexual passion does not satisfy; their fantasy world soon falls apart. 'We are not living the lives we were meant to lead', she muses, leaving him to reflect on his inchoate desire to be 'woken up', brought back to life, by a muse-like fantasy woman – a clichéd role that Della decides she does not want to play. 'Judgment' focuses on Rick's ex-wife Nancy (Cate Blanchett), who sketches the disintegration of their marriage, Rick's emotional inexpressiveness, his distraction from personal and professional fulfilment and his inability to commit to marriage, children, or their shared future. The Tower focuses on Helen (Freida Pinto), an ethereal model, whose sensuality is coupled with a spiritual bent; her eschewal of a sexual relationship with Rick leaves him fascinated yet dissatisfied, desiring something more that he cannot grasp or define. This desire leads him to Karen

(Teresa Palmer), the High Priestess, whose free-spirited openness to experience, to sexuality and adventure arouses Rick but again leaves him unsure what her ambiguous combination of sexual provocation and arbitrary desire actually means. She plays with life and identity, open to everything but attached to nothing, drawing Rick in but also keeping him at a distance, one among many lovers, passion and intimacy shadowed by boredom and distraction. Like Kierkegaard's seducer, Rick becomes fascinated with a married woman, Elizabeth (Natalie Portman) ('Death'), who throws over her marriage for an affair with Rick, the two of them playing at an intimacy that is both desired and disavowed. When she discovers she is pregnant, unsure whether to Rick or to her husband, the reality of sexual intimacy – and Elizabeth's implied abortion – becomes too confronting for Rick, and their relationship falls apart. Finally, an ethereal figure, Isabel (Isabel Lucas), briefly glimpsed earlier in the film, now returns, and the implied balance between sensual self-expression, openness and spiritual calm suggests the possibility that Rick will finally find peace, reconciling those conflicting desires for immanent experience and self-transcendence that have driven his meandering quest. Whether this final relationship promises happiness or disappointment is left ambiguous: the film concludes with images of a desertscape, a highway, of sky and light, accompanied by the Exodus theme and Rick's final questioning word – 'begin'.

'I never knew I had a soul; the word embarrassed me' (*Song to Song*)

This theme is taken up virtually unchanged in *Song to Song*, the third film in the 'weightless' trilogy.[35] Set amidst the music scene in Austin, Texas, it returns to the love-triangle motif familiar from

Days of Heaven, doubling this triangle between two sets of couples, synthesizing fragmentary moments in the intertwining relationships of Faye (Rooney Mara) and BV (Ryan Gosling), Rhonda (Natalie Portman) and Cook (Michael Fassbender). The protracted couplings and periodic dispersions of the two couples are shown in Malick's fragmentary vignette style, intercut with sequences of musical performance, the creating of songs, improvised cameo appearances by musicians and artists and a sensuous, physical rendering of interpersonal intimacy coupled with expressions of emotional distance and subjective ambiguity.

The film extends the experimental narrative presentation of romantic/erotic love, while exposing the inability of *Song to Song*'s 'weightless' figures – with the exception of the film's central couple, Faye and BV – to transcend the sphere of the aesthetic/erotic. If *Knight of Cups* is the story of Rick's troubled quest to find the pearl of wisdom via experiences of erotic transcendence, *Song to Song* is the story of Faye's desire to find erotic fulfilment, artistic recognition and emotional satisfaction through musical creativity and romantic love. The film frames these couples as sharing intersecting life paths – with Cook as Mephistophelian seducer – the one couple (Cook and Rhonda) experiencing self-destruction via the path of sensual excess, the other (Faye and BV) leaving the seductive world of music behind to find fulfilment in a rural domestic setting far removed from the 'immediate sphere of the erotic' (which, as Kierkegaard suggests (1959: 43–134), is centrally concerned with music).[36]

Unusually for Malick, *Song to Song* begins with a directly narrated, rather than intimated, voiceover, accompanied by an obscure image of Faye (Rooney Mara) cautiously opening her door for BV (Ryan Gosling), followed by rapid montage shots of Cook (Michael Fassbender) and BV: 'I went through a period when sex had to be violent. I was desperate to feel something real. Nothing felt real. Every kiss felt like half of what it should be. You're just reaching for air.' Shots of water and sand give way to slow-motion video capture of revellers dancing at a rock music festival, the handheld camera now following BV through the dynamic scene, showing him enjoying the Dionysian atmosphere of music, improvised performance and bodily self-expression.

Faye continues her narration, as we see her at a party conversing with musicians: 'I thought you had to know the right people, get close to them. The ones who could give me what you need.' Her desire to 'get through the fence', to be an artist, to achieve success, to experience that ecstatic self-transcendence through creating art, is also an attempt to find herself – her quest for musical success is a quest for enlivening experience that would alleviate her background state of ennui. This tone or mood is deftly evoked by Mara's subtle performances, her deadpan delivery, her physical liveliness coupled with a wary reserve or emotional reticence, as though her public persona as aspiring musician required keeping her private struggle with despair carefully concealed: 'I wanted experience. Any experience is better than no experience. I wanted to live. Sing my song.' Her voiceover is accompanied by sounds of birds, the murmur of the cityscape, shots of Faye on a motorbike with Cook, attending a party with him, a naked girl posing as a human decoration adorning a glass table.

Cook is introduced as the worldly seducer, the powerful music producer who can make and shape careers, the Mephistophelean deceiver who promises the world to Faye and BV but who will nearly destroy them through his own tormented desire to find satisfaction (rather than wisdom) via the road of excess.[37] The film presents sequences out of order, creating a confusing, non-linear pastiche of fragmentary images corresponding to the dispersed recollections of the main figures, whose attempts at comprehending their own pasts are as distracted as their momentary experiences. We are shown BV first meeting Faye (in a blond wig) at a daytime party, far more sedate and languid than the torrid nightclub scenes with Cook. The contrast between BV's openness and Cook's intensity, BV's guileless candour and Cook's seductive but dangerous drive, could not be starker. Faye describes her relationship with Cook as one of convenience, designed to help her succeed in the music world: 'I thought he could help me, if I paid my dues.' Patti Smith appears throughout the film, at first as a performer on stage – 'You are the future ... you will decide what happens with this world', she tells her audience during one of her performances – and later as Faye's guide and mentor, exemplifying the balance of life purpose, wisdom and creativity that Faye also desires.

Faye, for her part, remains an opaque figure, sharing her insights and impressions while remaining physically expressive yet emotionally guarded. She underplays the degree to which Cook has bewitched her and the degree to which she resists what draws her to BV. Nonetheless, her affection for BV, coupled with her sense of being beholden to Cook, sets the scene for the ambiguous three-way relationship that follows. Despite having defined contours at the beginning, these intersecting relationships become amorphous as the film unfolds. Faye and BV play together, improvising games, dressing up, sharing make-up, writing songs, 'rolling and tumbling' with each other. Faye and Cook, by contrast, circle around each other, like predator and prey, hesitating and lunging, drawing together and coming apart, their connection remaining both taut and loose, binding and detached. BV warns Faye not to trust Cook but she does. 'He said trust me. And I did. Whatever I wanted he'd make it happen.' Recalling Milton's Satan, Cook puts his malevolent charisma in the service of manipulation and deception. He offers his dark and cynical advice to Faye, his nihilistic evaluation of the seductive fantasy world to which he can offer her access: 'It's all for sale. All of it. Honours, titles, none of that exists. It's a stage-show; it's a free for all.' When Faye responds that he has too much pride, Cook replies, again echoing *Paradise Lost*: 'People aren't proud enough.' After a sequence showing Faye and Cook fighting, Faye narrates, 'People changed around him, did things. So did I.' His emotional game of seduction and subversion begins to take its toll. 'I wanted to be free the way he was', Faye remarks, 'I went on seeing him. I let myself be smashed.'

Under Cook's spell she embraces the romantic vision of self-annihilation through art and sensuous experience. Pointing to a wall-sized photographic portrait of the poet Rimbaud in her apartment, she explains to BV: 'He did everything. He exhausted every passion. He knew every form of love, suffering, madness ... in order to reach the unknown – he experimented.' Linking the late romantic visionary poet with the contemporary radical performer, the film intercuts a vignette of John Lydon (former Sex Pistol and leader of PIL) proclaiming that rules are just there to please your parents, so throw them out the window. Faye follows suit and denounces morality as arbitrary ('They scare you with names like wicked'), pledging her allegiance to an experimental, aesthetic mode of existence, embracing (like Milan Kundera's characters) the 'unbearable lightness of being' experienced through erotic encounter.

Against shots of Faye and BV about to take a hot air balloon ride, she confesses her desire to leave the earth, to break all bonds, to be free, 'weightless': 'I want to escape from every tie, every hold, to have life at any price. Not to settle, to go up higher, free', against images of the drifting balloon and an aeroplane soaring high above. A few scenes later, the threesome – BV and Cook having formed a brotherly bond, and Faye dividing her attentions as the three of them holiday together in Mexico – take a trip together on a private jet, flying Icarus-like as high as possible, the three friends and lovers, improbably, defying gravity and floating playfully around the plane's interior. Cook's quasi-Nietzschean declaration – 'Let us decide what is right and wrong' – coupled with Faye's retrospective moment of insight – 'I knew everything came from that hour … I wish it could have lasted forever' – announce the caesura that will bring them crashing back down to earth.

Cook meets the second major female figure in the story, Rhonda (Natalie Portman), in a diner, where she is working part-time as a waitress between jobs as a kindergarten teacher. Their colour-coded attire announces their sexual attraction (Cook's deep-purple shirt rhyming with Rhonda's pink top and purple apron). He takes her for a ride in his Ferrari, visiting a concert where they hang out with musicians (Flea from Red Hot Chilli Peppers and rock legend Iggy Pop) as she is swiftly inducted into his world. He seduces her into various sexual games, offers her widowed mother a new house and asks Rhonda to marry him, promising that she can get out whenever she wants. Faye, meanwhile, maintains her relationship with BV but feels guilty about not telling him about Cook. Cook and BV's bond begins to fray, as BV discovers Cook has been taking credit for BV's work, taking over the copyright for his songs. Cook uses contracts, and the promise of fame, as lures to manipulate Faye and BV. His money, power and charisma are put into service to seduce others, especially Rhonda, who becomes his sexual toy and personal protégé, luring her away from her own life and remoulding her sense of self – via experimentation with sex and drugs – in his own image, a godlike affirmation of himself as creator and master of all around him.

In one striking scene we see Cook securing hallucinogenic mushrooms from a tattooed green-skinned man, announcing to Rhonda, 'This is dipped in God', before they take it together. 'Here I reign … ', Cook murmurs in voiceover, amidst shots of musicians, dancers and performers in a nightclub, ' … King. Who sees us? The world wants to be deceived.' The two relationships intersect in contingent ways but are united by a pervasive desire for 'something more' – something transcending the immediate satisfaction of desire, the sensuous, erotic search for meaning.

Other relationships come and go. BV starts up a liaison with his former girlfriend, performer Lykke Lai, who seems interested in starting over, playing music with BV, but leaves when it becomes clear he cannot commit. Faye starts an affair with a beautiful European artist Zoey (Berenice Marlohe). Her creativity and sensuality seduce Faye but Zoey tires of her and leaves. Like the arresting snakeskin art work on her wall, Zoey sheds her skin and moves on; or like the close-up image of a whirlpool in the pond of her garden, which expresses her seductive energy, she draws Faye into her world, a powerful vortex with an empty core. BV begins a relationship with Amanda (Cate Blanchett), whose attraction to BV falters after an awkward lunch meeting; BV's mother effectively blocks any happiness for them by insisting to BV that 'she is not for you'. Amanda turns out to bear a rather Oedipal resemblance to BV's mother, whom he at one point jokingly describes as a 'stone fox' (although any such psychological currents remain submerged throughout the film).

Moments of insight occur to the characters but do not really crystallize into action or decision. Faye's narration is something of an exception, for she is the only character who attempts to examine herself, to reflect upon the state of her soul, something she had hitherto dismissed as an embarrassment concealing an underlying anxiety: 'I roll and I tumble', she confides, 'I never knew I had a soul; the word embarrassed me. I've always been afraid of myself. I thought there was no one there'. The idea that one's self has both finite and infinite dimensions – 'I never knew I had a soul' – is a moment of existential reckoning for Faye. She confesses her sense of having become lost, of having fallen, desirous of self-transformation: 'Touch me. Fallen so low. Had to find my way out … to life'. This homely confession of existential insecurity, a vernacular declaration of despair, sets

the scene for the process by which she does come to recognize her
'soul'. She eventually escapes with BV from the weightless cycle of
desire – a Kierkegaardian repetition without transcendence – finding
light and life away from the 'immediate sphere of the erotic' defining
their weightless sojourn through the music scene in Austin under the
arresting spell of Cook.

The ephemeral, drifting nature of these contingent relationships –
'from song to song, kiss to kiss' – takes on a darker, tragic quality with
the self-destruction of Rhonda (Natalie Portman). As Faye begins to
acknowledge her condition, confessing that she had revolted against
goodness, thought it had deceived her, thought that she was better
than others, didn't need what made life sweet for them, Rhonda, in
a parallel movement, continues her downward spiral, being drawn
by Cook further into his world of intoxicating sensuality. Her
experimentation with limit experiences aims to annihilate that part
of herself still seeking love and reconciliation: 'There is something
else', she remarks at one point, 'Something that wants us to find it',
her voiceover hinting at a moment of spiritual awareness giving way
to a joyless but poignant encounter with a prostitute, an enactment
of Cook's personal fantasy. Rhonda talks with the woman afterwards
about her difficult life and future direction, as the woman, in tears,
talks about how this must all be part of God's plan. Both women
remain unsure of their own paths and individual futures, not to
mention the contingent events that brought them into contact.

Rhonda senses the darker impulses driving Cook in his relationship
with her but seems powerless to resist his demands or bring their affair
to an end, despite realizing 'what he is' and accusing him of killing her
love. She finds her sense of self becoming distorted, sullied, disturbed
('I'm afraid of myself. Hatred in me. Makes me evil'). Poignant
images of Rhonda alone, looking dazed and confused, possibly on
drugs, accompanied by ululating vocal chants, set the mood for her

tragic demise. She calls out to her mother in voiceover, who we see wandering frantic and alone in an empty carpark. 'Where am I now?' she asks. We see striking images of Cook lying in a solarium, sunning himself, as though already in the underworld, and then of Faye's mother crying alone in an empty carpark. The film cuts to a shot of Rhonda lying inert at dusk in the shallows of their swimming pool: 'You know how destroyed I was', her voice echoes. Cook discovers her, weeps and carries her away, as we hear her last words to her mother, 'Forgive me' – suggesting her death was not accidental but a suicide.

Faye and BV meet again at a party and decide to start over again, to make music together, finding a new beginning for themselves and their love. This time they are no longer bound to the desire for fame, but approach each other with a sense of acknowledgement and gratitude, of openness and forgiveness. Faye recounts her experiences with erotic love as a sensuous and moral lesson with a metaphysical slant: 'I played with sex, a gift. I played with it. I played with the flame of life.' Patti Smith appears live on stage, performing to an adoring crowd, reinforcing Faye's insights by reciting lines from William Blake's poem *The Divine Image* (Songs of Innocence). She sings her song, channelling Blake, 'In My Blakean Year':

> Mercy has a human heart,
> Pity a human face.
> Love a human form divine,
> Peace a human dress.
> To mercy, pity, peace and love
> For praying their distress,
> But mercy shall embrace,
> Mercy shall embrace

BV and Faye leave the sphere of the aesthetic, begin their journey though the ethical and return to the everyday as transfigured. What

Faye and BV were searching for through music, the experience of self-transcendence through art and romantic-erotic encounter, might be found, the film hints, through love understood in a more grounded sense of personal, emotional and existential (spiritual) care. Art is a path to transcendence through sensuous representation and heightened experience, music a form of physical transport and collective Dionysian rapture; but as Nietzsche observed à propos Greek tragedy, it also requires the form-giving power of self-reflection and metaphysical insight. The 'weightless' trilogy reveals the personal quest for sensual and existential fulfilment solely through romantic-erotic love to be misguided, unless grounded in a more communal, self-transcending form of love. After the numerous failed attempts at the 'formation of the couple', we are left with the fragile possibility of a pair who may find a path to happiness through romantic love coupled with artistic self-expression, now within an ethically transfigured world of everyday experience.

Aesthetic theodicy and narrative abstraction

Faye's story structures and concludes the film, which eschews the allegorical framing devices defining *To the Wonder* and *Knight of Cups*. Because it lacks a structuring mythic framework (like 'The Pilgrim's Progress' or the 'Hymn of the Pearl'), *Song to Song* is perhaps the most lyrical of the three films in the trilogy. Despite its focus on recognizable elements of conventional romantic narrative, it is also the most demanding on viewers and critics alike. *Song to Song* too received harsh criticism, despite it being the most 'secular' film in the trilogy. My suspicion is that this was due to not only its fragmentary narrative and paratactic visual style but its lack of explicit mythic or allegorical framing to organize and direct emotional engagement through its loosely episodic, highly elliptical mode of presentation.

Thanks to their extreme form of narrative abstraction, all three films raise what we might call the problem of aesthetic theodicy and audience disengagement. On the one hand, there is an attempt to offer something like an 'aesthetic justification of existence' (Nietzsche): an aesthetic theodicy, centred on the experience of romantic-erotic love, one that invites the possibility of an aesthetic conversion towards a morally richer, self-transcending conception of love. On the other, all three films experiment with an attenuation of narrative style and subversion of conventions that removes the familiar aesthetic markers and psychological triggers that typically solicit emotional engagement and support spectator identification. Such an aesthetic-experimental-cum-moral-allegorical strategy, however, risks alienating the very spectators who would be the 'target' subjects of this kind of transformative aesthetic experience. Malick's attenuation of character and narrative 'thickness' is such that emotional engagement is reduced to a minimum in favour of sensuous immersion, paratactic association and diffuse expressions of mood. Such a strategy, I suggest, is not dynamically directed enough to engage audiences in such a way that would make the 'aesthetic theodicy' truly effective: for those with eyes to see and ears to hear, the message is clear; but for those who do not hear or see 'the glory', or who are already immersed in the aesthetic sphere, there is only perplexity and puzzlement, or for some, boredom and frustration.

Consider the religious aspect of Malick's trilogy: for the believer, the world already reveals itself as an expression of divine love, of the 'glory shining through all things', all aesthetically evident in Malick's late work. For the aesthete, there are, to be sure, occasions here for aesthetic pleasure, but this autonomous aesthetic experience is mitigated, even ruined, by the intrusion of 'alien' non-aesthetic elements (existential, moral, philosophical and religious concerns). For the unbeliever, or for the aesthetic sceptic, such images, while visually arresting, do not sustain attention or commitment to the narrative over time; they remain lacking in substance, value or meaning, and so cannot generate the kind of aesthetic-moral effect that is their ultimate aim.

We might call this the aesthetic 'preaching to the choir' problem that confronts the late Malick's more 'religious' works. The 'weightless' trilogy risks aesthetic 'failure', from this point of view, insofar as it only partially offers the aesthetic pleasure or emotional involvement that it seems to promise, but also needs to fulfil cinematically in order to articulate the Kierkegaardian aesthetic-moral 'conversion' that may be its ultimate aim. Abstract, elliptical and impressionistic films, such as these late Malick works, risk failing to engage viewers at the level of narrative meaning necessary for the moral uptake of their allegorical significance. Although they may serve as occasions for aesthetic contemplation, poetic revelation or moral-spiritual conversion for the happy few, for the restless many they can only suggest but fail to yield any dramatic revelation of the moral-spiritual significance of love that remains, as it does for the characters in the 'weightless' trilogy, something obscurely desired but rarely fulfilled.

***

Malick's late films allegorize a host of related philosophical and religious myths concerning love. They explore metaphysical, theological and existential dimensions of the movement from erotic to agapic love, from the aesthetic sphere of immanence to the religious experience of transcendence. They do so, moreover, in ways that show the unity, rather than the separation, of these forms of love and spheres of existence, suggesting the need to reconcile the 'subjective' sphere of aesthetic and the 'objective' sphere of the ethical through the leap towards the religious sphere. In so doing, they present viewers with a cinematic version of Kierkegaard's 'Either/Or choice': a choosing to choose that points to religious faith from within the medium of the aesthetic (cinema, albeit of a highly 'abstract', impressionistic, mood-evoking kind).

This experiment in Kierkegaardian edification raises intriguing questions. Can the religious itself be expressed through the medium of cinema? Or does it require, as Kierkegaard found, an experimental form of aesthetic expression that brings us to the threshold of the religious, without necessarily disclosing faith as such? (For faith is an existential, rather than an aesthetic, experience.) Are the late Malick films updated Platonic myths, Kierkegaardian edifying or upbuilding discourses, aimed at a sceptical world captivated by the aesthetic possibilities of cinema but less receptive to its ethical, let alone religious, possibilities? These questions, I suggest, drive the later Malick's 'religious turn' towards an experimental, Christian-existentialist poetics of revelatory cinematic expression. They also remain open questions in evaluating Malick's work as instances of cinematic ethics.

To be sure, this choice of Christian-existentialist allegory seems unpopular and no doubt partially responsible for the negative reception of these films. This choice plays into the criticisms made of their gender, race and class politics and the complaint that they attenuate emotional engagement to the point where they risk aesthetic failure as narrative films. This is a risk that Malick chooses freely, a moral commitment or act of artistic faith perhaps, precisely as a critical response to the dominance of the aesthetic and ethical spheres in cinematic culture today (roughly speaking, either distracting spectacle and cynical manipulation or didactic moral and political pedagogy, both of which return us to the Kierkegaardian Either/ Or). These are films that offer phenomenologically rich evocations of contemporary subjectivity expressing both desire and despair in the characters' frustrated quests for love, freedom and acknowledgement. They hint that the movement from the finite to the infinite, from the subjective feeling of love to its existentially transfiguring effects, as both an aesthetic experience and as an ethical-religious 'duty'. They suggest that transforming our sense of love – its varieties, meaning and possibilities – remains a promise that cinema, despite our distraction and despair, might one day fulfil.

Conclusion: Malick's Cinematic Ethics (a philosophical dialogue)

I have sought to do two things in this book: the first is to present a case for rethinking the idea of 'film as philosophy' via a close study of Malick's cinematic work; the second is to show how my own 'apprenticeship' in film-philosophy has been profoundly shaped by my engagement with these remarkable films. Indeed, my encounter with Malick prompted me to transform my approach to the question of 'film as philosophy' and continues to shape my thinking on the relationship between philosophy and film. Using Malick as my case study, I have argued that we ought to modify our notion of 'philosophical contribution' in order to emphasize the manner in which these films can afford us complex varieties of aesthetic and ethical experience. And I have claimed, further, that this conception of 'cinematic ethics' ought to be expanded to include the ways in which moral and metaphysical concerns are also addressed by forms of religious/theological reflection (e.g. Nagel's 'cosmic question') that find aesthetic expression in Malick's work. At the same time, I have analysed the challenge Malick's later films face, in combining experimental narrative form with moral-religious experience: namely, how far can one attenuate or minimize narrative, rendering emotional engagement too diffuse, and risk 'imaginative resistance' in response to religious themes or content, before such films risk aesthetic failure to engage audiences in respect of their moral-ethical, as well as existential-religious, concerns.

There are other problems that one could raise about this project, or criticisms concerning Malick's cinema more generally. I would summarize these in the following three questions:

(1) Does Malick's cinema work lapse into naive romanticism, aesthetic pretentiousness or religious mysticism?

(2) The question of Malick's 'religious' turn: Are his later films still philosophical?

(3) Is a cinematic response to nihilism enough? This question becomes acute in the case of cinema, which appears, according to Malick, implicated in the loss of belief, conviction or meaning defining our moral-cultural scepticism.

My own responses to these three questions tend to be qualified and mixed, and they remain open to revision depending on the films in question. So one way of articulating some of these nuances and complexities is to frame my responses in the form of a dialogue between a *rationalist sceptic* critic of Malick and a *romantic idealist* defender of his work. My caveat to the reader is that there may be truth in any or all of these contributions and that it is no philosophical flaw to entertain a number of different perspectives at once, especially when it comes to evaluating film – in this case Malick's – as philosophy or, more precisely, as ethics. As to the conclusion of this debate, only the reader can decide, preferably with close reference to Malick's remarkable body of work.

***

RS: You have made a strong, even impassioned case for taking Malick as a philosophical filmmaker, an artist whose work has an ethical or moral purpose, perhaps even as a religious filmmaker. I respect your conviction about the aesthetic merits of Malick's films, despite their controversial or 'difficult' qualities. But there are some important critical issues here that you have avoided. One of them is that Malick, for many critics, fails as a filmmaker because of the aesthetic (and perhaps moral-intellectual) flaws in his films: namely, their naive romanticism, their aesthetic pretentiousness and their religious mysticism.

To start with, romanticism is a troubling approach to understanding art, let alone responding to social reality. We no longer live in a world that can naively accept notions of nature as inherently good, or art as improving our souls, or of subjectivity as the source of all truth, or of love conquering all. The very attempt to present such themes or ideas on screen betrays an anachronistic romanticism that simply does not cohere with contemporary theoretical (or ethico-political) claims concerning art and film, let alone subjectivity and culture. Many of the tropes Malick champions seem ideologically questionable historico-cultural constructs. For many, the ideas in Malick's work (including philosophers like Heidegger) are out of date at best and retrograde or dangerous at worst. How can you defend Malick's naive rehabilitation of romanticism?

RI: Your criticisms certainly capture some of the reasons why Malick remains a polarizing artist. Many critics admire his earlier films, but as you say some regard him as having entered a phase of sterile repetition or even self-parody. However, I don't find the reasons given for dismissing Malick's work on these grounds to be persuasive (I leave aside questions of taste, which is not something for us to debate here).

The charge of naive romanticism is often confused; sometimes critics fault Malick for naivety, sometimes for his romanticism, without clarifying what this means. To put things plainly, I don't think 'romanticism' – a capacious term covering a plurality of meanings – is inherently problematic, especially as contrasted with, say, modernism. On the contrary, the artistic, intellectual, and cultural movements associated with romanticism have provided a powerful counterpoint to Enlightenment rationalism and then to modernist currents of art and scientific-industrial culture, for well over two centuries. Neo-romanticism, in the form of a renewed emphasis on experience, subjectivity, the body, affect, emotion, nature, imagination and cultural particularity (difference), remains a powerful current of thought (certainly in regard to film).

If you are implicitly opposing romanticism to modernism here, you ought to show why we should be rehabilitating modernism instead (as many theorists seem wont to do). You would also need to show why romanticism is supposed to be either naive or dangerous (or both) or why those elements of romanticism in Malick's work – be it a responsiveness to the beauty of nature, a valorization of subjective experience, an expressive emphasis on mood or the idea that art offers some kind of redemption – are inherently problematic. Modern art and culture, including film, continue to be shaped by the dialectical play between modernist and romantic impulses. So I don't see any problem in regarding Malick as a romantic filmmaker, provided we articulate what this means in his body of work, which I have tried to show in my readings of individual films.

As for naivety, it suggests an unknowingness, ignorance or lack of self-reflection regarding art, ethics, culture or history that I don't find evident in Malick's films. If anything, in addition to romanticism there is also a subtly modernist aspect to his work that is relevant here, namely the manner in which these films reflect upon their own cinematic, historical, artistic and philosophical conditions. This provides a salutary corrective and aesthetic enhancement to his work, which, in my view, neutralizes the charge that it is naively romantic. Today one can only be a critical romantic, or maybe a modernist romantic, which is another way of describing Malick's self-conscious, reflexive romanticism.

RS: Romanticism is one thing, but aesthetic value is another. Some might argue that you haven't really addressed the aesthetic value of Malick's work. Indeed, there are critics who criticize Malick's films for their aesthetic pretentions: their pseudo-philosophical insights, their moralizing tone and their artistic overreach. Pauline Kael was on to this aspect of Malick from the start, and you can read contemporary reviews by Amy Taubin and others that continue this critique. The problem is not just that his films are obscure or 'difficult'; it is that they do not succeed as narrative films and can't be redeemed as arthouse experiments. Unlike his earlier and mid-period efforts, Malick's later films move away from whatever 'philosophical' perspectives he might have once held (an existentialist kind of philosophy, say that of Heidegger) and towards religious forms of 'mysticism' – religious mystification masquerading as artistic experimentation. How can one redeem Malick from the charges of naivety, pretentiousness and mysticism that, for many, are the chief reasons for rejecting his work?

RI: The complaint about aesthetic pretentiousness is easily made but more difficult to defend. It is rare to find any theoretical articulation of the aesthetic concept of 'pretention', which I would define as the failed attempt to match artistic execution with intellectual ambition; an aesthetic flaw that involves the failure of a work to meet its own aesthetic, moral or cultural aims or purposes. To substantiate such a claim requires close and careful critical analysis and interpretation of a work, showing how, in specific respects, a work fails in this achievement of correspondence or coherence between intention and execution. I've not found many convincing examples of this kind of critical analysis on the part of Malick critics, many of whom tend to reach for the charge of artistic pretentiousness, which usually amounts to little more than an expression of personal distaste ('I don't like it!') masquerading as an aesthetic judgement. To defend Malick on this score becomes a matter of offering close critical interpretations of his work, which make the case for the aptness of cinematic style or technique for narrative, aesthetic or whatever other moral-philosophical aims the work might have.

I am quite happy to ignore such complaints and prefer to deal with the more interesting criticisms of Malick that offer a (moral rather than aesthetic) critique of his films' alleged 'religious mysticism'. The first thing is to clarify what this means, for there are those for whom any kind of religious thought or experience would count as 'mysticism', and is therefore to be rejected. But I find this kind of 'new atheism', as applied to art or cinema, to be dogmatic and misguided; it lacks any historical, cultural or intellectual perspective on the meaning of religious thought and cultural practices, especially in regard to art, hence is both philosophically and aesthetically vacuous. If we accept a broad account of religion, however, and its relationship with art, especially cinema (as in S. Brent Plate's work, for example), then we can get decent debate underway on the question of Malick's so-called 'religious mysticism'.

It is curious that one would not ordinarily criticize an author or a poet (like Walker Percy or William Blake), a composer (like Berlioz, who claimed to have transcended religion) or a film director (like Bresson or Apichatpong) for the presence of, or their commitment to, religious theme or values in their works. Yet this is a frequent criticism – usually implicit or veiled – made against Malick in respect of his Christianity. I don't think one need share an artist's religious – or for that matter moral or political – views in order to appreciate their work. In fact, opening oneself up to this perspective may not only illuminate their art but offer a new way of thinking ethically as well. Many theorists today tend towards a rather dogmatic, extreme form of *aesthetic moralism*, which prescribes an identity, or at least consonance, between an artist's moral, ethical and political-ideological views and their artistic works, as well as a consonance between an artist's views, values or their identity and those of the viewer, spectator, critic or recipient. On this view, I should reject or refrain from judging Bresson or Apichatpong because I am neither a Catholic nor a Buddhist. I find this kind of dogmatic aesthetic moralism objectionable but cannot go any further into this issue here.

Suffice to say that one needn't be a Christian, or even remotely religious, to appreciate films that may have Christian or religious elements. Even atheists can appreciate Bresson! It could be that these elements, for some critics and viewers, present an obstacle to understanding or enjoyment; they may generate what philosophers of art call 'imaginative resistance' in the viewer that prevents an open or receptive aesthetic (and moral) engagement ('uptake') with regard to these works. I do think this happens with Malick, especially his later films, perhaps more than other contemporary filmmakers. Nonetheless, there is always the possibility that one might be transformed by what one sees, even if this does not agree with one's assumptions or prejudices (in the hermeneutic sense) or one's moral-ethical (or even political) views. Indeed, experiencing such works may be a way of opening oneself up to a dimension of experience that may be unfamiliar yet important to understand. I hope that such critics can extend the same hermeneutic charity towards Malick's work as towards the work of filmmakers from other cultural and religious traditions. To fail to do so would be a betrayal of what I think cinematic art, as medium of ethical experience, can make possible, namely expanding our horizons of experience via the sensuous and imaginative encounter with a variety of complex and diverse cinematic worlds.

RS: Most critics today are champions of cultural difference and supportive of diversity of all stripes. But there may be good reasons why critics – and especially philosophers of film – have issues with Malick's 'religious turn'. Put simply, art should not preach; the overt religiosity – particularly Christianity – in Malick's cinematic works is therefore difficult to take (at least for some critics). There is also the issue of whether such films should still be regarded as 'philosophical'. How can you approach Malick as a 'philosophical' filmmaker when his work is concerned with religious values and theological issues?

RI: This is one of the most challenging aspects of Malick's later films, which are not 'philosophical' in a narrow or technical sense. They're not really akin to moral thought experiments; they don't make arguments; they don't explicitly explore topics or issues that we would ordinarily define as moral or ethical. At the same time, they do engage in reflective considerations concerning the conditions of the medium and of composing cinematic worlds (as Neer and Pippin have shown). But what if the problem here is that we are assuming these films need to fit within a given framework or definition of philosophy? That cinema is philosophical only to the extent that it coheres with recognizable forms of critical argument, theoretical discourse or conceptual reflection? My view is that we are on stronger ground talking of Malick's *ethical* cinema; but this also means expanding our notions of what counts as 'ethics' so as to include aspects of religious experience and moral-spiritual transformation. This may sound alarm bells for narrowly rationalist philosophers or strictly secular theorists, but I do think it is an important question explicitly raised by Malick's later work.

Take these films' focus on love. The phenomenon of love is not just an interpersonal experience but many other things besides: a philosophical topic, a moral problem, an existential possibility, a psychological issue, a sexual adventure, a cultural phenomenon, even a form of religious experience. So why can't this phenomenon – in all its facets – be a legitimate subject for cinematic exploration? Why can't films exploring love, especially our privileging of romantic-erotic love compared with other forms of love, thereby acquire philosophical as well as moral or religious significance? These were some of the questions that motivated my response to Malick's recent trilogy. So that is why I think we can still call his films philosophical, or rather ethical, where this emphasis on ethical experience also raises the question of how we should think about the relationship between film, philosophy and religion.

RS: This kind of pluralist approach may work for some, but for many critics, there is something troubling about claiming that religion can contribute to philosophy (or vice versa). Whatever the case, how can you maintain that Malick's cinema – or any kind of art – can provide an adequate response to what you describe as the problem of (moral-cultural) nihilism: the pervasive moral-cultural scepticism about meaning and value, the loss of belief, conviction or basic trust in our world? That seems like a very tall order, especially for narrative cinema.

RI: Putting things simply, I would maintain that cinema *can* play an important role in responding to these larger moral-ethical questions of value and meaning. Like Nietzsche, I do think that art – including cinema – can provide a 'counter-movement' to nihilism, at least in more sober, modest, localized terms than what Nietzsche had in mind (with Wagner and tragedy). Perhaps we could call this, echoing Bordwell and Carroll, a 'piecemeal' (rather than world-founding or 'grand') artistic and ethical response to nihilism, which is all that individual works of art can ever offer. That said, the fact that narrative cinema involves the artistic practice of world-creation, of composing fictional worlds that we can participate in imaginatively, emotionally and reflectively, is one of the main reasons why I think it has a special role to play in this regard.

Malick strikes me as a filmmaker deeply concerned with our condition today, about the loss of belief or conviction in what makes life valuable and what makes our struggling planet still a meaningful world. His films offer experiential encounters with worlds inhabited by figures seeking 'the glory' that subtly illuminates our mundane reality, if only we can transform our relationship with ourselves, with others, and maybe with something transcendent. Whatever one makes of such views, I think that one can find meaningful ways of experiencing and engaging with moral-ethical questions through Malick's work. That is why I think Malick remains a philosophical filmmaker, an ethical and religious artist, whose work enriches us aesthetically and existentially.

RS: You have offered an eloquent defence of Malick, even if I do not share your belief in the transformative power of his work. Maybe it is my 'imaginative resistance', or my intellectual temperament, which makes any talk of 'aesthetic theodicy' seem alarming. It will be fascinating to see what Malick's next film (*Radegund*) brings, which apparently returns to a more 'structured' filmmaking style. I trust it will offer a more emotionally engaging and aesthetically satisfying form of narrative cinema (another war movie too!) than the 'weightless' trilogy.

RI: Malick's trilogy has pushed the limits of narrative abstraction, impressionistic allegory and poetic fragmentation about as far as they can go. Audiences can only take so much experimentation, and there comes a point where the 'beholder's share' becomes onerous. For me, and for some viewers, these late films are remarkable works that perhaps will take more time to absorb and understand, that may come to be regarded as breakthrough works from an aesthetic and, perhaps, moral-ethical point of view. For others, they do not succeed as narrative films in the conventional sense, for they generate imaginative resistance in audiences, so their apparent moral-ethical aspects fail to be taken up successfully. However his next films turn out, I feel grateful for the aesthetic and ethical experiences I have had with his work. These have profoundly shaped my engagement with film-philosophy, but also given me ways to see, think and feel the world anew.

RS: I am pleased that we can agree to at least that much, whatever my doubts or misgivings may be about Malick's later work. Perhaps, like with good poetry, these are films requiring time to digest, repeated viewings or readings, with an open heart and mind. Speaking of poetry, watching Malick sometimes reminds me of Rilke's poem 'Archaic Torso of Apollo', with its devastating concluding lines:

> for here there is no place
> that does not see you. You must change your life.[1]

Notes

Introduction

1 Cavell thanks Malick in the first edition of *The World Viewed* published in 1971, two years before Malick's first feature film, *Badlands*, was released. Malick was apparently better versed in Heidegger's philosophy than Cavell himself, who worried that Malick would receive an unfavourable response from his Oxford examiners: 'Those closest to me included Terrence Malick whose academic major – "concentration" in Harvard patois – was philosophy and whose expert honours thesis on a text of Heidegger's I would be assigned to advise. Malick had taken a semester in Germany to attend Heidegger's classes, and he knew, and we discussed the facts before he began writing, both that he had read and studied more Heidegger than I had and at the same time that I was the only member of the philosophical faculty at that time who respected and had studied any at all of Heidegger's work, hence that he was likely to receive an unsympathetic judgment from the two readers who would be assigned to examine him, having in effect to be instructing his instructors, something I was hoping his thesis might itself recognizably begin to accomplish' (Cavell 2010: 426).

2 Cf. Malick's remarks in a *Sight and Sound* interview from 1975: 'I was not a good teacher; I didn't have the sort of edge one should have on the students, so I decided to do something else. I'd always liked movies in a kind of naïve way. They seemed no less improbable a career than anything else. I came to Los Angeles in the fall of 1969 to study at AFI [American Film Institute]; I made a short called *Lanton Mills*. I found the AFI very helpful; it's a marvellous place.' Quoted in Michaels (2009: 102).

3 See Davies' entry on Malick in the *Routledge Companion to Philosophy and Film* (2009a) and the Routledge Philosophers of Film volume dedicated to *The Thin Red Line* (Davies 2009b).

4 Cf. Critchley's dismissive remark on *The New World*, published with the revised version of his 'Calm' essay on *The Thin Red Line*, namely that 'the less said about it [i.e. *The New World*], the better' (2009: 27).

Chapter 1

1 Cf. Malick's remarks from one of his rare interviews: 'The critics talked about influences on the picture and in most cases referred to films I had never seen. My influences were books like *The Hardy Boys, Swiss Family Robinson, Tom Sawyer, Huck Finn* – all involving an innocent in a drama over his or her head. … I wanted the picture to be set up like a fairy tale, outside time, like *Treasure Island*. I hoped this would, among other things, take a little of the sharpness out of the violence but still keep its dreamy quality.' Walker (1975: 82–83), quoted in Michaels (2009: 102–103, 105).

2 Tucker (2011: 80–100) provides an exception to this rule, offering a distinctly Heideggerian approach to *Badlands* as exploring the 'worlding of the world'.

3 That the film was generally understood to be a romantic lovers-on-the-run tale is evinced by the curiously inappropriate imagery selected for the film's DVD release, both versions of which attempt to evoke a romantic passion and sexual frisson that is simply absent in the film.

4 See Barnett (2016: 117–137) for a Kierkegaardian reading of *Badlands* as depicting 'selves in despair, longing for personal fulfillment but ironically (and even pitiably) frustrated in attaining it – a perspective that accords with the theological anthropology of one of Malick's intellectual touchstones, Søren Kierkegaard' (137).

5 See McCann (2007: 77–87) for a discussion of the 'fetishisation of nature' in *Badlands* and *Days of Heaven*.

6 As Malick explains, 'Kit doesn't see himself as anything sad or pitiable, but as a subject of incredible interest, to himself and to future generations. Like Holly, like a child, he can only really believe in what's going on inside of him. Death, other people's feelings, the consequences of his actions – they're all sort of abstract for him. He thinks of himself as a successor to James Dean – a rebel without a cause – when in reality he's more like an Eisenhower conservative.' Walker (1975: 82–83), quoted in Michaels (2009: 104). See also Maher (2014: 86).

7 See Brant (2016: 138–158) for a theological reading of the film, emphasizing its presentation of a natural theology.

8 Cf. 'And ye shall teach them your children, speaking of them when thou sittest in thine house, and when thou walkest by the way, when thou liest down, and when thou risest up. And thou shalt write them upon the door posts of thine house, and upon thy gates: That your days may be multiplied, and the days of your children, in the land which the Lord sware unto your fathers to give them, as the days of heaven upon the earth' (Deuteronomy 11:19–21).

9 As Kendall notes: 'Ruth is the story of a destitute young woman called Ruth who is essentially saved by a rich man, named Boaz. Boaz first glimpses Ruth in his fields, after she "has been on her feet from early this morning until now, without resting even for a moment." Boaz "said to his servant who was in charge of the reapers, 'To whom does this young girl belong?'" (1.5). Boaz then asks Ruth to stay and continue working his fields. Ruth is relieved by and respectful of his willingness to help her. Later, Ruth relates the incident to her mother-in-law, Naomi, with whom she lives, and Naomi encourages her to place herself at Boaz's feet as she sleeps on the threshing floor (3.4). Though Naomi is suggesting that Ruth seduce Boaz so as to secure his aide [*sic*], the scene is not unduly manipulative and Boaz does not simply have sex with her. He takes appropriate steps to marry her in the eyes of the community' (Kendall 2011: 156).

Chapter 2

1 See Millington (2010) for a thorough study of the confusing attribution of voiceovers in the film. I also succumbed to this confusion, assuming that the questions posed at the beginning of the film – just prior to the first shot of Witt paddling his canoe, a beatific smile on his face, having gone AWOL on a Melanesian island – were attributable to him, the first character as such we see on screen. The film suggests that it is Witt's voiceover that we hear, but then complicates the attribution of voiceover to character by mismatching audio and visual sequences. This suggests that it is not individuals with their private thoughts at issue here but rather a shared or collective form of experience, distributed among different men, each of whom has a different attitude towards war but who is not clearly individuated by this experience.

2 See Sinnerbrink (2014) for a more detailed discussion of Heidegger on cinema. See Mosely (2018) for a critique of existing film-philosophical accounts of 'Heideggerian cinema' and an alternative account of what an authentic Heideggerian approach would look like (in relation to 'cinematic excess' and 'dead time' in Antonioni's *L'eclisse*).

3 Interestingly, most Malick scholars who claim him as a Heideggerian filmmaker pass over *Badlands* and *Days of Heaven*, despite Stanley Cavell's remarks – the first to link Malick and Heidegger – that *Days of Heaven* shows us the play of presence and absence and revealing of world that one finds in Heidegger's thinking of Being (Cavell 1979: xiv–xvi).

4 See Rossouw (2017).

5 It is the spiritual or religious dimensions of this experience, notably in the case of Witt, that 'Heideggerian' readings of the film tend to overlook. I would suggest that *The Thin Red Line* does not focus solely on existential finitude (à la Heidegger) but also on the possibility of existential *infinitude*: the infinite or transcendent dimension of subjectivity that Witt alludes to in his debates with Welsh.

6 Actually Train, although usually attributed to the dead Witt.

7 Critchley's essay was reprinted, in slightly edited form, in two important volumes: Read and Goodenough's volume on *Film as Philosophy* (2005) and Davies' volume on *The Thin Red Line* (2009).

8 Critchley thus discusses the ways in which Malick departs from James Jones' gritty 1963 novel and the 1964 film version by Andrew Marton.

9 Critchley also mentions Blanchot's short story *L'Instant de ma mort* ('The instant of my death') in this context. See Blanchot and Derrida (2000).

10 As I discuss presently, this issue will also affect Pippin's reading of the film, which also disavows the 'Heideggerian' significance of the film's 'vernacular metaphysics'.

11 Cf. Doll's (Dash Mihok's) remark to Staros: 'We wanted to thank you, sir. For asking to make that flanking move. For watching out for us. Keeping us together. We're all sorry to see you go. We feel like you got a rotten deal.' Contra Pippin, it is hard to imagine why the soldiers would say this to Staros unless they regarded him as the initiator of the move that not only saved lives but enabled them to achieve their military objective.

12 Having exhaustively quoted misattributions from many critics and commentators on the film, Millington (2010) expresses surprise that none seemed to have focused on Train. Unfortunately he goes no further with this observation.

Chapter 3

1 Critchley does not reveal the basis for his dismissal of the film, which I suspect has much to do with the ways in which it resists the kind of 'philosophical' reading that *The Thin Red Line* seemed to invite.

2 What the 'mocking tone' in film reviews suggested would arise again with the release of *The Tree of Life* in 2011.

3 A point well made by Critchley: 'If we cast the Japanese in the role of the Trojans, and Guadalcanal in the place of Troy, then *The Thin Red Line* might be said to recount the pre-history of American empire in the same way as Homer recites the pre-history of Hellenic supremacy' (2009: 12).

4   This is counter to Neer's secular 'modernist', anti-philosophical interpretation of the film (2011). I address his approach to the film in what follows.

5   Michaels notes that 'Malick had been working with Benicio del Toro for some time on a biopic about Che Guevera when the project foundered for lack of financing' (2009: 81).

6   *Pocahontas and John Smith* (1924, Bryan Foy), *Captain John Smith and Pocahontas* (1953, Lew Landers), *Pocahontas* (1994 animated film, Toshiyuki Hiruma Takashi), Disney's *Pocahontas* (animation film, 1995) and the Disney sequel, *Pocahontas II: Journey to a New World* (1998).

7   *Pocahontas* (USA 1995). At least one commentator has claimed that the Disney version is a primary reference for Malick's *The New World*, a claim based upon the emphasis on the romance between Pocahontas and Smith and the appearance of actors (Irene Bedard and Christian Bale) from the Disney version in Malick's film (in which Bedard plays Pocahontas' mother and Bale her husband, John Rolfe) (Macdonald 2009: 100–101).

8   I draw here on the accounts of Buscombe (2008), D'Entremont (2007). See also Woodward (1969).

9   Popular usage substitutes the Algonquin term for 'chief' (*Powhatan*) for the name of Pocahontas' father (Wahnunsunackock). Pocahontas' actual name was Matoaka.

10 As noted by Michaels (2009) and Martin (2007). For a historian's critique of the historical distortions in Malick's romantic rendering of the tale, see D'Entremont (2007).

11 Frampton likewise criticizes the film as philosophy movement for focusing on plot and character rather than images and their cinematic qualities and elaborates on the dangers of avoiding 'cinematics' in favour of philosophical 'content' (2006: 8–11).

12 Neer's piece appeared after my book (Sinnerbrink 2011a) had gone to press, which meant I could not reference it in my chapter on *The New World*. See Donougho (2011) for an alternative, Heideggerian approach to the 'worlding of world' in *The New World*.

13 A point that Stanley Cavell had been concerned about in his account of how Malick's Heideggerian thesis topic would be received by his examiners (Cavell 2010: 426).

14 See Sinnerbrink (2009) for a discussion of ambivalent responses to *The New World*.

15 As Adrian Martin notes, this verse is an example of Malick's use of pre-existing versions of the Pocahontas tale, in this case reworking 'a poem by that great on-the-spot theorist of silent film, Vachel Lindsay (1917)', entitled, 'Our Mother/Pocahontas' (2007: 215). Lines from Lindsay's

poem – 'We rise from out of the soul of her' and 'Because we are her fields of corn' – are directly referenced in the voiceover to Malick's film. *The New World* also resonates with the kind of imagery, sympathy for Pocahontas and renunciation of English/American and Western European ancestry to be found in the Lindsay poem (2007: 215). Malick, however, submits it to a subtle rewriting: Lindsay takes Pocahontas to be the 'sacred mother' figure, whereas in *The New World* Pocahontas is a seeker *searching* for her Mother, 'the "spirit"' whom she invokes in order to sing the story of our land' (Martin 2007: 215).

16 The film also features a suitably romantic-aquatic signature piece, 'Aquarium', from Saint-Saëns' *Le Carnaval des Animaux*.

17 The Prelude to *Das Rheingold* begins with the three Rhine maidens swimming beneath the surface of the water. They mock the ugly Alberich, a Nibelung dwarf, who steals the famous Rhine gold they were supposed to guard. In stealing the Rhein gold, which can only be acquired by abandoning love in favour of wealth and power, he fashions a magic ring that gives its bearer the power to rule the world. As Neer observes, it is not difficult to discern the parallels in Malick's recasting of this mythic scene to the Virginian tidewater region, which commences with Native American water maidens and the arriving colonists (including, ironically, John Smith) embodying Alberich's rejection of nature and love in favour of power and wealth.

18 The other piece of music used to articulate the relationship between Pocahontas/Rebecca and Smith is the slow movement from Mozart's Piano Concerto No. 23.

19 Neer draws attention to the parallel between the close shot of Pocahontas' mother's face, with a serene expression and her hands outstretched in a gesture of worship, and another close shot of the face of 'Savage' (Jon Savage), ranting about religion and evil, his expression maniacal, face twitching, spittle flying. The two faces are visually paralleled but utterly different in affective charge and expressive meaning. This is a good example of how formal similarity between images does not necessarily translate into expressive symmetry or consonance of meaning.

Chapter 4

1 Taken from Malick's press release on the film before its public release.
2 Cf. the famous voiceovers in *The Thin Red Line*: 'Maybe all men got one big soul where everybody's a part of. All faces are the same man, one big self.

Everyone looking for salvation by himself. Each like a coal drawn from the fire'. (Train) 'Who were you that I lived with, walked with? The brother, the friend? Strife and love, darkness and light – are they the workings of one mind, features of the same face? Oh my soul. Let me be in you now. Look out through my eyes. Look out at the things you made. All things shining'. (Train) The phrase 'All things shining' comes from James Jones' war novel, *The Thin Red Line*, upon which the Malick film is (loosely) based. The 'one big soul' recalls Emerson's 'over-soul', that which unites men, nature and God. See Emerson (1906: 149–167).

3 As discussed in last chapter, Neer (2011) takes issue with the imposition of philosophical readings that do violence to the film's aesthetic and cinematic complexity, offering a finely nuanced interpretation of the film that nonetheless makes what I would describe as 'crypto-philosophical' claims.

4 Scott Foundas (2011: 61) asked why Malick's *The Tree of Life* received such a hostile response at Cannes, whereas Apichatpong Weerasethakul's 2010 Palme d'Or winning *Uncle Boonmee Who Can Recall His Past Lives*, 'another meditative film about nature, death, and possible afterlives', did not.

5 Most of the composers used in these sequences are not 'classical' but contemporary (Zbigniew Preisner, Giya Kancheli, John Tavener and Mother Tekla). The 'Creation' sequence concludes with the *Domine Jesu Christe* movement from Berlioz's *Grande messes des morts* (or *Requiem*) Opus 5 (1837).

6 As Peter Bradshaw (2011) remarked, '[p]eople would repeatedly reproach me for my own laudatory notice; this film, they said, was pretentious, boring and – most culpably of all – Christian. Didn't I realise, they asked, that Malick was a Christian?'.

7 See, for example, McCracken (2011) and Cashill (2011).

8 See, for example, Olszewski (2011).

9 Steritt (2011) offers an 'aestheticist' reading of the film that takes issue with Malick's alleged 'theodicy'. As I discuss below, Pfeifer (2011) contrasts two contrary perspectives that the film attempts to reconcile: that of the idealist, for whom *The Tree of Life* is an ineffable, aesthetic and emotional revelation of beauty and spiritual truth, and that of the analyst, for whom the film is a self-reflexive cinematic meditation on memory, childhood and history.

10 One might venture another allusion here: the fact that Malick's extraordinary 'creation' sequence in *The Tree of Life* recalls the wonderful evolution of life sequence from Walt Disney's *Fantasia* (1940), set to Stravinsky's *Rite of Spring* – just the sort of film that the young Jack might have seen and remembered.

11 Having sketched these two contrasting perspectives, Pfeifer then claims that *The Tree of Life* ends up endorsing them both, which results in an

unstable oscillation between sublime epiphany and self-reflexive irony and a self-undermining questioning of the possibility of aesthetically revealed spiritual truth. The evidence Pfeifer offers for this reading, however, remains rather thin: a general parallel with author David Foster Wallace's work and a sketchy claim that the contrast between images of Jack as child and as an adult show, in a self-reflexive manner, the impossibility of beauty resisting the flow of time.

12 For further discussion of the ethical potential of a cinema of belief, see Sinnerbrink (2016a, b, c).

13 The Tree of Life is mentioned in the Book of Genesis, after Adam and Eve eat the forbidden fruit of the Tree of Knowledge and hence are cast out of the Garden of Eden: 'And the LORD God said, Behold, the man is become as one of us, to know good and evil; and now, lest he put forth his hand, and take also of the tree of life, and eat, and live forever' (Genesis 3:22, King James Version). The film evokes this quest to retrieve the fruit of the Tree of Life (eternal life), but within the limits of our natural and historical existence.

14 See Candler (2016) and Nunziato (2016) for illuminating theological interpretations of *The Tree of Life*. See Handley (2014) for an 'ecotheological' reading of the film, drawing on both Kierkegaard and Dostoevsky. In an excellent recent article, Caruana (2018) offers a persuasive Kierkegaardian reading of the film, one that articulates lucidly, via Kierkegaard on repetition and belief in Job, the kind of existential concern with 'world loss' that I attempted to describe via the film's moral-aesthetic response to nihilism.

15 Thomas Wilfred was an American-Danish artist who was a pioneer in creating 'Lumia' images or visual music: works of art composed of light, colour and form, using the colour organ or 'Clavilux'.

16 Rybin points out that Malick has composed the story of Jack's childhood through flashbacks that go well beyond what the adult Jack could remember (or what the young Jack could have experienced directly), exposing and exploring the inherent ambiguity of the flashback as a way of communicating recollections of the past in a manner that overflows individual memory. In this way, *The Tree of Life* could be read, Rybin argues, as 'a philosophical inquiry into the very nature of the flashback as a source of meaning in film' (2012: 176).

17 Rybin (2012: 172) also notes that, unlike a Kempis, 'Malick is ultimately concerned to show us how both the ethereally spiritual and the brutally natural are intertwined'. See also McAteer's (2011) illuminating discussion of the theology informing the way of nature/way of grace duality in *The Tree of Life*.

18 One intrepid viewer has shown that the Western Union telegram Mrs O'Brien receives states that her son's death took place in Mexico, on 6 February 1968, in an automobile accident (rather than by committing suicide, as Malick's brother Larry did while living in Spain and studying guitar under Andres Segovia) – or being killed in Vietnam, as I, along with other commentators, conjectured. See Schwartz (2011).

19 This image of the lost brother will recur at the end of the film, during Jack's epiphanic vision, his experience of spiritual reconciliation through love.

20 Much of this footage is taken from a project Malick had conceived in the twenty-year gap between *Days of Heaven* and *The Thin Red Line*, an experimental documentary piece on the origin of life in the universe entitled Q, which eventually appeared as *Voyage of Time* (2016).

21 What looks like a Troodon spares an injured Parasaurolophus.

22 Berlioz: 7. Domine Jesu Christe (Requiem Op. 5, Grande Messe des Morts).

23 Panentheism, in contrast to both traditional theism (God as separate from nature) and pantheism (God as identified with nature), unites both the immanent and the transcendent; God is both expressed in nature but also not reducible to it, embraces the natural universe but also the realm of the intelligible or non-natural. It has become a 'third way' in theology since German idealism and romanticism, particularly among thinkers wishing to reconcile Christianity with a scientific understanding of the universe (see Culp 2017). Although I cannot go further here, it would be worth exploring the question of Malick's theology as a contemporary version of panentheism as articulated in works like *Voyage of Time* (and others).

Chapter 5

1 See the volume Barnett and Clark (2017) for illuminating interpretations of Malick's work from theological and religious perspectives.

2 As Caruana (2018: 72) asks: 'Why did we not see the Kierkegaard connection with Malick earlier?' A question that I have also put to myself over recent years! My sense is that this is related to the hesitation and reluctance to engage with the religious-theological dimension of Malick's work and the difficulty of articulating the relationship between film, philosophy and religion in contemporary film theory/philosophy of film.

3 The film had originally been titled 'Lawless' but Malick allowed John Hillcoat to use it for his 2012 crime drama. 'Weightless' was announced as the title of the film in March 2015 (and confirmed in 2016) but the title

was later changed to *Song to Song*. I take the term 'weightless' trilogy from Michael Rewin's (2017) review of *Song to Song*.

4 See Tomasulo and McKahan (2009: 1–23) and Kierkegaard (1972). Antonioni's critique of 'sick eros' in his trilogy is oriented by an atheistic existentialist humanism, whereas Malick's version is shaped by a Platonic theory of love and Christian existentialism (Kierkegaard).

5 A parallel noted in Brody's review (2013).

6 This 'empty' or generic form of character presentation is the deeper sense of the criticism that the later Malick films border on 'self-parody' in their depiction of characters in love.

7 According to the Rotten Tomatoes website, *To the Wonder, Knight of Cups* and *Song to Song* attracted positive reviews from only 46, 47 and 43 per cent of critics, respectively, and they all scored an underwhelming audience approval rating of 37 per cent.

8 For similar approaches to Malick's later films, emphasizing Kierkegaardian existentialism and Christian theology, see Calhoun (2017), Camacho (2017), Caruana (2018), Goodman (2013), Hamilton (2016), McAteer (2013) and Urda (2016). I agree with the Christian existentialist approach to these later Malick films but think they are more ambivalent about the prospects of 'perfecting' the Platonic-Christian ascent from erotic to agapic love via a commitment to faith in the modern secular world. Malick's films also emphasize the *insufficiency* of romantic love, failing an anchoring in communal and religious (agapic) love, to fulfil its promise of self-transformation.

9 I discuss this further in Sinnerbrink (2016b).

10 See my discussion of the idea of cinematic ethics in the Introduction. I discuss this idea further in Sinnerbrink (2016c: 1–24).

11 See Nietzsche (*Birth of Tragedy*, Section 5): 'we have our highest dignity in our significance as works of art – for it is only as an aesthetic phenomenon that existence and the world are eternally justified.'

12 Plato is an acknowledged influence on Kierkegaard's thought, evident through the use of mythos or story, rather than argument or logos, to articulate philosophical truth; the undermining of authorial authority via the use of dramatic dialogue, diverse literary forms, authorial pseudonyms and rhetorical devices designed to provoke independent thought; and by a conception of the self as encompassing both immanent and transcendent (or finite and infinite) dimensions that must be reconciled by being related to an objective Good (namely God). See Carlsson (2007), Howland (2007) and Rudd (2012).

13 Cf. 'Man is a synthesis of the finite and the infinite, of the temporal and the eternal, of freedom and necessity, in short it is a synthesis. A synthesis

is a relation between two factors. So regarded, man is not yet a self'
Kierkegaard (1968: 146). Kierkegaard describes despair as 'a disrelationship
in the relation which relates itself to itself' (i.e. the self) (1968: 147), a
disrelationship that can only be overcome via grounding the self in its
relationship with the infinite, namely God (Kierkegaard 1968: 147).

14 'The despair lies in relating oneself with infinite passion to a single
individual, for with infinite passion one can relate oneself – if one is not in
despair – only to the eternal' (Kierkegaard 2009: 54).

15 See, for example, Kierkegaard, 'The Immediate Stages of the Erotic or the
Musical Erotic' and 'Diary of the Seducer' (1959: 45–134 & 299–440).

16 Cf. 'the aesthete uses artifice, arbitrariness, irony, and willful imagination to
recreate the world in his own image. The prime motivation for the aesthete
is the transformation of the boring into the interesting' (McDonald 2017).

17 M. Gail Hammer (2017: 251 ff.) argues that both *To the Wonder* and
Knight of Cups 'disentwine the chiasm of nature and grace that structures
The Tree of Life', and that Malick's cinematography and montage craft
'a visual phenomenology that transgresses the rules of visual discourse
and narrative expectations of Hollywood films' (2017: 251). In a
variation on the idea of 'cinematic excess', Hammer maintains that the
'visual transgression' of Malick's visual and narrative style corresponds
phenomenologically to the 'excessive' (incoherent and dissonant) character
of subjective experience and that this is the manner in which the divine
is manifested through an aesthetics of excess (what she calls, drawing
on Peirce, a 'phaneroscopy', a scrutiny of the chaotic visual array of
appearances) (2017: 251–252 ff.).

18 In response to a query from one of the editors of the *Theology and Terrence
Malick* volume, the producers of *Knight of Cups* replied that the 'Tale of
Western [Occidental] Exile' is in fact the source text of the quotation from
the 'Hymn of the Pearl' recited in the film (Hammer 2017: 270, fn. 2). As
Hammer notes, however, Surhrawardi's 'Hymn' contains 'no reference to
a prince, a journey to Egypt, the falling asleep (and into slavery), and then
finally remembering his princely task – all of which are elements of the
"Hymn of the Pearl" in the Acts of Thomas' (2017: 270, fn. 2).

19 As de Vitis (2018) remarks: 'The meaning of the cycle has been much
debated. Experts now (generally) agree that they present a meditation on
earthly pleasures and courtly culture, offered through an allegory of the
senses.'

20 See Hammer (2017: 263–264) for a discussion of the role of the Tarot Card
figures and the need to supplement these via the Platonic and Christian
theological myths of love in Malick's aesthetic presentation of the presence
of the divine in the everyday.

21 In what may or may not be a nod towards Malick's biographical background, in one scene we see Neil lying in bed alone reading a copy of Heidegger's *Being and Time*!

22 Marina succumbs to the awkward attentions of a carpenter, who in an earlier scene gifts her a dulcimer (a reference to the 'Abyssinian maid' in Coleridge's *Kubla Khan*?). They have a passionless erotic encounter, in an anonymous hotel room. Marina's reluctant desire and guilty conscience colours the dismal encounter, their brief coupling symbolized by the carpenter's chest tattoo of a skull caught in a spider's web.

23 The text closely paraphrases St. Isaac of Syria, *Directions on Spiritual Training* (1990: 633).

24 I would like to thank Anat Pick and Libby Saxton for bringing this point to my attention.

25 These sequences parallel those in *Knight of Cups* showing Rick's wife Nancy (Cate Blanchett), whom we see treating and caring for her impoverished and afflicted patients. The use of non-professional actors/real people in these sequences could be criticized on ethical grounds: the contrast between using a recognized actor (Bardem) playing a fictional priest (Quintana) listening to the stories of troubled members of a disadvantaged underclass (featuring people of colour, recovering drug addicts and people with disabilities) might raise charges of exploitation or manipulation of disenfranchised others for the sake of artistic expression. The footage was shot by Eugene Richards, hired by Malick because of his extensive photojournalism experience working with poverty and racial issues in the American South, and has recently been released as a documentary drama, *Thy Kingdom Come* (2018). The religious motivation to depict both spiritual and physical suffering, while stressing the redemptive power of love and dignity of individuals, could be seen as clashing with the ethical question of consent while avoiding exploitation, and with political considerations concerning the depiction of race, poverty and social suffering.

26 One of the common criticisms of Malick's films concerns the question of gender representation, the depiction of female characters embodying stereotypical gendered traits (expressed through movement, dance and gesture) or embodying a female saviour or 'manic pixie dream girl' stereotype (a woman whose creativity or joie de vivre enlivens and redeems a male character in despair, or who exists to 'teach broodingly soulful young men to embrace life and its infinite mysteries and adventures' (Nathan Rabin)). Many female characters veer close to this account, but in most cases they are presented as viewed from a (flawed or limited) male character's perspective (e.g. Private Bell's wife Marty (Miranda Otto) in *The Thin Red Line*, or Jack's mother (Jessica Chastain)

in *The Tree of Life*, as seen from Jack's perspective as a boy, and most
of the female love interest/Tarot card characters in *Knight of Cups*).
Moreover, the female characters also offer contrasting perspectives,
which often clash with those of the male characters or show up the
latter's limitations (e.g. Rick's ex-wife Nancy (Cate Blanchett) in *Knight
of Cups*). The 'fantasy' figures such female characters represent for the
male characters is thrown into relief by the presentation of their own
perspectives, their own struggles for self-knowledge or finding oneself
through love. In *Knight of Cups*, for example, Della (Imogen Poots) calls
attention to Rick's (Christian Bale) 'manic pixie dream girl' fantasy image.
She accuses Rick of being weak and claims that she has to shock and wake
him, bringing him back to life: 'You think I could make you crazy, crack
you out of your shell. Make you suffer.' *Song to Song*, as I argue, is Faye's
story, not that of the male characters; it thus represents an important
gendered contrast with the more or less exclusively male character
perspectives structuring *Knight of Cups*.

27   Cf. The *Song of Solomon* 4:12: 'A garden enclosed is my sister, my spouse; a
spring shut up, a fountain sealed.' As Timmerman (2013) notes, 'the deeper
allusion' here 'is to the literary idea of the *hortus conclusus*, the "enclosed
garden."'... embedded within the notion of the *hortus conclusus* is both the
idea of the female body as a site of enclosure and the "enclosed" spatial
quality of the female social experience.'

28   The film uses a recording of Plato's *Phaedrus* recited by Charles
Laughton, which can be heard on YouTube: https://www.youtube.com/
watch?v=b7ANslOvACE (consulted 15 May 2018). The original citation
is from the famous 'Myth of the Charioteer' in Plato's *Phaedrus* (1892:
246a–253c): 'Thus far I have been speaking of the fourth and last kind of
madness, which is imputed to him who, when he sees the beauty of earth,
is transported with the recollection of the true beauty; he would like to fly
away, but he cannot; he is like a bird fluttering and looking upward and
careless of the world below' (249d).

29   *To the Wonder* explicitly uses the Platonic-Christian metaphor of love as
an 'ascent' from the sensuous to the spiritual, for example in image of the
lovers' ascent up the steps of Mont Saint-Michel, accompanied by Marina's
voiceover: 'We climbed the steps/To the Wonder'. As Camacho notes, we
can take this as 'an allusion to the Platonic "ladder of love" – that image for
the way in which we, as finite beings possessed of an infinite desire, might
ascend through love to a lasting possession of the good and the beautiful in
their widest possible scope' (2017: 235–236).

30   Cf. 'Every movement of infinity comes about through passion, and no
reflection can bring a movement about' (Kierkegaard 1968: 53).

31 The wonderful shot in *The Tree of Life* of Mrs O'Brien walking on the salt plains and giving thanks against a background of mountains and sky – the camera both hugging the dazzling earth and tilting up at the illuminated heavens – combines both immanent and transcendent movements at once.

32 There are eight chapters in *Knight of Cups*, organized according to seven cards (and one fictitious one) belonging to the Tarot deck: I. The Moon (Della (Imogen Poots)); II. The Hanged Man (Rick's brother Barry (Wes Bentley) and father (Brian Dennehy)); III. The Hermit (Tonio (Antonio Banderas)); IV. Judgment (Nancy (Cate Blanchett), Rick's physician ex-wife); V. The Tower (Helen, a model (Freida Pinto)); VI. The High Priestess (Karen (Teresa Palmer), a free-spirited stripper); VII. Death (Elizabeth (Natalie Portman), a married woman with whom Rick has an affair and who may be pregnant to him); VIII. Freedom (Rick and Isabel (Isabel Lucas), a sensuous, spiritual woman with whom Rick finally finds peace).

33 Like the other two films, this is inflected, moreover, via a Christian theological account of transcendent, but also humanized, divine love, rather than the Platonic account of the intellectual love of the Good achieved through philosophical wisdom.

34 *Knight of Cups* also resonates with one of Malick's longstanding obsessions: Walker Percy's Southern existentialist novel *The Moviegoer* (1961), which Christian Bale was advised to read in order to prepare the role of Rick. The protagonist, Binx Bolling, is a materially successful but spiritually alienated Korean War veteran cum New Orleans stockbroker, a womanizer and a moviegoer, searching for meaning and purpose – what he calls 'the wonder' – as he approaches his thirtieth birthday, setting off on a picaresque 'quest' for his true self, amidst the revelry of New Orleans' French Quarter. Movies offer a world more authentic than the inauthenticity of his everyday world, from which he remains distant and aloof, isolated in a despair that he both recognizes as familiar and struggles to overcome, finding possible redemption in his relationship with his beautiful but depressive cousin, Kate Cutter. This Kierkegaardian-inspired novel was the subject of a screenplay Malick wrote in the 1980s but later abandoned; key elements of the novel have subsequently been worked into his most recent films.

35 According to Malick, the title 'weightless' is taken from Virginia Woolf's *The Waves* (1931): 'How can I proceed now, I said, without a self, weightless and visionless, through a world weightless.' In *Song to Song*, as Malick explains in his rare appearance at the SXSW Film Festival (March 2017): 'I think you want to make it feel like they're just bits and pieces of [the characters'] lives. [As Woolf asks,] can you live in this world just moment to moment, song to song, kiss to kiss [and] try to create these different moods for yourself and go through the world "without a self,"... and living one

desire to the next? And where does that lead, what happens to you in that sort of [spontaneous life]?'.

36 The 'immediate sphere of the erotic' in *Either/Or, Volume I* focuses on Mozart's *Don Juan*.

37 In order to prepare Cook's character, Malick advised Fassbender to channel the character of Satan from Milton's *Paradise Lost*.

Conclusion

1 From the Stephen Mitchell translation (1995: 68).

References

Badlands (1973), [Film], Dir. Terrence Malick, USA: Warner Bros. and Williams Pressman.

Baggini, J. (2003), 'Alien Ways of Thinking: Mulhall's on Film', *Film-Philosophy*, 7 (24). Available online: http://www.film-philosophy.com/vol-2003/n24baggini (accessed 1 May 2008).

Barnett, C. B. (2013), 'Spirit(uality) in the Films of Terrence Malick', *Journal of Religion & Film*, 17 (1): Article 33. Available online: http://digital-commons. unomaha.edu/jrf/vol17/iss1/33 (accessed 29 June 2018).

Barnett, C. B. and Elliston, C. J. (eds) (2017), *Theology and the Films of Terrence Malick*, New York and London: Routledge.

Barrett, C. B. (2016), 'The Obscurity of Self – Or Why Bruce Springsteen Gets *Badlands* Wrong', in C. B. Barnett and C. J. Elliston (eds), *Theology and the Films of Terrence Malick*, 117–137, London and New York: Routledge.

Bazin, A. (1997), 'Cinema and Theology', in *André Bazin at Work: Major Essays and Reviews from the Forties and Fifties*, trans. Alain Piette and Bert Cardullo, 61–72, New York and London: Routledge.

Bazin, A. (2009), '*Diary of a Country Priest* and the Robert Bresson Style', in *What Is Cinema? André Bazin*, trans. T. Barnard, 139–159, Montreal: Caboose Books.

Bersani, L. and Dutoit, U. (2004), *Forms of Being: Cinema, Aesthetics, Subjectivity*, London: BFI Books.

Blanchot, M. and Derrida, J. (2000), *The Instant of My Death/Demeure: Fiction and Testimony*, trans. E. Rottenberg, Stanford, CA: Stanford University Press.

Bradshaw, P. (2011), '*The Tree of Life* – Review', *The Guardian*, 7 July. Available online: http://www.guardian.co.uk/film/2011/jul/07/the-tree-of-life-review (accessed 18 July 2017).

Brant, J. (2016), 'The Unique Difficulty of *Days of Heaven*', in C. B. Barnett and C. J. Elliston (eds), *Theology and the Films of Terrence Malick*, 138–158, London and New York: Routledge.

Brody, R. (2013), 'The Cinematic Miracle of "To the Wonder"', *New Yorker Magazine*, 10 April. Available online: https://www.newyorker.com/culture/richard-brody/the-cinematic-miracle-of-to-the-wonder (accessed 12 March 2018).

Brody, R. (2016), 'Terrence Malick's Metaphysical Journey into Nature', *The New Yorker*, 8 September. Available online: https://www.newyorker.com/culture/richard-brody/terrence-malicks-metaphysical-journey-into-nature (accessed 5 October 2018).

Buscombe, E. (2008), 'What's New in *The New World?*', *Film Quarterly*, 62 (3) Spring: 35–40.

Calhoun, D. H. (2017), 'Who Has Eyes to See, Let Him See: Terrence Malick as Natural Theologian', in C. B. Barnett and C. J. Elliston (eds), *Theology and the Films of Terrence Malick*, 66–98, New York and London: Routledge.

Camacho, P (2017), 'The Promise of Love Perfected: Eros and Kenosis in *To the Wonder*', in C. B. Barnett and C. J. Elliston (eds), *Theology and the Films of Terrence Malick*, 232–250, New York and London: Routledge.

Campbell, N. (2007), 'The Highway Kind: Badlands, Youth, Space, and the Road', in H. Patterson (ed.), *The Cinema of Terrence Malick: Poetic Visions of America*, 2nd Edition, 27–39, London and New York: Wallflower Press.

Candler Jr, P. M. (2016), '*The Tree of Life* and the Lamb of God', in C. B. Barnett and C. J. Elliston (eds), *Theology and the Films of Terrence Malick*, 205–217, Abingdon and New York: Routledge.

Carlsson, U. (2007), 'Love as a Problem of Knowledge in Kierkegaard's Either/Or and Plato's Symposium', *Inquiry*, 53 (1): 41–67.

Caruana, J. (2018), 'Repetition and Belief: A Kierkegaardian Reading of Malick's *The Tree of Life*', in J. Caruana and M. Cauchi (eds), *Immanent Frames: Postsecular Cinema between Malick and von Trier*, 69–85, Albany: State University of New York Press.

Cashill, J. (2011), 'Critics Don't Get *Tree of Life*', *American Thinker*, 25 June. Available online: https://www.americanthinker.com/articles/2011/06/critics_dont_get_tree_of_life.html (accessed 18 July 2017).

Cavell, S. (1979), *The World Viewed: Reflections on the Ontology of Film*, Enlarged Edition, Cambridge, MA, and London: Harvard University Press.

Cavell, S. (2010), *Little Did I Know: Excerpts from Memory*, Stanford, CA: Stanford University Press.

Cooper, S. (2006), *Selfless Cinema? Ethics and French Documentary*, London: Legenda.

Cousins, M. (2007), 'Praising *The New World*', in H. Patterson (ed.), *The Cinema of Terrence Malick: Poetic Visions of America*, 192–198, London: Wallflower Press.

Critchley, S. (1997), *Very Little … Almost Nothing: Death, Philosophy, Literature*, Revised Edition, London and New York: Routledge.

Critchley, S. (2002), 'Calm – On Terrence Malick's *The Thin Red Line*', *Film-Philosophy*, 6 (38). Available online: http://www.film-philosophy.com/vol6-2002/n48critchley (accessed 30 June 2017).

Critchley, S. (2005), 'Calm – On Terrence Malick's *The Thin Red Line*', in R. Read and J. Goodenough (eds), *Film as Philosophy: Essays on Cinema after Wittgenstein and Cavell*, 133–148, Basingstoke: Palgrave Macmillan.

Critchley, S. (2009), 'Calm – On Terrence Malick's *The Thin Red Line*', in D. Davies (ed.), *The Thin Red Line*, Philosophers on Film, 11–27, London and New York: Routledge.

Culp, J. (2017), 'Panentheism', *Stanford Encyclopedia of Philosophy*, Available online: https://plato.stanford.edu/entries/panentheism/(accessed 24 October 2018).

d'Entrement, J. (2007), '*The New World* (movie review)', *The Journal of American History*, 94 (3) December: 1023–1026.

Davies, D. (2009), 'Terrence Malick', in Paisley Livingston and Carl Plantinga (eds), *The Routledge Companion to Philosophy and Film*, 569–580, New York and London: Routledge.

Davies, D. (2009), *The Thin Red Line*, Philosophers on Film, London and New York: Routledge.

Davies, D. (2009a), 'Terrence Malick', in P. Livingston and C. Plantinga (eds), *The Routledge Companion to Philosophy and Film*, 560–580, London and New York: Routledge.

Davies, D. (2009b), *The Thin Red Line*, Philosophers on Film, London and New York: Routledge.

Days of Heaven (1978), [Film], Dir. Terrence Malick, USA: Paramount Pictures.

Deleuze, G. (1989), *Cinema 2: The Time-Image*, trans. H. Tomlinson and R. Galatea, Minneapolis: University of Minnesota Press.

De Vitis, M. (2018), 'Explainer: The Symbolism of the Lady and the Unicorn Cycle', *The Conversation*, 8 February. Available online: https://theconversation.com/explainer-the-symbolism-of-the-lady-and-the-unicorn-tapestry-cycle-91325 (consulted 14 May 2018).

Diary of a Country Priest [*Journal d'un curé de campagne*] (1951), [Film], Dir. Robert Bresson, France: Union Générale Cinématographique (UGC).

Donougho, M. (2011), '"Melt Earth to Sea": *The New World* of Terrence Malick', *The Journal of Speculative Philosophy*, 25 (4): 359–374.

Downing, L. and Saxton, L. (eds) (2010), *Film and Ethics: Foreclosed Encounters*, Abingdon and New York: Routledge.

Ebert, R. (2011), 'The Tree of Life', *Chicago Sun-Times* (Chicago), 2 June. Available online: https://www.rogerebert.com/reviews/the-tree-of-life-2011 (accessed 18 July 2017).

Emerson, R. W. (1906), 'The Over-Soul', in *Essays. First and Second Series*, 149–167, London: J.M. Dent.

Flanagan, M. (2007), '"Everything a Lie": The Critical and Commercial
Reception of Terrence Malick's *The Thin Red Line*', in H. Patterson (ed.), *The
Cinema of Terrence Malick: Poetic Visions of America*, 125–140, London and
New York: Wallflower Press.

Foundas, S. (2011), 'Suffer the Children', Cannes Festival report, *Film Comment*,
July August. Available online: https://www.filmcomment.com/article/cannes-
2011-report-2/ (accessed 18 July 2017).

Frampton, D. (2006), *Filmosophy*, London: Wallflower Press.

Furstenau, M. and McAvoy, L. (2003), 'Terrence Malick's Heideggerian Cinema:
War and the Question of Being in *The Thin Red Line*', in H. Patterson (ed.),
The Cinema of Terrence Malick: Poetic Visions of America, 173–185, London
and New York: Wallflower Press.

Goodman, D. R. (2013), 'To the Wonder', *Journal of Religion and Film*, 17 (2):
Article 13: 1–5.

Hamilton, J. M. (2016), '"What Is This Love that Loves Us?": Terrence Malick's
To the Wonder as a Phenomenology of Love', *Religions*, 7 (76): 1–15.

Hammer, M. Gail (2017), '"Remember Who You Are": Imaging Life's
Purpose in *Knight of Cups*', in C. B. Barnett and C. J. Elliston (eds),
Theology and the Films of Terrence Malick, 251–274, New York and
London: Routledge.

Handley, G. (2014), 'Faith, Sacrifice, and the Earth's Glory in Terrence Malick's,
The Tree of Life', *Angelaki*, 19 (4) December: 79–93.

Heidegger, M. (1993), 'What is Metaphysics?' in D. F. Krell (ed.), *Martin
Heidegger: Basic Writings*, Revised and Expanded Edition, 93–110, San
Francisco, CA: Harper and Row.

Heidegger, M. (2010), *Being and Time*, trans. J. Stambaugh, Albany: State
University of New York Press.

Howland, J. (2007), 'Plato and Kierkegaard: Two Philosophical Stories', *The
European Legacy*, 12.(2): 173–185.

Hynes, E. (2017), 'Make It Real: Form and Void', *Film Comment*, January/
February. Available online: https://www.filmcomment.com/article/terrence-
malick-voyage-of-time/ (accessed 5 October 2018).

Jones, K. (2011), 'Light Years', *Film Comment*, July–August. Available online:
https://www.filmcomment.com/blog/light-years-kent-jones-tree-of-life-
review/ (accessed 18 July 2017).

Kael, P. (1977), 'Sugarland and Badland', in *Reeling*, 300–306, London: Marion
Boyars.

Kael, P. (1982), *5001 Nights at the Movies*, London: Zenith.

Kendall, S. (2011), 'The Tragic Indiscernibility of *Days of Heaven*', in T. D.
Tucker and S. Kendall (eds), *Terrence Malick: Film and Philosophy*, 148–164,
New York and London: Continuum.

Kendrick, J. (2017), 'An Improbable Career: The Films of Terrence Malick', in C. B. Barnett and C. J. Elliston (eds), *Theology and the Films of Terrence Malick*, 3–28, New York and London: Routledge.

Kierkegaard, S. (1959), *Either/Or Volume I: A Fragment of Life*, trans. D. F. Swenson and L. M. Swenson, Princeton, NJ: Princeton University Press.

Kierkegaard, S. (1968), *Fear and Trembling* and *The Sickness unto Death*, trans. W. Lowrie, Princeton, NJ: Princeton University Press.

Kierkegaard, S. (1972), *A Literary Review: Two Ages. A Novel by the Author of "A Story of Everyday Life,"* trans. A. Dru, New York: Harper Torchbooks.

Kierkegaard, S. (2009), *Works of Love*, trans. H. and E. Hong, Foreword by G. Pattinson, New York and London: Harper Perennial Modern Thought.

Knight of Cups (2015), [Film], Dir. Terrence Malick, USA: Dogwood Films, Waypoint Entertainment.

Livingston, P. (2006), 'Theses on Cinema and Philosophy', in M. Smith and T. E. Wartenberg (eds), *Thinking through Cinema: Film as Philosophy*, 11–18, Malden, MA and Oxford: Blackwell Publishing.

Livingston, P. (2009), *Cinema, Philosophy, Bergman: On Film as Philosophy*, Oxford: Oxford University Press.

Loht, S. (2013), 'Film as Heideggerian Art? A Reassessment of Heidegger, Film, and His Connection to Terrence Malick', *Film and Philosophy*, 17: 113–126.

Loht, S. (2014), 'Film as Ethical Philosophy, and the Question of Philosophical Arguments in Film – A Reading of *The Tree of Life*', *Film and Philosophy*, 18 (164): 183.

Loht, S. (2017), *Phenomenology of Film: A Heideggerian Account of the Film Experience*, Lanham: Lexington Books.

MacDonald, I. (2009), 'Nature and the Will to Power in Terrence Malick's *The New World*', in D. Davies (ed.), *The Thin Red Line*, Philosophers on Film, 87–110, London and New York: Routledge.

Maher Jr., P. J. (ed.) (2014), *One Big Soul: An Oral History of Terrence Malick*, Raleigh, NC: Lulu Press.

Malick, T. (1969), 'Translator's Introduction', in M. Heidegger (ed.), *The Essence of Reasons*, trans. T. Malick, xi–xviii, Evanston, IL: Northwestern University Press.

Martin, A. (2006), 'Things to Look Into: The Cinema of Terrence Malick', *Rouge*, 10. Available online: http://www.rouge.com.au/10/malick.html (accessed 15 September 2017).

Martin, A. (2007), 'Approaching *The New World*', in H. Paterson (ed.), *Poetic Visions of America: The Cinema of Terrence Malick*, 212–221, 2nd Edition, London: Wallflower Press.

Martin, A. (2007), 'Approaching *The New World*', in H. Patterson (ed.), *The Cinema of Terrence Malick: Poetic Visions of America*, 2nd Edition, 212–221, London and New York: Wallflower Press.

McAteer, J. (2011), *Video et intellectum* (weblog), 'The nuns taught us there are two ways through life: The way of nature and the way of grace', 21 July. Available online: https://filmphilosopher.wordpress.com/2011/07/21/%E2%80%9Cthe-nuns-taught-us-there-are-two-ways-through-life-the-way-of-nature-and-the-way-of-grace-%E2%80%9D/ (accessed 3 October 2012).

McAteer, J. (2013), 'I Love, Therefore I Am: *To the Wonder* as Existential Apologetic', *Christian Research Journal*, 36 (4). Available online: http://www.equip.org/article/i-love-therefore-i-am-to-the-wonder-as-existential-apologetic/ (accessed 12 March 2018).

McCann, B. (2007), '"Enjoying the Scenery": Landscape and the Fetishisation of Nature in *Badlands* and *Days of Heaven*', in H. Patterson (ed.), *The Cinema of Terrence Malick: Poetic Visions of America*, 2nd Edition, 77–87, London and New York: Wallflower Press.

McCracken, B. (2011), 'The Tree of Life' Review, *Christianity Today*, 27 May. Available online: https://www.christianitytoday.com/ct/2011/mayweb-only/treeoflife.html (accessed 18 July 2017).

McDonald, W. (2017), 'Søren Kierkegaard', *Stanford Encyclopedia of Philosophy* (1996/2017). Available online: https://plato.stanford.edu/entries/kierkegaard/ (consulted 9 April 2018).

McNab, G. and Lubezki, E. (2011), 'The Light Fantastic', *Sight and Sound*, BFI, 21 (7) July: 22–23.

Michaels, L. (2009), *Terrence Malick*, Urbana and Chicago: University of Illinois Press.

Millington, J. (2010), 'Critical Voices: Points of View in and on *The Thin Red Line*', *Cineaction*, 81: 28–38.

Mitchell, S. (1995), *Ahead of All Parting: The Selected Poetry and Prose of Rainer Maria Rilke*, ed. and trans. Stephen Mitchell, New York: Random House.

Morrison, J. (2007), 'Making Worlds, Making Pictures: Terrence Malick's *The New World*', in H. Patterson (ed.), *The Cinema of Terrence Malick: Poetic Visions of America*, 2nd Edition, 212–221, London and New York: Wallflower Press.

Morrison, J. and Schur, T. (2003), *The Films of Terrence Malick*, Westport, CT: Praeger.

Mosely, M. J. (2018), 'Another Look at Heideggerian Cinema: Cinematic Excess, Antonioni's Dead Time and the Film-Photographic Image as Copy', *Film Philosophy*, 22 (3): 364–383.

Mulhall, S. (2002), *On Film*, London and New York: Routledge.

Mulhall, S. (2008), *On Film*, 2nd Edition, London and New York: Routledge.

Nagel, T. (2010), 'The Religious Temperament', in T. Nagel, *Secular Philosophy and the Religious Temperament: Essays 2002–2008*, 3–17, Oxford: Oxford University Press.

Neer, R. (2011), 'Terrence Malick's New World', Issue #2 (12 June), nonsite.org. Available online: https://nonsite.org/feature/terrence-malicks-new-world (accessed 14 June 2017).

Nunziato, J. (2016), 'Eternal Flesh as Divine Wisdom in *The Tree of Life*', in C. B. Barnett and C. J. Elliston (eds), *Theology and the Films of Terrence Malick*, 218–231, Abingdon and New York: Routledge.

Olszewski, T. (2011), 'The Tree of Life, Reviewed', *Washington City Paper*, 3 June. Available online: https://www.washingtoncitypaper.com/arts/film-tv/article/13040887/the-tree-of-life-reviewed (accessed 18 July 2017).

Orr, J. (2007), 'Terrence Malick and Arthur Penn: The Western Re-myth', in H. Patterson (ed.), *The Cinema of Terrence Malick: Poetic Visions of America*, 2nd Edition, 63–76, London and New York: Wallflower Press.

Patterson, H. (2003), *The Cinema of Terrence Malick: Poetic Visions of America*, London: Wallflower Press.

Patterson, H. (2007), 'Two Characters in Search of a Direction: Motivation and the Construction of Identity in *Badlands*', in H. Patterson (ed.), *The Cinema of Terrence Malick: Poetic Visions of America*, 2nd Edition, 40–51, London and New York: Wallflower Press.

Pfeifer, M. (2011), 'Either and Or: On Terrence Malick's *Tree of Life*', *Senses of Cinema*, Issue 60. Available online: http://www.sensesofcinema.com/2011/feature-articles/either-and-or-on-terrence-malicks-tree-of-life/ (accessed 03 October 2012).

Pippin, R. (2013), 'Vernacular Metaphysics', *Critical Inquiry*, 39 (2) (Winter): 247–275.

Plantinga, C. (2012), 'Art Moods and Human Moods in Narrative Cinema', *New Literary History*, 43 (3): 455–475.

Plate, S. Brent (2012), 'Visualizing the Cosmos: Terrence Malick's *The Tree of* Life and Other Visions of Life in the Universe', *Journal of the American Academy of Religion*, 80 (2) (June): 527–536.

Plato (1892), *Phaedrus*, trans. B. Jowett, Oxford: Oxford University Press.

Read, R. and Goodenough, J. (eds) (2005), *Film as Philosophy: Essays on Cinema after Wittgenstein and Cavell*, Basingstoke: Palgrave Macmillan.

Rewin, M. J. (2017), '*Song to Song* and Malick's Weightless Trilogy', *Brooklyn Magazine*, 17 March. Available online: http://www.bkmag.com/2017/03/17/song-to-song/ (accessed 12 March 2018).

Rhym, J. (2010), 'The Paradigmatic Shift in the Critical Reception of Terrence Malick's *Badlands* and the Emergence of a Heideggerian Cinema', *Quarterly Review of Film and Television*, 27 (4): 255–266.

Rossouw, M. (2017), 'There's Something about Malick: Film-Philosophy, Contemplative Style, and the Ethics of Self-Transformation', *New Review of Film and Television Studies*, 15 (3): 279–298.

Rudd, A. (2012), *Self, Value, and Narrative: A Kierkegaardian Approach*, esp.
    Chapter 2, 'The Teleological Self: Plato and Kierkegaard', Oxford: Oxford
    University Press.
Russell, B. (2006), 'The Philosophical Limits of Film', in N. Carroll and J.
    Choi (eds), *Philosophy of Film and Motion Pictures: An Anthology*, 387–390,
    Malden, MA and Oxford: Blackwell Publishing.
Rybin, S. (2012), *Terrence Malick and the Thought of Film*, New York: Lexington
    Books.
Schwartz, N. (2011), *The Niles Files*, 'Terrence Malick's Song of Himself V –
    The Tree of Life: Los Demiurgos', Comment by Anonymous, 9 November.
    Available online: http://nilesfilmfiles.blogspot.com/2011/06/song-of-himself-
    terrence-malicks-tree.html (accessed 03 July 2012).
Scott, M. M. (2017), 'Light in the Darkness: The Problem of Evil in *The Thin
    Red Line*', in C. B. Barnett and C. J. Elliston (eds), *Theology and the Films of
    Terrence Malick*, 172–175, New York and London: Routledge.
Shaw, D. (2012), *Morality and the Movies: Reading Ethics through Film*, London
    and New York: Continuum.
Silverman, K. (2003), 'All Things Shining', in D. L. Eng and D. Kazanjian (eds), *Loss:
    The Politics of Mourning*, 332–342, Berkeley: University of California Press.
Sinnerbrink R. (2006), 'A Heideggerian Cinema? On Terrence Malick's
    The Thin Red Line', Film-Philosophy, 10 (3): 26–37. Available online:
    http:/www.film-philosophy.com/2006v10n3/sinnerbrink.pdf (accessed
    30 September 2017).
Sinnerbrink, R. (2009), 'From Mythic History to Cinematic Poetry: Terrence
    Malick's *The New World* Viewed', *Screening the Past*, 26, December. Available
    online: http://www.screeningthepast.com/2015/01/from-mythic-history-
    to-cinematic-poetry-terrence-malick%E2%80%99s%C2%A0the-new-
    world%C2%A0viewed/ (accessed 21 March 2017).
Sinnerbrink, R. (2011a), *New Philosophies of Film: Thinking Images*, London and
    New York: Continuum.
Sinnerbrink, R. (2011b), 'Song of the Earth: Cinematic Romanticism in Terrence
    Malick's *The New World*', in T. D. Tucker and S. Kendall (eds), *Terrence
    Malick: Film and Philosophy*, 179–186, London and New York: Continuum.
Sinnerbrink, R. (2012a), 'Cinematic Belief: Bazinian Cinephilia and Malick's',
    The Tree of Life, Angelaki, 17 (4): 95–117.
Sinnerbrink, R. (2012b), '*Stimmung*: Exploring the Aesthetics of Mood', *Screen*,
    53 (2) Summer: 148–163.
Sinnerbrink, R. (2014), '*Techne* and *Poiesis*: On Heidegger and Film Theory',
    in A. van Den Oever (ed.), *Téchne/Technology. Researching Cinema and
    Media Technologies, Their Development, Use and Impact*, 67–82, Amsterdam:
    University of Amsterdam Press.

Sinnerbrink, R. (2016a), 'Belief in the World: Aesthetic Mythology in Terrence Malick's *The Tree of Life*', in J. Beever and V. W. Cisney (eds), *The Way of Nature and the Way of Grace: Philosophical Footholds in Terrence Malick's* The Tree of Life, 89–103, Evanston, IL: Northwestern University Press.

Sinnerbrink, R. (2016b), *Cinematic Ethics: Exploring Ethical Experience through Film*, London and New York: Routledge.

Sinnerbrink, R. (2016c), 'Historical Moods in Film', *Screening the Past*, 10. Available online: http://www.screeningthepast.com/2016/10/historical-moods-in-film/ (accessed 24 December 2016).

Sinnerbrink, R. (2016d), '"Love Everything": Cinema and Belief in Malick's *The Tree of Life*', *Symposium: Canadian Journal of Continental Philosophy*, 'Varieties of Continental Philosophy and Religion', 20 (1) (Spring): 91–105.

Sinnerbrink, R. (2018), 'Two Ways through Life: Postsecular Visions in *Melancholia* and *The Tree of Life*', in J. Caruana and M. Cauchi (eds), *Immanent Frames: Postsecular Cinema between Malick and von Trier*, 29–46, Albany: State University of New York Press.

Smith, M. (1995), *Engaging Characters: Film, Emotion, and the Cinema*, Oxford: Oxford University Press.

Smith, M. (2006), 'Film, Art and Ambiguity', in M. Smith and T. E. Wartenberg (eds), *Thinking through Cinema: Film as Philosophy*, 33–42, Malden, MA and Oxford: Blackwell Publishing.

Song to Song (2017), [Film], Dir. Terrence Malick, USA: Buckeye Pictures, FilmNation Entertainment.

St Isaac of Syria (1990), 'Directions on Spiritual Training, Text 53', in J. Manley (ed.), *The Bible and the Holy Fathers for Orthodox: Daily Scripture Readings and Commentaries for Orthodox Christians*, Crestwood, NY: St Vladimir's Seminary Press.

Stadler, J. (2008), *Pulling Focus: Intersubjective Experience, Narrative Film, and Ethics*, New York and London: Continuum.

Sterritt, D. (2011), 'Days of Heaven and Waco: Terrence Malick's *The Tree of Life*', *Film Quarterly*, 65 (1): 52–57.

Taubin, A. (2011), 'All Movies Great and Small', *Film Comment*, July–August. Available online: https://www.filmcomment.com/article/cannes-2011-report-1/ (accessed 3 October 2012).

The New World (2005), [Film], Dir. Terrence Malick, USA: New Lone Cinema.

The Thin Red Line (1998), [Film], Dir. Terrence Malick, USA: Fox 2000 Pictures.

The Tree of Life (2011), [Film], Dir. Terrence Malick, USA: Cottonwood Pictures, River Road Entertainment.

Timmerman, J. (2013), 'Terrence Malick, Theologian: The Intimidating, Exhilarating Religiosity of "The Tree of Life" and "To the Wonder"': Mubi,

Notebook Feature', 22 July. Available online. https://mubi.com/notebook/posts/terrence-malick-theologian-the-intimidating-exhilarating-religiosity-of-the-tree-of-life-and-to-the-wonder.

To the Wonder (2012), [Film]. Dir. Terrence Malick, USA: Brothers K Productions, Redbud Pictures.

Tomasulo, F. P. and McKahan, J. G. (2009), '"Sick Eros": The Sexual Politics of Antonioni's Trilogy', *Projections*, 3 (1) (Summer): 1–23.

Tucker, T. D. (2011), 'Worlding the West: An Ontopology of Badlands', in T. D. Tucker and S. Kendall (eds), *Terrence Malick: Film and Philosophy*, 80–100, New York and London: Continuum.

Tucker T. D. and Kendall, S. (eds) (2011), *Terrence Malick: Film and Philosophy*, New York and London: Continuum.

Urda, K. E. (2016), 'Eros and Contemplation: The Catholic Vision of Terrence Malick's *To the Wonder*', *Logos*, 19 (1) Winter: 130–147.

Walker, B. (1975), 'Malick on *Badlands*', *Sight and Sound*, 44 (2): 82–83.

Wartenberg, T. E. (2007), *Thinking on Screen: Film as Philosophy*, London and New York: Routledge.

Wheatley, C. (2009), *Michael Haneke's Cinema: The Ethic of the Image*, New York and Oxford: Berghahn Books.

Winter Light [*Nattavardsgästerna*] (1963), [Film], Dir. Ingmar Bergman, Sweden: Svensk Filmindustri (SK).

Wittgenstein, L (1953), *Philosophical Investigations*, trans. G. E. Anscombe, ed. P. M. S. Hacker and J. Schulte, London: Routledge and Kegan Paul.

Woessner, M. (2011), 'What Is Heideggerian Cinema? Film, Philosophy, and Cultural Mobility', *New German Critique*, 38 (2) (113): 129–157.

Woodward, G. S. (1969), *Pocahontas*, Norman: University of Oklahoma Press.

Index

emotional 15, 34, 35, 133, 164–5,
167, 170, 172, 203, 205, 208–9,
217
ethical and moral 7, 47, 203–4,
210, 214
ethical attitude 10, 54–5, 125, 166,
168, 187
ethical disorientation 164, 178
ethical experience 4–5, 13–16, 18–19,
54–5, 165, 203–4, 208, 215–16,
218
cinema as medium of 5, 7, 15, 19,
75, 128, 168, 214
existentialism. *See* phenomenology
existential themes 18–19, 21–2, 26–8,
34–6, 44–9, 52, 54–8, 129–31,
153, 158–9, 173
authenticity 21, 27–8, 43, 45–6,
52–3, 127–8, 143, 171
care 116, 125, 166, 177, 202
Christian existentialism 163, 169,
175, 205, 227 n.4, 227 n.8
despair 132, 134, 139–40, 142–4,
149, 162–3, 170, 180, 195,
199–200, 227–8 n.13, 228 n.14
distraction 164–5, 167, 170–1,
173, 183, 186, 195, 208–9
expression 5–7, 10–11, 14–16, 19,
21–2, 24–5, 30–4, 36, 44,
65–6, 68, 70, 76, 96, 106, 108,
110, 116–17, 120, 125, 129,
157–60, 162–3, 165–72, 171,
174, 185–6, 190, 193–4, 196,
202–4, 208, 223 n.19. *See also*
communication

figures. *See* character
film aesthetics 11–12, 18, 30, 56–8,
81–2, 85, 88, 223 n.19. *See also*
cinematic technique
formalism 11–12, 58, 82

self-reflexive 20–3, 28, 33–4, 42,
66, 69, 86–7, 93–6, 123, 156,
175, 187, 189–90, 211, 215,
224 n.9
film and philosophy 4, 6, 38–40, 49,
73, 81–2, 85, 98, 115, 118, 122,
129, 208
differences between 4–5, 45, 49
film in the condition of
philosophy 22–3, 89–90, 94, 98
film as philosophy 1, 4–7, 9, 36,
50–1, 75, 81–2, 89–94, 98, 114,
119, 124, 162, 208
film as philosophizing 89–90, 92
film-philosophy ix, 5, 14, 43, 49,
56, 83, 89, 97, 112, 161, 218
ethical turn in 14
philosophy of film 89
film world. *See* world, cinematic and
extra-cinematic worlds
finitude 10, 43, 45–8, 51–6, 67, 70,
75–6, 96, 108, 133, 159, 171,
199, 221 n.5, 227 n.12, 227–8
n.13
freedom 20–1, 103, 175, 178–9, 185

gaze 95–6, 99, 189
Gelassenheit. *See* releasement
(Gelassenheit)
genre 8–9, 13, 18, 35, 45, 56–7, 61–2,
65–6, 94, 119, 153
gesture 35–6, 165, 167, 170, 174
grace 116–19, 126–9, 132–3, 136–9,
144, 146, 150, 159, 172, 185.
See also transcendence

Heidegger, Martin viii, x, 1–3, 5, 8–11,
12–13, 20, 38–49, 54–8, 65, 67–
71, 73–4, 76, 81, 83–5, 87–8,
91–2, 99, 112, 119, 127–8, 135,
162, 210, 212, 218 n.1

Malick, Terrence
  critical reception x, 2, 9–10,
    13, 19–20, 34, 39, 44–5, 52,
    73–4, 76, 100–1, 113–14, 116,
    119–21, 152–4, 165, 202, 205,
    215, 227 n.7
  as filmmaker and philosopher
    viii–ix, 10, 40, 44, 81, 85, 87–8,
    99, 119, 210, 215, 217
  life 1–5, 226 n.18
  literary influences 20, 219 n.1,
    231–2 n.35
  philosophical influences 1–2, 8,
    40–2, 82–4, 88, 99
  philosophical writing 73, 84–5
    (*see also* Heidegger, Martin,
    The Essence of Reasons (*Vom
    Wesen des Grundes*))
  religious turn 162, 205, 209, 215
  style x, 9, 16, 18, 23, 35–6, 39, 44,
    58, 74, 81, 88–9, 92–3, 117,
    134–5, 142, 145, 150, 162–3,
    171–2, 174
  memory 116, 118, 123, 149
  collective-historical 116, 118, 123,
    133–7, 144, 195
  cosmic 116, 118, 143–8, 157
  involuntary 143
  personal 116, 118, 123, 132–3,
    139, 142–4, 146–7, 188, 195,
    224 n.9
metaphilosophy 6–7
metaphysical themes 10, 18, 42, 51–2,
    63, 68–9, 115, 120–1, 151–4,
    204
modernism 69, 87, 89, 91, 142, 211–
    12. *See also* film aesthetics,
    self-reflexive
modernity 58, 127–8
montage. *See* cinematic technique,
    editing

mood 18, 22, 30, 33–4, 36, 47–50, 51,
    70, 76, 96, 136, 141, 148–50,
    153, 163–7, 170, 172, 186.
    See also existential themes;
    phenomenology
  ethical aspects of 165–7
moral imagination 7, 16, 166
mortality. *See* finitude
Mulhall, Stephen 22, 40, 50, 89, 94,
    114
music and sound 23–4, 31, 36, 38–9,
    82, 92, 110, 115, 117, 120, 122,
    124, 131–6, 139–41, 142–3,
    145–7, 149–50, 155, 171–2,
    193–5. *See also* cinematic
    technique; film aesthetics
  Das Rheingold (Wagner, Richard)
    94–5, 102–3, 104–9, 223 n.17
mysticism
  aestheticist 8, 82
  religious 138, 160, 209–10,
    212–13
myth 19–21, 24, 27–8, 30–6, 86–7,
    97, 131, 134, 144, 174, 182,
    202–3
  cultural 21–2, 34, 36, 78–80, 94–5,
    100
  historical 35–6, 77, 100–1, 110
  poetic 18–20, 75–8, 101, 107,
    109–10, 118, 133, 144, 146,
    151, 157, 159
myth of the new 97–101

naivety. *See* romanticism
narration. *See* voiceover
narrative 56, 60, 81–3, 86, 88–9, 91,
    115, 140
  experimental, minimalist, or
    fragmented 13, 18–19, 24, 115,
    182–3, 202, 203, 208–9, 212
  narrative interpretation 81–2, 112